TITLES IN THIS SERIES

THE
DOCTRINE
OF
HUMANITY

CHARLES SHERLOCK

CONTOURS *of*

CHRISTIAN

THEOLOGY

GERALD BRAY
General Editor

InterVarsity Press
Downers Grove, Illinois

InterVarsity Press
P.O. Box 1400, Downers Grove, IL 60515-1426
World Wide Web: www.ivpress.com
E-mail: email@ivpress.com

InterVarsity Press® is the book-publishing division of InterVarsity Christian Fellowship/USA®, a student movement active on campus at hundreds of universities, colleges and schools of nursing in the United States of America, and a member movement of the International Fellowship of Evangelical Students. For information about local and regional activities, write Public Relations Dept., InterVarsity Christian Fellowship/USA, 6400 Schroeder Rd., P.O. Box 7895, Madison, WI 53707-7895, or visit the IVCF website at <www.intervarsity.org>.

All Scripture quotations, unless otherwise indicated, are taken from the New Revised Standard Version of the Bible, copyright 1989 by the Division of Christian Education of the National Council of the Churches of Christ in the USA. Used by permission. All rights reserved.

The Bible quotations in chapter two are Charles Sherlock's own translation.

ISBN 978-0-8308-1535-7

Printed in the United States of America ∞

Library of Congress Cataloging-in-Publication Data

Sherlock, Charles, 1945-
   The doctrine of humanity/Charles Sherlock.
     p. cm.—(Contours of Christian theology)
   Includes bibliographical references and indexes.
   ISBN 0-8308-1535-X (alk. paper)
    1. Man (Christian theology)   2. Image of God.   I. Title.
II. Series.
BT701.2.S48   1997

233'.5—dc20
                                     96-43775
                                       CIP

| **P** | 23 | 22 | 21 | 20 | 19 | 18 | 17 | 16 | 15 | 14 | 13 |
| **Y** | 23 | 22 | 21 | 20 | 19 | | | | | | |

For Sharon, who made me run and jump,

and Greg, who helped me see

Contents

Series Preface

Contours of Christian Theology covers the main themes of Christian doctrine. The series offers a systematic presentation of most of the major doctrines in a way which complements the traditional textbooks but does not copy them. Top priority has been given to contemporary issues, some of which may not be dealt with elsewhere from an evangelical point of view. The series aims, however, not merely to answer current objections to evangelical Christianity, but also to rework the orthodox evangelical position in a fresh and compelling way. The overall thrust is therefore positive and evangelistic in the best sense.

The series is intended to be of value to theological students at all levels, whether at a Bible college, a seminary or a secular university. It should also appeal to ministers and to educated laypeople. As far as possible, efforts have been made to make technical vocabulary accessible to the non-specialist reader, and the presentation has avoided the extremes of academic style. Occasionally this has meant that particular issues have been presented without a thorough argument, taking into account different positions, but when this has happened, authors have been encouraged to refer the reader to other works which take the discussion further. For this purpose adequate but not exhaustive notes have been provided.

The doctrines covered in the series are not exhaustive, but have been chosen in response to contemporary concerns. The title and general presentation of each volume are at the discretion of the author, but final editorial decisions have been taken by the Series Editor in consultation with IVP.

In offering this series to the public, the authors and the publishers hope that it will meet the needs of theological students in this generation, and bring honour and glory to God the Father, and to his Son, Jesus Christ, in whose service the work has been undertaken from the beginning.

Gerald Bray
Series Editor

Preface

What does it mean to be human?

Any answer involves two interacting foci. One is our world-view, even if it is not explicitly formed; in the case of this book, it is biblically based Christian faith. The other is our life experience: family relations, where and when we live, language(s) spoken, what we do, and all the many other factors touching everyday life.

For someone living in a Los Angeles suburb, human life is shaped by a mixture of Spanish and English language and cultures, and is strongly influenced by the motor car and television. An Indian villager may find life dominated by constant concern over water supply, Hindu or Muslim religious life – and television. Someone who works as a banker in Switzerland will be at home with two or more languages, find life-threatening hunger unthinkable, and have easy access to a rich cultural heritage (and television from four nations in six languages). A midwife in China will think in Asian ways, and be formed deeply by experiences peculiar to women. And the human existence of each of these individuals would be very different if they had lived a hundred or a thousand years ago.

How then do you respond to the question of what it means to be human? This book aims to help you shape your own answer, in the light of the Christian faith. My hope is that through reading and reflecting on it, you will be enabled to integrate the treasure of Christian perspectives on being human with your own distinctive life and lifestyle.

My own life experience inevitably affects my writing, so let me say something about myself. I am male, a middle-aged Australian of English and Irish descent, married to my Anglican parish priest (and co-theologian), with two adult sons. Originally from Sydney, then Canberra, the inner suburbs of Melbourne have been my home for twenty-five years, though I have lived for a year at a time in Taiwan, the United States, and England. Melbourne, though a city at the end of the earth, is a place where over 150 languages are spoken. My part of it contains not only Anglican, Baptist and Roman Catholic churches, but Greek and Oriental Orthodox parishes, an Islamic mosque, bookshop and butchers, New Age crystal shops, and many people who describe themselves as having no religion. Asides about Australia recur throughout this book; it is important that the particularity of this context be acknowledged.

My own approach to being human is also affected by close involvement, as an Anglican deacon and priest, with many who experience the underside of Australian society and Christianity. At a different level, it is influenced by ecumenical dialogue, especially as a member of the Anglican–Roman Catholic International Commission. All of these influences are framed through the eyes of a faith shaped from birth in a Christian home, influenced by evangelical Christianity in my student years, and matured through professional life as a statistician, theological teacher and writer. This book is thus written from the perspective of mainstream Christian faith. It is a product of reflection on what it means to be human as known in a particular life. You, the reader, are invited to test your own experience of being human against the witness of the Scriptures, for it is only in the conjunction of this witness and experience that a truly contemporary doctrine of humanity can be lived.

I would like to express my thanks to the many human beings who have shaped my reflection and learning in the writing of this book. My parents passed on to me the immeasurable treasure of the grace of Jesus Christ, Emily living out what it means, through much suffering, to hold to an uncluttered passion for truth, and Charles showing the meaning of care for people in all their complexities, potential and need. Jonathan and Peter have pushed me to take with full seriousness the boundaries of faith, society and life, in the bonds of affection. Peta has helped me begin to learn the task of doing theology in the bonds of love between woman and man.

Thank you to Lorri and Bruce Ellis for giving time hospitably to the discussion of the issues of this book; to Mark Burton, Jonathan Bright, and Fay and Greg Magee for reminding me of the importance of humour; to Cathy Laufer for willingness to read, mark, and return manuscripts swiftly; and to Hayden Robson and Colin Lee for patient friendship without strings.

I am grateful for the patience and guidance of David Kingdon, who did much more than arrange for a book to be commissioned and published.

Introduction

Given the sparkling variety of people in our world, can any
single answer be formed to the question of what it means to be
human? The Bible's unique testimony is that to be human
means to be made 'in the image of God'. This visionary,
enigmatic answer is explicated in Christian understanding by
pointing to Jesus Christ, who is both 'the image of the invisible
God' (Col. 1:15) and the image of perfect humanity (Heb. 2:14–
18). In his life, death and resurrection we see what being human
means at its deepest and fullest, but even then we find ourselves
lost for words.[1] A simple formula cannot do justice to the
wonderful mystery of human life.

Exploring human nature entails an unending journey of
living, a journey unique to each person, yet also undertaken in
the company of others. This book seeks to present the
perspectives of mainstream Christian faith upon human living,
as revealed to us in the Christian Scriptures, centred in Jesus
Christ. It is designed particularly as a textbook for theological

students, and so will consider biblical data, historical and contemporary interpretations of it, and theological perspectives upon both. But human life cannot be discussed in the abstract; the reality of life as it is actually experienced must be taken with full seriousness, even by those whose immediate task is the discipline of study. To help with this, when referring to other works on this subject, I have sought to indicate the background of the author concerned, so that the particularity of each contribution is appreciated.[2]

Reflecting on the subject of human nature is like moving around the different areas of an ellipse with two foci. Exploring the biblical affirmation that humans are 'made in the image of God' constitutes Focus 1 of this book, its theological focal point. At first sight this may appear to constitute a rather technical approach to what is a human subject. As Carl Henry has written, however, 'The importance of a proper understanding of the *imago Dei* can hardly be overstated. The answer given to the *imago*-inquiry soon becomes determinative for the entire gamut of doctrinal affirmation. The ramifications are not only theological, but affect every phase of the . . . cultural enterprise as a whole.'[3]

The other focus is the reality of human existence, the tragi-comedy of amazingly gifted creatures made for eternal glory, yet deeply mired in sin, frustration and need. This focus has both communal and personal dimensions, and needs to be considered from both perspectives. We live as social creatures, part of the human race (Focus 2a), but experience life as unique individuals (Focus 2b). Ideally both foci belong together, as they did in Jesus Christ, bringing the ellipse into a perfect circle. In reality, they often seem to be so far apart that the ellipse collapses into a flat line with no content. To commence this exploration of what it means to be human, both foci need to be brought into more detailed view.

The God in whose image we are made

'God' for many people means an abstract force, power or influence. For others 'God' is like the communication cord on a train – for emergency use only. Believers have their understanding of God shaped by the religious tradition from which they have come, and in which they stand. Since we are made in the image of God, the view we have of God will considerably affect our understanding of ourselves as human beings. For example, someone for whom God means an impersonal power will tend to think of human life in terms of abstract force. Conversely, the way in which anyone envisages God says a good deal about his or her personality, experience of life, and priorities. Many of these concepts and ideas are unconscious, formed by our surroundings, culture, friends and family without our realizing it is happening. This does not make them bad, misleading or wrong; but much of what we think about God and being human is taken for granted, and needs to be scrutinized if we are to discern the truth.

Christian faith is grounded in the God revealed in and through the Scriptures.[4] The centre and climax of their presentation of God is Jesus Christ. Christians not only look to Jesus for teaching about God, but acknowledge him to be their Lord, as God come to live with us (1 Cor. 12:1-3; Jn. 1:1-18). Christians pray to and through Jesus, find their sins forgiven through him, look to him to direct their living, and even believe that all that exists involves the activity of Christ (Heb. 10:19-25; Col. 1:15-20). In short, Jesus Christ is 'the image of the invisible God' (Col. 1:15), 'the likeness of God' (2 Cor. 4:4), the one human being who shows us what true humanity, and true divinity, are like. Taking this seriously has led Christians to acknowledge that God is the kind of God who from all eternity could assume our human nature in a personal life. Such a view calls for drastic revisions of some overly philosophical views of God!

Jesus lived some 2,000 years ago: how may we today know God as revealed in him? Jesus promised the Holy Spirit to those who put their trust in him. Through the Spirit they would know the power of his life, death and resurrection, and the true presence of God among them, in their life together (Rom. 8:1-11). To know God through the Spirit is impossible, however, unless the Spirit shares in the very being of God. It took some time for this to be realized by the first Christians; they were more concerned with the practical reality of the Spirit's work in them. Nevertheless, the implication of the God of Jesus being known through the Spirit of Jesus is that this Spirit must be as divine as can be. And if the Spirit is God, then the God of the Bible is the kind of God who can act in every nook and cranny of our lives, and of all life, 'for the Spirit searches everything, even the depths of God' (1 Cor. 2:10).

What sort of God do we know through the Spirit? Jesus spoke of God as his own Father, who welcomes all Jesus' disciples as children. This 'new birth from above' into the divine family takes place through the Spirit (*cf.* Jn. 3:5–7). As Paul wrote, 'When we cry "Abba! Father!" it is that very Spirit bearing witness with our spirit that we are children of God, and if children, then heirs, heirs of God and joint heirs with Christ' (Rom. 8:15–17). Christians thus know the privilege of prayer through Jesus Christ, in the Spirit, to their Father in heaven. God is revealed in this way as 'the God and Father of our Lord Jesus Christ' (Eph. 1:3; 1 Cor. 1:3). This heavenly Father cares for all the children of God, and is generous, forgiving, fair and faithful (Mt. 6:1–18). This picture contrasts markedly with the popular idea of God as a distant, unconcerned deity who is indifferent to human needs.

Putting all this together, Christian faith names God as 'Father, Son and Spirit', the holy Trinity. Thus baptism, the sign and seal of Christian identity, is into (lit.) 'the name of the Father and of the Son and of the Holy Spirit' (Mt. 28:20). Again, Christians pray not so much 'to' a distant deity, but in and through Christ, in the Spirit, to their heavenly Father. The nature of the one true God is thus far deeper, holier and more beautiful than the plain, featureless deity many people think of as 'God'. Divine unity is more like the harmony of a close family or group of friends than the stark sameness of a block of ice. Only of this trinitarian God can we say, 'God is love' (1 Jn. 4:16). And when it comes to thinking about being human as being 'made in the image of God', this vision of God makes a great deal of difference. From the beginning of our discussion it is vital to be clear about how we image God, before we begin to explore what being made in the image of God as human beings may mean.

Now it is time to turn to the other focus of the ellipse, lest the study fail to be grounded in the reality of life as we know it today.

Human life in today's world

Human societies have been classified into three 'worlds' in recent decades. By the 'First World' is meant the countries of Western Europe, and nations which have developed from its culture, especially the USA, but also others such as Canada, Australia and New Zealand. What characterizes them is their common roots in the movements known as the Reformation, Renaissance and Enlightenment, and their inheritance of the Industrial Revolution, with succeeding developments in transport and communications, public health, and education, which most of their citizens take for granted. The 'Second World' refers to Eastern Europe, influenced less by the Reformation and Renaissance, but dominated until recently by the socialist revolutions of the earlier part of this century. The view of being human commonly held in the First World stresses the rights of the individual; that held in the Second World focuses (at least in theory) on the needs of the wider community. The one emphasizes private life; the other has tended towards totalitarianism.

The term 'Third World' has become synonymous with poverty, oppression and deprivation, but more properly it refers to nations whose identity came to be subsumed under that of colonizing European powers. In these areas of the world much of human life is dominated by ancient ways of living, whether tribal (as in Africa), or philosophical and intellectual (as in China); or by particular religious traditions (as in the Indian subcontinent and the Arabic world). In each case, however, these inheritances interact with trends derived from Europe, and all three 'worlds' exist side by side in most countries. Australia is a case in point, with its indigenous peoples, immigrant and refugee communities, and distinctive urban and rural lifestyles.

I have drawn attention to these major variations in the contemporary world for two reasons. The first is to illustrate the sheer variety of human existence, the complex web of interactive traditions and the multitude of overlapping subcultures in which we experience life. It is impossible to keep every possibility in mind at each stage of the discussion, but the variety of approaches must not be forgotten. This particularly applies to the way in which we read and interpret the Scriptures in trying to understand ourselves. Other areas of Christian belief may allow for less ambiguity, to the extent that they deal with realities which transcend any particular human experience. But the doctrine of humanity can never be studied without our own context coming to the fore; it is like a fish trying to think objectively about water![5] The second reason for the above sketch, simplistic though it may be, is to draw attention to the major influences on ideas about what it means to be human. We now turn to a brief outline of these, to set the context for a fuller discussion with our eyes as wide open as possible.[6]

The *Reformation* focused several significant emphases in European assumptions about being human, primarily but not exclusively in Protestant areas. First was a strong stress on the significance of each person before God, without the necessity of any human mediation, although human institutions, both social and ecclesial, were acknowledged and used as God's good provision for the ordering of corporate life. Secondly, along with this went an emphasis upon the particular vocation to which each Christian was called, not just clergy, monks or nuns. But vocation was not seen as earning one's salvation, for the Reformers denied that human nature by itself was capable of coming to know God in any saving way. Sin did not merely 'deprive' us of the good, while leaving us capable of playing some part in responding to the grace of God. Rather, sin 'depraved' us, so that we can become right with God only through faith in Christ, and need new birth through the Spirit to do so. Thirdly, the use of everyday language for liturgy, and the availability of the Scriptures in languages other than Latin, meant that education and learning began to spread beyond the upper classes of society. Finally, the Reformation's stress on the sanctity of the 'secular' world changed attitudes to nature, freeing thinkers to begin to explore this world as a place where God's truth was available.

This last, desacralizing shift went hand in hand with the flourishing of the arts and literature in a movement which interacted with the Reformation, the *Renaissance*. The latter, however, had its basis in a rediscovery of the majesty of humankind in and of itself, rather than primarily in scriptural revelation about human existence defined in relation to God.

The *Enlightenment* followed both movements in the eighteenth century. It continued the Reformation emphasis on the significance of the individual, but tended to displace the gospel of grace by stress upon the adequacy of human reason. This came about in part because religious differences were perceived as leading causes of the disastrous wars which racked Europe in the seventeenth century. The rejection of the authority of the church gradually became a rejection of any theological authority. Human reason came to be regarded by many as the only adequate resource for guiding human life. To the extent that this represented a genuine self-confidence in the human spirit, and the overthrow of tyrannous ideologies, it was welcomed by many Christians, especially those who were persecuted because they rejected state control of religion. Yet such an exaltation of reason also tended to squeeze God out of human affairs. David Kelsey argues that it was not until human beings came to think of themselves as independent, self-existent 'subjects' that theologians began to consider 'human nature' as a study in its own right.[7] The ongoing influence of the Enlightenment continues in the modern stress on the liberty and rights of the individual, seen at its best in the democratic impulse, but also in 'secular humanism', where humankind is the measure of all things.

Enlightenment ideas would possibly not have come to dominate so much of the modern world, however, without the *Industrial Revolution*. By this is meant the rapid series of discoveries and inventions from 1700 onwards, which brought about mass production. Critical here was the discovery of a process of smelting iron to make steel, and the invention of the steam engine, both made in England, and by active Christians.[8] It is hard to put ourselves back to the time when the only power available was that of human or animal muscles, supplemented to some extent by the use of water-wheels and windmills. Iron and steam, soon to be accompanied by electricity and the internal combustion engine, had profound effects on human society in the nineteenth century. Slowly but surely they changed the way we think about human life. To take a simple example, consider the way 'light' works as a symbol. Where light is available at the flick of a switch, the transition from day to night, summer to winter, is far less significant than where candles and oil lamps

22

are the only ways of banishing the darkness of night. In the world of 1990, the theological claim that 'Christ is the light of the world' thus carries nuances quite different from those it carried in 1790. Again, the liturgical use of candles is today wholly symbolic, whereas only a century or so ago it had practical functions as well. Such examples could be multiplied; the point is that most of the time we simply accept them, without realizing how significantly they affect our imagination, our reading of the Scriptures, and especially our self-understanding as human beings.

The coming of industry also led to profound social changes, particularly the rapid growth of large cities, the gradual end of subsistence lifestyles (continuing, with much pain, in slum areas today) and the spread of suburban living. Combined with Enlightenment ideas, the Industrial Revolution enabled the rapid development of capitalism, the mechanization of armaments, and the rapid expansion of scientific research. As a result, many have come to see human beings as themselves capable of providing answers to life's problems through the sciences, especially medicine and technology. This worldview is widespread today, not only in the relatively few people committed to secular humanism, but far more widely in the everyday assumptions made by nearly everyone.[9]

The Industrial Revolution also fuelled the colonial expansion of European powers which characterized the nineteenth century. *Colonialism* saw European technical and administrative skill spread over much of the world. This commonly took the form of exploiting the resources of Africa, Asia and India for the benefit of Europe, although it also brought the benefits of literacy (in previously oral cultures) and modern medicine. Along with the expansion of European culture went the spread of the Christian faith, so that Christianity was becoming a universal religion in practice as well as in claim, encompassing people of every place and language. The rapid development of new forms of *communication* has further shifted human consciousness. Steam ships and trains unified nations internally (especially the USA), or were instrumental in defining their boundaries, while mass newspapers helped to forge common bonds among citizens. Air transport has brought the world as a whole together, while radio and television have fostered the (often deceptive) sense that we all are neighbours in a 'global village'. In the last few years, the amazingly rapid growth in information technology via computers, fax machines, mobile phones, e-mail and the internet has given many of its users the sense that this village has now arrived. As one involved in journalism, I am well aware of the benefits of the information superhighway, but am also concerned about the decreased amount of actual human contact that it often involves. Whatever the future holds with regard to communication, many children now at school are growing up with assumptions about human nature and life very different from those of their grandparents.

The general standard of *education* has risen sharply since 1945, especially in the First World. My grandparents, storekeepers and homemakers, considered primary school sufficient for most of their children; my own parents knew themselves privileged to have been able to complete high school (one did so at night); yet my children's generation regards a tertiary qualification as almost essential. Even though functional illiteracy is growing in some educationally rich nations, being human today entails a keen awareness of events and trends, both local and global, in a manner inconceivable by earlier generations. On the other hand, local cultural patterns are increasingly being subsumed into a general culture dominated by television and the English language, especially under American influence. A distinct youth culture (with many sub-cultures) has developed, as the beginnings of work and marriage are deferred in favour of education – or unemployment and homelessness. Sexual permissiveness has become commonplace as contraception has become widely available, and moral values have broken down with the spread of both material prosperity and desperate poverty.

Yet empires, both commercial and national, were built on the sweat and suffering of factory labour and exploited native peoples. Such abuses saw many people of conscience begin not merely to seek to change the way societies worked, but to look for new forms of human corporate life. A revolutionary spirit began to sweep the world, fuelled by the ideas of Marx and Engels. The labour movement has become a permanent feature of the First World, while totalitarian Communism ruled the Second World until very recently. Though varied in particular times and places, democratic, anti-discriminatory ideals now permeate human thinking. For example, the internationally co-ordinated actions taken against apartheid in South Africa would have been unthinkable a hundred years ago, but carried widespread assent in the late twentieth century. There are sharp limits to such actions, however: the Tian An Men Square massacre in Peking, and the brutal events in the former Yugoslavia and the old Soviet Union, drew little practical response from the rest of the world, for example. Nevertheless, that such events are widely noticed and protested about is evidence of the gaining replacement of nationalist by egalitarian ideals in many places.

The rapid spread of industry, and the resulting enormous demand for energy resources, has affected the way we think about the world in which we live. Air and water pollution, and long-term factors such as the thinning of the ozone layer, are major contemporary issues, and raise many questions about life in industrial societies. Rejection of the expansionist mentality behind much modern living has led many in the West to be more open to eastern ideas. Ecology has thus become linked with spirituality for some, while bringing changes in such daily issues as rubbish disposal, recycling and energy consciousness for many more. Ecology concerns the future of the planet, its plant and animal life, and the human race as a whole, but it is not always easy to link these general issues with everyday life. Most people see political or economic issues as remote from their daily concerns, unless they themselves are directly involved. Each of us, however, is a woman or a man, and sexuality touches us at the most intimate level. Because of this personal focus, *feminism* represents another significant move-ment affecting human life today. In the past it was commonly assumed that the model for humanity is individual and male; such an idea would now be labelled as sexist by many. The ideals of feminism look towards co-operative rather than competitive personal relationships; it thus shares some traits with socialism, but is more characteristically linked with ecology and spirituality.

The phrase 'the doctrine of man' betrays the assumption that normative humanity is male (Appendix 2 discusses inclusive-language issues). It is a doctrine which has often been dominated by individualistic perspectives, and has rarely included women in its purview.[10] Where this has been the case, women are usually discussed in a special section, implying that they are a special form of human, but not quite as 'norm'-al as men.[11] Such an approach poses sharply the question which formed the title of a book by Dorothy L. Sayers, *Are Women Human?*[12] The reformulation of the doctrine of humanity today needs to do more than talk about women, or involve them only as bringing a special perspective. The doctrine must involve a truly common search, itself embodying the fellowship in and for which we were and are made, men and women together, in the image of God.

All these factors, issues and movements raise both questions and opportunities for Christian theology, not least in reflecting on what being made in God's image means today. None of us can avoid having attitudes, both conscious and unconscious, that shape our approach to the many facets of the world in which we live, especially our own place in its life and history. An element of tentativeness is thus appropriate for particular theological responses given in particular contexts to the question of what being human means. Where such responses remain wholly tentative, they can become so vague as to lose all shape. If one focus of our study must be human life today, in both its social and personal dimensions, the other and more fundamental one must be the question of what the Scriptures mean in their affirmation that we are 'made in the image of God'. That question forms the first Focus of this book.

FOCUS 1

MADE IN THE
IMAGE OF GOD

1

THE IMAGE OF GOD IN ANCIENT ISRAEL

To be human is to be 'made in the image of God'.[1] This is the basic premise from which ancient Israel's understanding of being human proceeds. What does this enigmatic phrase mean, however? The actual formula occurs in only a few texts: in the Hebrew Scriptures, three to be precise, the second and third of them variations on the first, fundamental reference. As with a number of doctrines, that of the 'image of God' thus has a small textual base, yet its importance in the Scriptures and Christian thought far exceeds this.

Foundation texts: a preliminary survey

The significance of our being made in the image of God is emphasized by its placement in the first chapter of the Scriptures. In Genesis 1 the structure of creation is unfolded, as the 'six days, morning and evening' of God's work are described, reaching their climax in the seventh day of rest. At the end of the six days of divine work, and placed as its high point, we read of the creation of human beings.[2]

Genesis 1:26–28

[26]Then God said, 'Let us make humankind ['ādām] in our image [ṣelem], according to our likeness [dᵉmût]; and let them have dominion over the fish of the sea, and over the birds of the air, and over the cattle, and over all the wild animals of the earth and over [all] the earth.
[27]So God created humankind [hā'ādām] in his image [ṣelem],

in the image [ṣelem] of God he created [him];
male and female he created them.
[28]God blessed them, and God said to them, 'Be fruitful and multiply, and fill the earth and subdue it; and have dominion over the fish of the sea and over the birds of the air and over every living thing that moves upon the earth.'

The content of this foundational text is expanded in Genesis 2, from the perspective of the origin of human life rather than creation as a whole (this is taken up below). But the text itself is repeated, in summary form, in Genesis 5:2–3, after the exclusion of Adam and Eve from Eden, and following the tragedy of Cain and Abel. It introduces the genealogy of the first humans, setting the scene for the flood narrative (Gn. 6 – 9).

Genesis 5:1–2

[1]This is the list of the descendants of Adam ['ādām]. When God created humankind [ha'ādām], he made [him] in the likeness [dᵉmût] of God. [2]Male and female he created them, and he blessed them and named them 'Humankind' [hā'ādām] when they were created.

The final text from the Hebrew Scriptures which mentions our being made 'in the image of God' also reiterates Genesis 1:26–28. It comes at the end of the flood narrative, as part of God's blessing of Noah before making a covenant with him and his posterity that reopens hope for the human race.

Genesis 9:6–7

> [6]"Whoever sheds the blood of a human,
>   by a human shall that person's blood be shed;
>   for in his own image [*ṣelem*]
>   God made humankind [*hā'āḏām*].
> [7]And you, be fruitful and multiply, abound on the
> earth and multiply in it.'

Being made 'in the image of God' is thus the way we are described at three critical turning-points in the Genesis account: at the highpoint of God's creative activity, at the beginning of the new stage of human history after the tragic events of Eden, and in the midst of God's new beginning with the human race after the judgment of the flood. In placing these texts at such key positions, the opening book of the Bible emphasizes that the concept of being made in the image of God is of fundamental importance to what it means to be human. The actual phrase may not recur again in the Hebrew Scriptures, but it undergirds all that is said and disclosed about human nature from this point on in Israel's history, and in the broader human canvas against which Israel's story is told. Further, it is taken up in the New Testament, and deepened in the light of Christ, in and through whom human nature is orientated to future hope as well as past glory.

Despite their importance, however, none of these passages tells us what the 'image of God' actually *is.* Scholars have interpreted it in a number of ways, examined in more detail in chapter 3 below.[3] Before looking at the texts more closely, the second (or second part of the first) commandment should be considered.

Exodus 20:4–5 (Deuteronomy 5:8–9)

> You shall not make for yourself an idol [lit. 'graven image', *pesel*], whether in the form [*temûnâ*] of anything that is in heaven above, or that is on the earth beneath, or that is in the water under the earth. You shall not bow down to them or worship them.

Here the concept of an image for God recurs, though the Hebrew terms used are different. Israel, and all who enter into

Israel's covenant with God, are called to reject any form of idolatry (the giving of honour and allegiance to any creature, rather than to God). The prohibition of image-making here is related to the denial of any depiction of God, who transcends physical limitation.[4] Traditionally, Jews (and, later, Muslims) understood this imperative so strictly as to avoid all forms of pictorial art, as well as statues.[5] Christians have generally not been so strict, because the incarnation of Christ, the express image of God, has been understood as giving permission, or even requiring, such artistic expression of theology, as in the Orthodox tradition. Even when such art is used, however, considerable care is taken to avoid the merest whiff of idolatry.[6]

Given this deep sensitivity to the danger of idolatry, in what sense can we speak of humankind as the 'image of God'? In the first place, though it is clearly legitimate to *describe* human beings in image terms, attempts to *define* the image of God precisely are fraught with danger. God cannot be defined, and any endeavour on our part to do so constitutes idolatry (*cf.* Is. 44:9–20). This prohibition does not remove the great privilege we have, given divine revelation, of speaking of and to God our Father, through Christ and the Holy Spirit. Yet it points to great caution in the way we think about the image of this indefinable God. To worship other than God is idolatry; to make a graven image is the practical form of idolatry, even though the 'graving' be mental rather than physical. More, trying to define the image of God is trying to define ourselves, since we are made in his image. The mystery of what it means to be human transcends such attempts to control either divine or human nature (*cf.* Ps. 8:4–8). Defining ourselves in terms of ourselves borders on pride, since it means exchanging the worship of the Creator for the worship of the creature (*cf.* Rom. 1:19–25). Even though human beings have been assigned by God the highest place in creation, creatures we remain. We belong to God, not God to us. Philip Hughes cites the English Reformer Hugh Latimer's preaching against images covered with gold, clothed in silk garments, and laden with precious gems and jewels:[7] '. . . whereas in the meantime we see Christ's faithful and lively images, bought with no less price than his most precious blood, alas, alas, to be an-hungered, a-thirst, a-cold, and to lie in darkness, wrapped in all wretchedness'. From such a perspective many approaches to what the image of God entails are ruled out. The Scriptures do not locate the image in some aspect or other of human life, or in any combination of aspects, but utilize the concept with some reserve. In short, if we are not told in the Scriptures what the 'image of God' *is*, we should not expect to know.

This observation points to the need for a more open exegesis of Genesis. Rather than asking, 'What is the image of God?' we are invited to explore the question, 'What does it mean to be made in the image of God?' In this way we acknowledge that we live as those who know our status as bearing the divine image. Rather than trying to tie this notion down, perhaps so that we may control both ourselves and God, the Scriptures call us to a pilgrimage of discovering both God and our own selves. And, as Augustine argued, only on such a spiritual journey may the meaning of the classic philosophical advice, 'Know thyself, and to thyself be true', take on a deeper, and truly Christian, meaning.[8] This, it seems to me, is one aspect of what Jesus was getting at in his famous phrase, 'Render . . . unto Caesar the things which are Caesar's, and unto God the things that are God's' (Mt. 22:21; Mk. 12:17; Lk. 20:25).[9] He had asked for a coin, and pointed out that it was stamped with Caesar's likeness and inscription. The coin is made in the image of Caesar, but human beings are made in the image of God. Jesus is not here asking for money, or seeking respect for religious sites as 'God's property' (as Ambrose later took him to imply), but calling for men and women to give their wholehearted allegiance to the One in whose image they are made.

With this caution in mind, it is now time to discuss the texts themselves. The exegesis which follows seeks to lay a basis for assessing the manner in which the image of God has been considered in the Christian tradition. It is by no means the last word on the subject, but does take a stand on a number of issues of contemporary interest. The argument needs to be assessed by each reader in his or her own context of being human; after all, the text matters more than any particular exegesis of it.[10]

Humanity as the climax of creation: Genesis 1:26–28

At least three facets of this text call for attention at this point, though they do not exhaust its meaning or significance.

First, God speaks in the plural: 'Let *us* make humankind in *our* image.'[11] Christians have sometimes seen an explicit reference to the Trinity here, yet this reads too much into the text. The word for 'God' (*ᵉlōhîm*) is itself a plural form, but only here in the Scriptures does it take a plural verb. Commentators suggest that the plural may derive from pre-Israelite forms, or that it is a plural of intensity or majesty, akin to the English 'royal we'. A more likely possibility is that it alludes to the concept of the 'heavenly assembly', the 'host' depicted as surrounding God in the heavenlies (*cf.* Pss. 8; 82).[12] From a more directly theological viewpoint, the concept of divine self-deliberation has been suggested: God 'reflects' before creating humankind.[13] Following on from this insight, and the highly original exegetical work of Karl Barth, the idea of plurality within God has been put forward, a notion not inconsistent with the revelation of God's triune nature as disclosed in Christ.[14] However it may relate to the doctrine of the Trinity, it is an interpretation which is coherent with the portrayal of the oneness of God in the Hebrew Scriptures: not a plain, undifferentiated unity, but dynamic and active. God is the sovereign Lord, whom 'heaven and the highest heaven cannot contain', yet who chooses to 'dwell on the earth' (1 Ki. 8:27). A number of terms are used in the Old Testament to speak of God's personal presence and activity on earth, such as the 'glory', 'angel', 'voice', 'wisdom', 'word' and 'spirit' of the Lord, all suggesting an internal dynamism within God.[15] It is terms such as these that New Testament writers quarried in exploring the significance of God's presence in Christ and the Spirit.

How significant is this for understanding what it means to be made in the image of God? Barth suggests that the plural corresponds to the plurality within the image of God in humanity: God created us as 'male and female', as a race in which there subsists an inherent plurality. Many assume that 'humankind' refers here to one original human person, Adam, presumably male, but the Hebrew vocabulary used in Genesis 1

34

does not carry such a meaning. The word *'ēt'ādām* (verse 27), including the accusative particle *'ēt*, is a collective noun meaning 'humankind', 'humanity', the race as a whole, rather than the proper name *'ādām*, 'Adam', which first occurs at Genesis 3:17.[16] Thus, although the plural pronoun in the divine address may allude to something in the nature of God, it more clearly alerts us to plurality within humanity. In the light of this, it can be concluded that being made in the image of God is not an aspect of or in each distinct person, but points to the personal relationships within which humanity lives.[17]

Secondly, as a further explication of this, being made as 'male and female' is closely associated with being made in the image of God. It is this aspect which is repeated in Genesis 5:2, so it is scarcely a chance reference. Barth explains it as denoting the 'fellowship' which distinguishes humanity: we are not made as fellow man and fellow man, or fellow woman and fellow woman, but as male and female, man and woman.[18] Some, however, deny that being male and female has anything to do with the 'image of God'. Hughes, for example, rightly rejects the notion of an original androgynous being (as in the Platonic tradition), but goes on to argue that gender is 'additional and not explanatory' of the image. However, he confuses gender with sexuality, relating 'male and female' exclusively to the (earlier) command to 'be fruitful and multiply'.[19] Further, having correctly observed that Genesis 1:27 refers to humanity in the plural, so marking the distinctness of male and female human persons, he fails to note that it also employs the singular, indicating their unity in diversity.[20] In reality, there is nothing else more alike in creation than women and men, who are nevertheless distinct. We do not relate as like with like only, but, as von Rad writes, 'By God's will, man was not created alone but designated for the "thou" of the other sex.'[21] As God is no plain, undifferentiated monad, but living and active, dynamic and personal, so is humankind: we are made for harmonious relationship.

This insight about the fellowship of men and women is developed further in later chapters, but it should be noted in passing that Barth was not primarily interested in affirming the equality of male and female. It is their *differentiation* in unity which he affirmed. Such differentiation is not restricted to gender, but can be seen in other varieties within the human race: language, skills, culture, occupation, interests and so on.[22] But these latter categories are all changeable, and can be learnt or developed. Maleness and femaleness are fundamental: we are made as both male and female, and also as male or female.[23] Thus being gendered is a basic facet of being human. Our being either a man or a woman emphasizes the distinct particularlity and value of each individual (*cf.* Gn. 9:6), while our being both men and women as human beings points to the relational nature of personal existence.

Thirdly, the relationship between humankind and other living creatures is denoted in verse 28 by the term 'have dominion' (*yrd*).[24] Humanity, formed at the climax of the six-day narrative, and as the result of divine reflection, is the only part of creation addressed by God, and told to 'be fruitful and multiply, and fill the earth and subdue it' (Gn. 1:28; 9:7; *cf.* Ps. 8:4–8). In the ancient world, as Westermann puts it, humans are made by the gods to 'relieve the gods of the burden of daily drudgery'. In the biblical account, however, 'Man is created not to minister to the gods but to civilize the earth.' The command to 'be fruitful' is God's blessing, not an automatic reality, and reinforces the kinship of humanity with the animals: 'the blessing . . . is something that binds man and beast together'.[25] Only when this is appreciated can the creation mandate to 'have dominion' and 'subdue' be understood aright. It has always been acknowledged in Christian thought, though the privileges involved have not uncommonly been emphasized at the expense of the responsibility which such dominion entails.

It is the distortion of human dominion over other creatures which allows ecologists such as Lynn White to accuse Christian doctrine of being a major source for the problems which have resulted from unrestrained exploitation of the earth.[26] In the light of this, some would translate the term by less dominating words, such as 'manage'; Carl Henry suggests that to 'subdue the earth' means 'to consecrate it to the spiritual service of God and man'.[27] Yet the term 'dominion' does carry hierarchical overtones; we do have considerable power over other aspects of creation, and it is dangerous both ecologically and theologically to deny it. The issue is what we do with this dominion, not whether it exists (see further in chapters 4 and 5). For the moment, note that nothing is said about locating dominion in the mind, reasoning power, or soul; it entails concrete relationships, not interior attitudes. Nor is the image of God defined by way of contrasting humanity and the animal world; the differences between them are the result of humanity's being made in the divine image.

It is also notable that in cultures of the ancient Near East 'it is the king who is the image of God, not mankind generally'.[28] In the biblical accounts, the giving of dominion to humanity universally over the animals and earth has a further consequence, that 'man is not created to exercise dominion over man'.[29] Finally, contemporary feminism argues that acceptance of the partnership between women and men is cognate with a more responsible 'gyn-ecology', since the assumption that men are the human norm often goes along with an exploitative attitude towards nature (see chapters 5 and 8 below). Genesis takes none of these paths, but emphasizes that dominion involves relationships and responsibilities incumbent upon the human race as a whole, men and women together.

This examination of these foundational texts shows that to be made in the image of God entails two dimensions of relationship. Being male and female speaks of a 'horizontal', social, relationship, while dominion has a 'vertical' reference, in a twofold direction. 'Upwards', we are to acknowledge our unique relationship with God, as creatures made to hear and respond in obedience to God's address. 'Downwards', we are designated as God's 'vice-regents', called to manage and utilize together the created world, not as wholly independent agents, but as persons accountable to our Creator.

Looking back over this exegetical work, it becomes clear that while we are not told what the image of God *is*, we are shown something of what being made in the image of God *involves*: living in a series of relationships.[30] These can be expressed as in Diagram 1.[31] The creation account in Genesis 1:1 – 2:4 is structured at what might be termed the 'macro' level, moving from the cosmic to the particular, having as its climax humanity created in the image of God. The text continues, however, in Genesis 2:4–25 at the 'micro' level, moving from the ground up (literally) to describe, in an unfolding pattern, the emergence of the human race. In short, if Genesis 1 describes creation from a broad, cosmological perspective, with human beings made as

---

God: self-related in 'unity in diversity' as the triune Lord

↕   relationship of obedience and praise

Humanity: self-related in 'unity in diversity' as male and female

↕   relationship of dominion

Creation

Diagram 1: The structure of the 'image of God' in Genesis 1

---

its climax, Genesis 2:4–25 describes creation from a human rather than cosmological perspective, with humanity at full maturity by its end. And both have a future orientation as well: the mystery of what it means to be human awaits further disclosure, signalled in each week's conclusion in the sabbath which reflects the divine holy rest of blessedness.

Creation: a human perspective: Genesis 2:4–25

No explicit mention is made of the image of God in Genesis 2, but the various facets of the above diagram can be clearly seen. As before, three points can be made.

First, humanity is described as having material reality: 'the LORD God formed man [*hā'ādām*] from the dust of the ground [*hā'ʿdāmâ*]' – 'earthlings' from 'earth', so to speak (Gn. 2:7). Our nature is firmly 'earthed' or 'grounded' in the world of nature, yet we owe our organic life as 'living beings' (*nepeš hayyâ*) to God's active giving of life (Gn. 2:7b).[32] It is important to note that *nepeš* is applied in the Scriptures to animal life generally, not to a 'soul' within us (see chapter 10). We may properly be described as 'spiritual' creatures, if by that is meant that we are made as 'spirited' beings with vitality and energy, made for relationship with God who is 'spirit'. But such a term must not be used to undermine the reality of our earthiness; we are 'dust, and to dust [we] shall return' (Gn. 3:19). If Genesis 1 describes us from the 'top down' in our diagram, Genesis 2 begins from 'bottom up', emphasizing our material commonality with all other creatures.

Secondly, a task is given to the human race (*hā'ādām*), to till and keep the garden which is the earth (Gn. 2:15).[33] This corresponds to the downward aspect of the dominion spoken of in Genesis 1:26–28. Likewise, the power of speech, of 'naming' – and thereby determining the respective roles of those named – expresses the exercise of this dominion over the animals (Gn. 2:19). The upwards aspect of dominion is marked by the tree of knowing (Gn. 2:16–17). In acknowledging this limit placed upon human activity, our obedience to the dominion of God as our Lord is indicated. In each of these ways the upward and downward vertical aspects of being made in the image of God are explicated.

Thirdly, we read that God says, 'It is not good that humanity should be solitary' (Gn. 2:18, my own rendering). Most translations imply that a single person is spoken of here, and that person a male: for example, 'it is not good that the man should be alone' (NRSV, even though this version is sensitive to gender-language issues). Some defend this translation on the grounds that any alternative would imply the creation of an androgynous being, which is nowhere even hinted at in the Scriptures.[34] The text, however, points in another direction: up to this stage in Genesis 2 the human creature, unlike its Creator, resembles a plain oneness. This is 'not good', and falls short of God's full creative intention (cf. Gn. 1:31). Further, such a 'solitary' being has needs which cannot be met from the animal kingdom; the 'naming' indicates the dominion which characterizes human relations with the beasts, rather than a fellowship between equals. What is needed is a co-partner, one to work with, not for, the other, as God does with us (cf. Ex. 18:4; Dt. 33:7).[35]

So God takes a new initiative, separating humanity (hā'ādām) into man ('iš) and woman ('iššâ), male and female persons; we can now speak of he and she. This explicates the 'horizontal' relationship within which we live as made in the image of God. How such a literary image corresponds to literal biological reality it is impossible to say; it is as unhelpful to suppose that pre-division humanity was male as it is to think of it as androgynous or hermaphrodite.[36] Rather, the text testifies powerfully to the unity in diversity of male and female in the exultant cry of the man, 'This at last is bone of my bones and flesh of my flesh' (Gn. 2:23). Or, as rabbinic tradition put it neatly, the woman was not taken from the head, to dominate, or from the feet, to serve, but from the side, to be a co-partner. The chapter continues with the remarkable comment, 'Therefore a man leaves his father and mother, and cleaves to his woman' (my translation). It concludes by stressing the togetherness of the now differentiated *hā'ādām*: the two 'become one flesh', and that with no shame (Gn. 2:24–25). This is the reverse of what we might expect. On the one hand, rather than some mystical vision of the human spirit, we have set before us the earthy reality of physical creatures made for deep relationship. On the other hand, it is the male who follows the female in establishing once more the unity in diversity of 'one flesh', the microcosm of humanity which is seen in marriage.[37]

One further note: children are not mentioned in Genesis 2. Marriage is here depicted as the one-flesh, exclusive relationship of a man and a woman, complete in itself; children are an added gift from the Lord. The command to 'be fruitful and multiply' (Gn. 1:28, repeated in Gn. 9:7) is a consequence of being made in the image of God, one aspect of exercising dominion, rather than directly tied to full human identity. Fruitfulness is wider than procreation, and in Genesis 1:28 it applies to all humanity, and each human within it, whether married or not. Procreation is thus a distinctive aspect of marital fruitfulness, but does not exhaust its meaning. This perspective is confirmed by Genesis 5:2, where humanity's being made in the image of God as male and female is reiterated, yet without mention of children. In the light of this, to limit the significance of gender to procreation is as restrictive as relating it only to sexual union; if the first is too narrow, the other is too hedonistic. On the one hand, being made as male and female (gender) is wider and deeper than sexuality. On the other, sexuality has procreation as a key purpose, a purpose which must not be rejected, but is not exclusive of others.[38]

In sum, it is only at the *end* of Genesis 2 that it is proper to speak of humanity's being fully 'made in the image of God', of which God can say, 'it is *very* good' (as in Gn. 1:31). There is thus an impressive coherence between the two creation accounts with regard to human nature, with their balancing macro/cosmological and micro/personal perspectives. This coherence can be seen in Diagram 2, an expansion of Diagram 1, combining both structures.

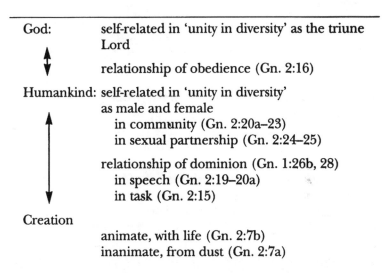

God:	self-related in 'unity in diversity' as the triune Lord
↕	relationship of obedience (Gn. 2:16)
Humankind:	self-related in 'unity in diversity' as male and female
	in community (Gn. 2:20a–23)
	in sexual partnership (Gn. 2:24–25)
	relationship of dominion (Gn. 1:26b, 28)
	in speech (Gn. 2:19–20a)
	in task (Gn. 2:15)
Creation	
	animate, with life (Gn. 2:7b)
	inanimate, from dust (Gn. 2:7a)

Diagram 2:   *The structure of the 'image of God' in Genesis 1 – 2*

Let me emphasize once more that nowhere are we told precisely what the image of God *is*. Rather, we have shown to us something of what it means to be made in the image of God. We are given a dynamic model of what being made in the image of God *involves*, not a static picture of its essence. It entails being called, as members of the human race (corporately male *and* female, and personally male *or* female), to live by obedience to God in human community, through creative stewardship. Thus the image of God can be seen only as we live it out, both as persons in community (chapter 4), and as individual people (chapters 7–10), and in both respects as those who are to grow up into the life of God.

Concern with the 'vertical' dimension is clearly indispensable here. The 'downward' aspect of this means that issues such as the environment (chapter 5) and culture (chapter 6) come into view. But its 'upward' aspect, our relationship with God, is of prime concern, since without this the other relationships become distorted. The grandeur, potential, privilege and responsibilities of humankind are depicted in the first two chapters of Genesis, as we have seen. By contrast, the capacity of human beings for deceit, corruption and despair is vividly portrayed in the third chapter. Without this latter perspective only a one-sided picture

41

of what it now means to be human has been given. To understand the whole story, a look at Genesis 3 is necessary.

The image distorted: Genesis 3:1–21

Genesis 3 opens with the woman showing full knowledge of the clear and simple task of obedience: all that was necessary was not to eat the fruit of one single tree. Yet the sin described in Genesis 3 was no mere peccadillo, an unlucky choice of fruit. Tiny though it may appear in itself, it entailed the wilful rejection of God as Lord, bringing dire consequences. The serpent's craftiness is particularly seen in the comment that the man and woman would be 'like God' (or 'gods') if they ate the forbidden fruit (Gn. 3:5). This suggests that human beings need to achieve something in order to be 'like God', whereas their status is *already* that of being made in the image and likeness of God. The terrible irony of the situation is reflected in the woman's thoughts: the tree was good; it was a delight to the eyes; and it was desirable. How could it not be so, as part of what God had declared to be 'very good'? But it would leave one wise only if left alone. Nevertheless, she ate, and the man followed suit (Gn. 3:6).

The consequences were immediate: they 'knew that they were naked' (Gn. 3:7); they could no longer relate to one another without shame, but needed to cover themselves.[39] The breakdown in the 'horizontal' relationship was by no means the most serious consequence. Far more serious was the breakdown in the 'upward vertical' relationship, between them and God; they 'hid themselves from the presence of the LORD' (Gn. 3:8). Their 'horizontal' division discloses a deep rivalry in the way that the man (*hā'āḏām!*) blames the woman (Gn. 3:12), while the 'downward vertical' relation is also corrupted, as the woman blames the serpent (Gn. 3:13). Thus, referring to Diagram 2, both 'vertical' and 'horizontal' relationships are corrupted. Human beings no longer *live* as those made in the image of God; sin distorts and mars it at every point. *The relationships, however, are not abolished.* Genesis 5:2 affirms that the 'horizontal' aspect of the image of God, the relationship between men and women, continues, even though partnership has turned into rivalry. Likewise, Genesis 9:2–6 affirms that the 'downward vertical' relationship remains, but dominion has become corrupted into exploitation. The flood wrought havoc on the ground (*hā'-ădāmâ*) because of human evil – a fate which God promised would never happen again (Gn. 8:21–22), but even so creation lives in fear and dread of humankind. Most crucially, the 'upward vertical' relationship also remains, but now works in condemnation rather than blessing: God continues to relate to human beings, as is obvious from the rest of the Scriptures, yet we remain incapable of knowing God by our own efforts (Rom. 1:18–24).

Our plight is not that the image of God has been abolished. It is far worse, namely that while its structures of relationship remain, they are distorted at every point or, as Anderson puts it, the image is 'inverted'.[40] We cannot get away from each other, from creation – or from God. And we find ourselves having lost the capacity to restore and renew these relationships. Such a plight is emphasized by the (just) series of curses God utters: the ground is cursed, child-bearing is sentenced to hard labour, work becomes toil, animals are set against us, and husbands rule wives (Gn. 3:14–19). The new state of things is seen in the 'naming' of the woman as 'Eve' (Gn. 3:20), by the man who now has himself a name, 'Adam' (Gn. 3:17). She is thereby placed below the man, having her 'desire' towards him, her role and identity defined by him, to be the 'mother of all living'. And yet, paradoxically, such a name breathes hope that even in a fallen creation there will be life that includes God's care even for rebels (Gn. 3:21). The human beings must leave Eden, however, over which a guard needs to be set (Gn. 3:22–24), lest our state of exclusion from the presence of God be rendered permanent by the eating of the tree of life. Even the administration of the curse is mixed with divine mercy – and it is God who takes the initiative to clothe the shamed sinners (Gn. 3:21).

Where then is the image of God now? The structures which show the (ontological) reality of being made in God's image remain, but are corrupted, inverted.[41] They work against their intended nature and purpose, dividing where they should unite, cursing where they should bless. This can be set out as in Diagram 3.

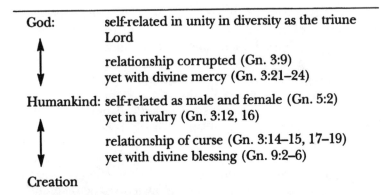

Diagram 3: The structure of the 'image of God' following Genesis 3

What does this inversion of the image mean today? To give a rather simplistic example, consider someone isolated on a desert island. He or she is still a human being, made in the image of God. But being isolated from others, and lacking the opportunity for the proper exercise of dominion, it makes sense to say that this person is in danger of becoming 'dehumanized'. The structures which long for fulfilment in relations with God, others, and creation remain; but their weakness is perhaps rather worse than their absence. In a similar manner, the modern experience of loss of identity through unemployment (where the 'downward vertical' structure is marred), male mid-life crises or the housewife isolation syndrome (corruptions of the 'horizontal' structure), let alone the angst shown about loss of the meaning of life itself (a tragic inversion of the 'upward vertical' relationship), graphically illustrates the plight of being made in the image of God, yet unable to live it out.

The opening chapters of the Scriptures thus portray the mystery, grandeur and tragedy of human existence. Made in the indefinable image and likeness of God, we find ourselves living in a cursed world, as fallen sinners in corrupted societies. But that is not the end of the matter; even in the midst of its sober account, Genesis offers signs of divine mercy and hope, pointing us to look forward for the full revelation of the meaning of human existence.[42]

Humankind in Israel's songs: Psalm 8; Job 28

The Hebrew Scriptures are full of stories about people: wicked, heroic, ordinary, spiteful, gracious, visionary, deceitful – and mostly unnamed. The saga of Noah, of Abraham, Lot, Sarah and Lot's wife, of Isaac and Rebekah, of Jacob and his wives and sons, of Joseph, Moses and Miriam, of Joshua, of judges such as Gideon and Deborah, of Naomi and Ruth, of Saul, Samuel, David, Solomon and Bathsheba, of the prophets and royal houses of north and south, of Nehemiah, Ezra and Daniel – this saga rolls along with a twofold theme throughout. Over and over is reiterated the human potential for divinely graced grandeur and sinful tragedy. Jeremiah diagnoses Israel's sorry plight as being due to 'a stubborn and rebellious heart' (Je. 5:23), while the psalmist can say, 'I treasure your word in my heart, so that I may not sin against you' (Ps. 119:11). Naomi and David stand as perhaps the clearest embodiments of this grandeur and tragedy; bitterness and selfishness respectively mix with obedience and blessing. The sheer volume of material must not be under-estimated; it offers a wealth of insight, for both crisis and calm, into both sides of our human condition, and into the justice and grace of God towards us. It is impossible to do more than undertake a rapid glance at two passages here. Both are songs, one from the psalter, the other typifying wisdom material.

Psalm 8 forms the closest parallel to Genesis 1 – 2 in its depiction of humanity. Having proclaimed the greatness of God in all the earth, the psalmist reflects on our dignity.

> 4. . . what are human beings ['$^{e}n\hat{o}\check{s}$] that you are mindful of them [Heb. singular],
> a mortal [ben-'$\bar{a}\underline{d}\bar{a}m$, 'son of humanity'] that you care for it? [my translation].
> 5Yet you have made them [singular] a little lower than God [Heb. 'the gods'],
> and crowned them [singular] with glory and honour.
> 6You have given them [singular] dominion over the works of your hands;
> you have put all things under their [singular] feet.

45

The text consistently uses singular pronouns, while modern translations (such as the NRSV, mainly cited above) resort to the plural to convey the idea that both corporate and personal meanings are intended. There are several translation issues: *ᵉnôš* usually refers to a particular male (*cf.* Ps. 9:19–20, where the stress falls on human vanity and weakness), but functions here in an inclusive manner; on the other hand, the more corporate *ben-'ādām* is interpreted in Christian citation in terms of Christ as *the* 'son of humanity' (*cf.* Heb. 2:5–7, where the NRSV maintains a generic reference and plural number); and what is meant by the plural 'the gods'? The tension in translation between singular and plural, male and female, is obviously tricky![43] Compare the NRSV with the *Book of Common Prayer* rendition, which at this point is more literal:

> ⁴What is man, that thou art mindful of him: and the son of man, that thou visitest him?
> ⁵Thou madest him lower than the angels: to crown him with glory and worship.
> ⁶Thou makest him to have dominion of the works of thy hands: and thou hast put all things in subjection under his feet.

Any translation is difficult. The main point is nevertheless clear: whatever the vicissitudes of human behaviour, whether of men or of women, and whatever our puny frailty in the face of the majesty of the heavens, we are regarded by God with the highest honour, and handed the task and responsibility of having dominion over all the earth. While difficult to sustain amid the realities of life, the faith of Israel regarding our elevated status before God continued to be exercised, even in song. Note, however, that it is faith not so much in human nature as in the Lord who has set us in such a privileged position.

The perspective of the wisdom literature is similar, though broader. Human wisdom is celebrated over and again in Proverbs, while its limits and accountability are emphasized in Ecclesiastes. In either case, 'The fear of the LORD is instruction in wisdom' (Pr. 15:33). A passage which holds both notions together is Job 28, a soliloquy which interrupts the main flow of the book's dialogue, and can therefore be cited in its own right.

The writer celebrates the skill of miners, even in distant places where survival is difficult (Jb. 28:1–11). Then the question comes,

> [12]But where shall wisdom be found?
> And where is the place of understanding?
> [13]Mortals do not know the way to it:
> and it is not found in the land of the living.
> [14]The deep says, 'It is not in me',
> and the sea says, 'It is not with me.'
> [15]It cannot be bought for gold,
> and silver cannot be weighed out as its price.

The comparisons continue: wisdom is priceless, hidden from the living and dead. Yet

> [23]God understands the way to it,
> and he knows its place.
> [24]For he looks to the ends of the earth,
> and sees everything under the heavens.

So the writer, having generously acknowledged human skill as well as human inability to know wisdom, attests Israel's faith, borrowing God's own words:

> [28]'Truly, the fear of the LORD, that is wisdom;
> and to depart from evil is understanding.'

In sum, the Hebrew Scriptures, while not directly utilizing the concept of the image of God outside the book of Genesis, continue to testify to both the creative grandeur and the deceitfulness of human nature. As human beings, we are made for growing and active relationship with God, to live as diverse partners in community, fellow stewards of creation, sharing the status of creatures with all the earth. We are made in and for hope, to look for the eternal rather than the transient. In spite of this, we continue to want to live in the past rather than in the light of God's future, to live for ourselves rather than for our Creator. So we corrupt our personal relationships and life in society, and exploit the earth in which we live. This double-sided perspective is the broad shape of the testimony of all the Scriptures, but, to discern its more specifically Christian parameters, we now consider the New Testament data.

2

THE IMAGE OF GOD
RENEWED IN CHRIST

To be a human being is to be made in the image and likeness of God. This privilege and dignity is not always seen or lived, however. Human life as we know it is marred, distorting the heritage of our created grandeur. Whether in relation to God, one another, or the world at large, we live as those made in the image of God, who constantly misuse and abuse those relationships. This is the testimony and heritage of Israel, a testimony received by the first Christians. Their understanding of what it means to be human was enriched and transformed in the light of Christ.

The early church strongly proclaimed the greatness of the human species, but with a future orientation rather than a past one, from the perspective of what we are to become rather than of what we were or are. At the same time, the gospel of Christ exposed more deeply the tragedy of our helplessness and corruption apart from Christ. The concept of the image of God is thus used in the New Testament in new ways. Indeed, Israel's testimony to the creation of the race as a whole in the image or likeness of God is spoken of only once (and that as a passing reference), in the most Jewish book of the New Testament, James: 'With [the tongue] we bless the Lord and Father, and with it we curse those who are made in the likeness [*homoiōsin*] of God' (Ja. 3:9). The major concern here is the ambiguous nature of the tongue, which can both bless and curse. The writer is not making a particular point about our being made in the likeness of God, but (as Bray puts it), 'Man remains the likeness of God, and for that reason must not be slandered by the misuse of the human tongue.'[1] In a passing allusion, the affirmation of Genesis that all people bear such a status is assumed by James to apply still.

Israel's witness to the creation of the human race as a whole in the image of God is thus not strongly affirmed in the New Testament, but it is certainly not contested. It pales into relative insignificance in the light of what God has in store for humankind: the focus is now on Christ, then on those who are 'in Christ', and their destiny. It is striking, for example, that the term 'image' (*eikōn*) is not used for humankind in the New Testament apart from reference to Christ. The argument of this chapter will be that in Christ, the perfect *eikōn* of God, the divine image is being renewed through the Spirit, until humanity is re-created into Christ's full dignity, according to the purpose of its Creator. The chapter endeavours to set out this distinctive Christ-centred perspective by examining those texts in the New Testament which shed light on the human condition, as created, under sin, renewed and restored. In the first place the focus falls on passages which speak of the image of God directly, then the canvas is broadened to consider others. The texts are considered in what was the likely order of writing, in order to gain some sense of the growing importance of the concept in the early church.

The somewhat stilted translations in this chapter are my own, for a number of reasons. First, the universal perspective of Paul's argument is obscured in most translations. In many texts he is not principally concerned with the fate of any human individual, but with the race as a whole; but the way in which the English language functions frequently hides this. Secondly, the use of generic masculine language raises the issue of gender inclusivity with particular force when speaking about being human. No-one suggests that women do not take part in the resurrection, for example, but retaining male generic terms in 1 Corinthians 15 makes this point difficult for many modern readers to feel. Thirdly, translations made for public reading, in order to make sense for readers and hearers, often supply verbs in many places where the text does not. This process entails deciding whether the verb carries a past, present or future reference, when there are often allusions to all three in the text. I acknowledge that my rendering is awkward, and hardly suitable for public reading, but it is vitally important that doctrine be grounded in the actual text of the Scriptures, rather than in particular translations.

The first (and earliest) text to be considered does not at first sight look like a promising beginning, but turns out to be of some significance.

New humanity in Christ glimpsed: 1 Corinthians 11:7

> A man [*anēr*] ought not to cover the head, being image [*eikōn*] and glory [*doxa*] of God; a woman [*gynē*] is the glory [*doxa*] of a man [*anēr*].

Sometimes this text is held to exclude women from the image, but Paul stops short of saying this; the statement that men are the image of God (literally 'subsisting as', *hyparchōn*) does not imply that women are not! The issue under discussion in this passage is the Corinthians' apparent disregard for any distinction between the genders.[2] Not only could this attitude lead to licence and immorality (lifestyles typical of ancient Corinth), so bringing disgrace on the church; it also contradicts the clear teaching of Genesis that women and men are different, a teaching reiterated by Jesus (Mk. 10:6). Among those 'baptized into Christ', who have put on Christ, as Paul has previously written, 'there is neither Jew nor Greek, neither slave nor free, neither male nor female, for you are all one in Christ Jesus' (Gal. 3:27–28). Race, social status and gender are not to form barriers between Christians, nor do they possess ultimate value; nevertheless they cannot be ignored, gender least of all.[3] Writing

51

to the Corinthians only shortly after he had penned Galatians, Paul here emphasizes that Christians must not confuse male and female, and that this needs to be recognized in congregational life.

The particular 'tradition' Paul commends the Corinthian church to maintain (1 Cor. 11:2) is some distinction in dress or hairstyle or both between men and women when engaged in public prayer and prophecy.[4] To argue his case he makes allusion to Genesis 1 – 2, but not in the clearest manner. In Genesis 1:26–28 (and 5:2), both men and women are said to be made in the image of God, while in Genesis 2:15–24, in which men and women are spoken of separately, there is no clear reference to the image of God (see the discussion in chapter 1). The basis of Paul's appeal is not this scriptural testimony but the Corinthians' understanding of what is 'disgraceful' (1 Cor. 11:6), or 'natural' (1 Cor. 11:14). Today, few Christians, at least in the western world, would regard the length of a woman's or man's hair as having any particular social or theological significance. Everyone is aware, however, that the way we dress says something about our ethics and social values, and that dress can obscure or exclude others (cf. Jas. 2:2–7; Mt. 6:16–18). Modes of costume vary, depending on the place, time and occasion, and there are sometimes disagreements among Christians over what constitutes appropriate dress for women and men (and young and old, and ministers and members) when leading public prayer. The need to maintain appropriate traditions for the sake of the gospel is the essential point Paul makes.

The significance of this text is not thereby exhausted. Paul may buttress his argument with appeals to the Corinthians' own perceptions of what is right, and allude to Genesis 1 – 2 in ways that stretch its original meaning, particularly to the picture of woman's being taken from man for man's sake and not vice versa (1 Cor. 11:8–9). The core of his position is more Christ-centred. Paul commences his discussion by using the different nuances of the 'head' metaphor as applied to Christ and God, and men and women, to argue for differentiation (1 Cor. 11:3).[5] Above all, he concludes the argument as he views both men and women in the light of Christ: 'Nevertheless, in the Lord woman is not independent of man or man of woman. For just as woman came from man, so now man comes from woman; but all things come from God' (1 Cor. 11:11–12).

Here the newness which Christ brings to the situation is affirmed. In creation, woman came from man initially, and with the coming of sin 'natural' behaviour entails the appearance of hierarchical modes of relationship (*cf.* Gn. 3:16). Yet even in creation, every man has been born from a woman. In Christ, while the differences between men and women remain, at least in this age, any sense of opposition or hierarchical relationship is transcended.[6]

In sum, this rather puzzling text, concerned with the practical matter of dress in the Corinthian Christian assemblies, reveals the continued significance for the early church of our being made in the image of God, as men and women. In this age, during which sin remains, behavioural adjustments need to be made for the sake of the gospel in particular circumstances. Yet the whole situation takes on new perspectives in the light of Christ. These are given substantial treatment in chapter 15 of this letter.

New humanity in Christ proclaimed: 1 Corinthians 15

Paul faced a denial of the resurrection of the dead by some at Corinth. He begins his response by pointing out the Christological implications: if the dead are not raised, neither is Christ, and the consequences of that are destructive of faith (1 Cor. 15:12–17). Direct and positive teaching about the Christian hope follows; it is more than a matter of individual survival beyond the grave, and entails a reconstitution of sinful humankind in Christ (1 Cor. 15:18–22). There is an order about this, reflecting priorities in creation and salvation: Christ, those who are his, the End, and the subjection of all things (1 Cor. 15:23–28). After a personal appeal, the main topic resumes, to answer the question, 'How are the dead raised?' (1 Cor. 15:35–44). The argument returns to the issue of the order in creation and salvation, with a more extended comparison and contrast of 'original' humankind (that 'in Adam'), and that restored in Christ (1 Cor. 15:45–49). It is this latter section which is of particular interest for the present study, since it focuses on the newness which Christ brings to the human race. It is important to note, however, that it is not the end of Paul's teaching. He concludes with a stirring panegyric on the victory of Christ over death, sin and the law, and an appeal to readers to live the resurrection life in the present (1 Cor. 15:50–58). In sum, Paul's argument discloses a deeper perspective on the human condition than was given to Israel, a perspective centred in Christ, and particularly in his resurrection and future appearing.

In the following translation of parts of 1 Corinthians 15, an asterisk indicates that English translations usually supply a verb at this point.

> [21]For since through humankind [di'anthrōpou] * death,
> also through humankind * resurrection of [the] dead.
> [22]For in that in Adam ['en tō 'Adam] all die/are dying,
> also in Christ ['en tō Christō] all shall be made alive.

Here the solidarity of the human race in death, all those 'in Adam', is attested. The reference to 'Adam' may include Adam as a particular individual, but the language, following that of Genesis 1 – 3, is wider and more universal. Adam here means in the first place hā'ādām, humankind, before any reference to 'ādām, 'Adam', can properly be made.[7] Further, Paul is not at this point trying to explain the origin of death. To supply the verb 'came' at the points marked * in verse 21, as do most English translations, shifts the emphasis in this direction by introducing a verb in the past tense, but that goes beyond Paul's point. On the other hand, to supply 'comes' or 'is', present-tense verbs, would dilute the reference to a past act, thus cutting the obvious and close ties with Genesis 3. That humankind as we know it is doomed to death is hinted at in Genesis 3, but in the Hebrew Scriptures death is 'explained in terms of life . . . one who dies is like water spilled on the ground, not to be gathered up again (2 Sam. 14:14)'.[8] It is in the light of the resurrection of Christ that we see death for what it really is, the 'last enemy' (verse 26). It is thus Christ, and Christ raised from death, who both reveals the stark horror of our plight – death in dread fullness – and offers a way out.

Paul returns to the general nature of the human condition in verses 45–49, after contrasting what is sown and what is raised.

[44]A living/alive body [*sōma psychikon*] is [being] sown,
a spiritual body [*sōma pneumatikon*] is [being] raised.
[45]Thus it stands written,
'The original/initial/protological humankind [*ho
    prōtos anthrōpos*] Adam, became living being [*psychē*]';
the last [final, eschatological; *ho eschatos*] Adam [is
    destined] for life-giving spirit [*pneuma*].
[46]But the spiritual [*to pneumatikon*] [is] not original,
but the living/alive [*to psychikon*], then the spiritual [*to
    pneumatikon*].
[47]Original humankind [*ho prōtos 'anthrōpos*] [is] dust of
    earth [*ek gēs choikos*];
the second humankind [*ho deuteros anthrōpos* [is] from
    heaven [*ouranou*].
[48]As the dusty one [*ho choikos*], so also the dusty [*hoi
    choikoi*];
as the heavenly one [*ho epouranios*], so also the
    heavenly [*hoi epouranioi*];
[49]Just as we have borne the image [*eikona*] of the dusty
    one,
we shall also bear the image [*eikona*] of the heavenly
    one.

The translation issues here are enormous! My rendition seeks
to make it clear that Paul is not at this point focusing on
particular individuals, but on the race as a whole. Compare the
slight difference in the two phrases used: *ho prōtos anthrōpos,
Adam . . . ho eschatos Adam*. In its first use the corporate
meaning is clear enough: *ho prōtos anthrōpos*, 'humanity', occurs
in apposition to the personal term *Adam*, conveying the
collective sense of the Hebrew *hā'ādām*, 'humanity'.[9] The
second reference, however, omits the word *anthrōpos*, and refers
to Christ, the 'eschatological Adam', as a representative person.
The double use of the term *Adam* thus gives Paul a way of
expressing the idea that Christ was *both* a particular *and* a
representative person. We belong as a whole race to 'original'
or 'protological' humanity, yet humanity in Christ is destined
for something even greater, for the life of 'spirit'. Note that Paul
is concerned here with no particular time except the distant
past (verses 45, 49) and the future (verse 49); to supply verbs in

verses 46–48 entails theological judgments which go beyond the text.[10] We are not to speculate about the precise details of either 'protological' or 'eschatological' humanity, but to look to Christ as the source and hope of human life, at both personal and corporate levels.

Paul then draws a further contrast between those in Adam and those in Christ. Earlier, in verses 21–22, it was between death and life: now the contrast is between the earthy, dusty, state of being (merely) 'alive', and the renewed, 'spiritual' state of resurrection in Christ. Genesis 2:7 is cited in verses 45–48 as applying to humankind as created, 'alive' and 'earthy', before sin has come into the picture. It reveals, Paul argues, that our present state is not the only reality; in Christ we are headed for a state in which, while remaining creaturely, we may share the life of God – 'spiritual' life. Such a state does not negate our being embodied, as verse 44 makes clear (*cf.* 1 Cor. 6:12 – 7:5). Rather, it throws new light on the significance of being embodied. We are given life, not just for its own sake, or as the final end of our race, but so that we might grow into the life of God. As Paul puts it, we are 'alive' ('psychic') in order that we might become 'spiritual' ('pneumatic'). We are finite, earthy creatures, endowed with 'life', made for relationship with God, for 'spirit'. Yet in our present condition we cannot achieve this; only one from heaven can bring us to our true end (verses 48–49).

It is in this context that the concept of 'image' comes to the fore. Created 'in the image of God', we experience this now as the 'image of the dusty one' (verse 49).[11] Our 'spirit' destiny thus eludes us; we remain dust-bound apart from receiving the new heavenly reality (verse 48). It is striking, however, that the language passes from the objective, disinterested third person, 'it', in verses 38–48, to the participatory, subjective first person, 'we', from verse 49 to the end of the chapter. Paul could analyse the human condition in both 'original' and 'heavenly' humanity at (so to speak) arm's length. But there comes a time when he must bring this rather technical discourse home, both for himself and for his readers, and for all who share life in Christ with him. 'We' language thus takes over. The new light of Christ has been allowed to shine on both the plight and the hope of the human race. For those 'in Christ' such a light becomes a personal hope and reality, to 'inherit the kingdom of God' (verse 50).

The human condition is seen as problematic, sometimes because we are finite and God is infinite, and sometimes because we are sinners and God is holy. Behind such analyses lie assumptions about the relationship between incarnation and atonement. In classical Christian theology the double movement of Christ's incarnation and ascension ('coming down' and 'going up') has been understood as overcoming finitude, enabled by Christ's death which meets the 'crucial' need for the forgiveness of sins.[12] Paul in 1 Corinthians 15 portrays both concerns as being met in Christ's resurrection, and our resurrection in Christ. This double provision is clearest in the concluding section of this great chapter. That our need for salvation in the light of divine holiness has been met was first shown in verses 21–22, and is now restated; Christ has overcome death and its sting, sin (verses 54–56). Further, the fact of our finitude, initially discussed in verses 44–49, has also been faced; Christ has opened the way to the imperishable, incorruptible, immortal life of heaven (verses 52–54). In Christ not only are death and sin put away, but the human race is re-created, and enabled to enter a state even greater than that which 'original humanity' knew: resurrection to 'spirit', to full life with God. In short, those in Christ have the promise that having borne the 'image of the dusty one', we will also bear the 'image of the heavenly one'. But if this is so, we must work for the Lord now, with steadfast hope and confidence (verse 58).

For Paul, then, and his Corinthian (largely Gentile) readers and hearers, the fundamental texts of the Hebrew Scriptures about the human condition continued to function effectively and authoritatively. The great difference is Christ. Christ's life, death and resurrection mean that the picture of humanity in Genesis 1 – 3 now speaks of hope made possible, rather than of grand beginnings spoiled. Instead of orienting human self-understanding towards the past, to what we once were, we are now oriented towards the future, to what in Christ we are to become. In such a light the present is transformed. This 'present seen from the future' perspective continues in Paul's second letter to the church at Corinth.

New humanity in Christ reflected in reconciliation: 2 Corinthians 3 – 5

It would seem that relations between Paul and the Corinthian church had become strained since the first letter was written. Before responding to a number of practical concerns, he finds it necessary to defend and explain his ministry (as he does once more in the closing chapters). The major interest is not theological anthropology, but these opening chapters shed considerable light upon it. Chapter 3 compares ministry under the Mosaic covenant with that of Christ: the one is associated with the letter that kills, the other with the Spirit who gives life. In particular, Moses' experience of a 'shining face', which needed to be veiled (*cf.* Ex. 34:29–35), is used to illustrate the different effects of law and Spirit.[13] Paul writes in a way which adds considerably to our understanding of the human condition.

> [17]Now the Lord is the Spirit, and where the Spirit of
> the Lord is, freedom!
> [18]And all of us, with unveiled faces,
> beholding/reflecting [*katoptrizomenoi*] the glory of the
> Lord,
> are being transformed [*metamorphoumetha*] into the
> same image [*eikona*]
> from glory to glory, even as from the Lord [who is]
> [the] Spirit.

The Spirit's presence and work in the Christian life have been mentioned in Paul's writing previously in relation to its beginning (Gal. 3:3–5; 1 Cor. 2:1 – 3:1), to our status as children of God (Gal. 4:6) who are to walk in and be led by the Spirit (Gal. 5:16–25), and to various charisms (1 Cor. 12:1–11). We have seen that Paul looks to the time when human life will become a fully 'spirit' life of unrestricted communion with God (1 Cor. 15:42–46). Now he relates all of this to the present transformation of those in Christ into the 'same image', 'from glory to glory'. This is not only a future expectation; it is a present reality, albeit one characterized by growth rather than completion. Through the operation of the Spirit, the future destiny of humankind is anticipated for those in Christ, who both 'behold' and 'reflect' (*katoptrizomenoi* carries both senses) the 'glory of the Lord'.

Paul goes on to describe his own practice of ministry as one undertaken in responsible freedom towards unbelievers who, because the gospel is 'veiled' to them, are kept from seeing

> [4]. . . the light of the gospel of the glory (*doxa*) of
>   Christ,
> who is [the] image [*eikōn*] of God.[14]
> [5]For we do not preach ourselves, but Christ Jesus as
>   Lord,
> ourselves [being] your slaves for Jesus' sake.
> [6]For it is God, who said, 'Out of darkness let light
>   shine',
> who has shone in our hearts to [give] the light
>   of the knowledge
> of the glory of God in the face of Jesus Christ.

Here the themes of creation and new creation come together in Christ, *eikōn* of God. Referring back to the diagrams used in chapter 1, in Christ the key 'upward vertical' relation – the relation between ourselves and God – has been restored, so that humankind receives new hope. The Spirit brings this hope into present experience through the preaching of the gospel of Christ, beginning the process of bringing humankind into the full glory of the Lord. This glory was glimpsed by Israel on Moses' face, but unbelief rendered it dangerous rather than helpful. It shines fully in the face of the risen Lord Jesus, and is seen and reflected in those in Christ.

This glory (a much used concept in these passages) is not fully present now. As Paul knew well from his own ministry, 'we have this treasure in earthen vessels' (2 Cor. 4:7). This 'earthy' life is transformed by the death of Jesus, through which we receive his life, and so the promise of resurrection (2 Cor. 4:10–14). The details of the personal aspect of this promise are spelled out in the following section, 2 Corinthians 4:16 – 5:15. The issue is more than one of giving finite mortals eternal life; it involves Christ dealing with sin, so that God and the human race may be reconciled. As Paul puts it in chapter 5,

[17]Therefore if anyone [is] in Christ, new creation/
   creature!
The old things have passed away; behold, new things
   have come into being.
[18]All these are from God, who reconciled us to himself
   through Christ
and gave to us the ministry of reconciliation;
[19]that is, God was in Christ reconciling [the] world to
   himself,
not counting to them their trespasses,
and entrusting to us the word of reconciliation.
[20]On behalf of Christ we therefore undertake
   ambassadorship,
God making appeal through us; we beseech on behalf
   of Christ:
be reconciled to God!
[21]Him who knew no sin, on behalf of us he made sin,
so that we might become [the] righteousness of God
   in him.

I have cited this passage in full because it brings together two
aspects of Christ's work on behalf of the human race which are
often separated. Some cite verse 17 without reference to what
follows; this gives the impression that the basic human problem is
creaturely finitude, and that Christ's resurrection applies without
regard to human response to God's reconciling work. In other
circles, only verse 21 is given full attention; here the wonder of
Christ's atoning death is emphasized, but the hope of restoration,
of new creation, is neglected. The divine work of reconciliation is
narrowed to apply only to the individual in her or his personal
relationship with God. On the broadest panorama, if the one has
been the tendency of the eastern theological tradition, stressing
Christ's resurrection and so corporate hope, the other has been
the tendency in the West, stressing Christ's death, and consequent individual forgiveness through it. Within Protestantism, if
the first has been the emphasis of proponents of a 'social gospel',
the other has been more characteristic of 'evangelicals'. Paul in
this letter, as in 1 Corinthians, holds both aspects together, calling
us to have a broader vision of human destiny than that of mere
restoration of the past, yet emphasizing the great cost to God of

bringing about this new creation. Reconciliation involves both personal response to the gospel, so that sins may be forgiven, and a corporate dimension, so that the new order of the Spirit may break into this creation.

New humanity in Christ – and the old: Romans 5:12–21

Paul's letter to the Romans sets out the nature and significance of salvation in Christ in perhaps the fullest manner in the New Testament. Romans 1 – 4 spells this out through the concepts of law and justification, against the background of human sinfulness. These opening chapters make it clear that both Jew and Gentile are sinners, that both are liable before God for their disobedience, and also that both are the objects of God's grace in Christ. As Paul writes, 'we have already charged Jews and Greeks alike, everyone, to be under sin' (Rom. 3:9) and again, 'since all have sinned and fall short of the glory of God, they are justified by his grace [as a] gift through the redemption which is in Christ Jesus' (Rom. 3:23–24).

It is striking that in this argument, the corporate, future focus is intertwined with the personal, present one. Paul's teaching certainly applies to every human being, but its force comes from his emphasis on the unity of Jew and Gentile in both sin and salvation. Further, the measure of what sin entails is to 'fall short of the glory of God'. This phrase alludes not only to the past (*cf.* 1 Cor. 11:7), but also to the future (*cf.* 2 Cor. 3 – 5). Our human plight is not only that we fall short of a standard given in the past, but that we fall short of what God is bringing us to become. Against such a background, Paul sets out in chapter 5 the results of Christ's justifying work. In doing so, the motif of reconciliation once more comes to the fore.

> [10]For if while we were enemies we were reconciled to God by the death of his Son,
> much more, now that we are reconciled, shall we be saved by his life.
> [11]Not only so, but we also rejoice in God through our Lord Jesus Christ,
> through whom we have now received reconciliation.

Reconciliation has as its background a situation of estrange-ment.[15] It refers here to the alienation of Jew from Gentile, an alienation now brought to an end in Christ. This particular tension is also a sign of the deeper human problem, our being enemies of God. The remainder of Romans 5 thus sets out Paul's perspective on our plight as human beings, caught up in the solidarity of sin. His main point is to stress the 'free gift' available in Christ, the grace which sets those in Christ in the right with God, bringing forgiveness, acquittal and life (Rom. 5:15–18). In setting out this argument Paul speaks of the negative side of being human.

> [12]As through one human [*henos anthrōpos*] sin entered
>   into the world,
> and through sin death,
> even so death spread to all humans in that (*eph hō*) all
>   sinned.

This verse has been the basis of much theological controversy, grounded in the 'great debate' in the early fifth century between Augustine of Hippo and Pelagius.[16] Before examining the issues involved, it should be noted that at first sight the text seems unremarkable: that all humans experience life as sinful, with death as its end, hardly needs to be argued. How did this state of affairs come about? In his earlier writing Paul stated that humanity 'in Adam' participates in death apart from Christ (1 Cor. 15:22), but no explanation for this state of affairs was given. In Romans 5, however, we are brought to face the question of the beginning of sin. Two major points emerge in Paul's teaching, both having considerable ongoing significance today.

First, sin 'entered' the world; to paraphrase Arius, 'there was a then when sin was not' – it had a beginning in time. It is perhaps surprising that such a point has not been made earlier in Paul's teaching, and that it is made here more in passing than as a substantial matter to be addressed in its own right. However, the concept of the beginning of sin does not seem to have been an issue at this stage in the early church. It did become significant in the second century after Christ, as the church spread into the Graeco-Roman world, and faced new intellectual challenges. In particular, the goodness of creation needed to be defended against gnostic ideas, and aspects of Hellenistic philosophy, which held that matter was evil.[17] If sin did not have a beginning, then creation has always been tainted with evil, for which God is to be held directly responsible. The creation is thus seen as other than 'very good', contradicting Genesis 1 – 2; and if creation is 'not good', then the incarnation is impossible, since God and evil cannot meet.

In contemporary terms, the notion of an historic fall is the critical point in relation to evolutionary concepts of humankind. According to the Scriptures, sin is neither the inevitable outcome of the struggle to survive (the pessimistic assumption of evolutionism), nor a stage in human development which we will leave behind as we evolve (the optimistic hope of evolutionism).[18] Sin is rather spoken of as something which had a beginning in time, and is an unnatural, ungodly 'development' in human history.[19] If the pessimistic assumption of evolutionism dishonours human freedom, its optimistic hope displays too shallow an understanding of the damaging consequences of sin, and its distinctive character of deliberate rebellion against God. How the committing of the first sin relates to a particular event in human history remains an open question, but abandoning the notion that 'there was a then when sin was not' entails accepting that nature as created involves evil, a position that effectively destroys the Christian view of God and creation.[20]

A great deal is therefore at stake for Christian faith in the way we understand sin and its beginning. It is important to note that to speak of a 'beginning' of sin is not the same as identifying an 'origin', which remains a profound riddle: 'They hated me without cause' (Jn. 15:25). Why human beings, created in the image of God, should reject their Creator (then and now) makes no sense, but to look for a 'cause' external to ourselves implies that it lies somewhere else in creation, implying either cosmic dualism, or that creation was made evil, both rejected in the Scriptures. Further, such a search encourages human beings to look for a scapegoat outside of themselves, and thus to shirk the necessity of repentance; this was precisely the initial reaction of Adam and Eve in Eden (Gn. 3:12–13).[21] In scholastic terms, the 'material' cause of sin is the good, but it lacks formal (patterning) and final (purposive) causes; sin is a desperately tyrannous, disordering, death-dealing, chaotic riddle, the result of deliberate human choice, puzzling and terrifying as that choice may be. The origin of sin is thus the mystery of the rebellious human heart, the 'infection' of a nature 'inclined to evil' (as Article IX of the Thirty-nine Articles puts it).[22] Human sin is a radical matter, a corruption at the root of our being; particular sins (see *e.g.* Rom. 1:21–32) are the fruit of the root sin, though this outcome is not automatic, but the result of deliberate human decision (Rom. 5:12–19). Conversely, the renewal of our corrupted nature (the 'flesh' in Paul's words), brought about by the regenerating activity of the Spirit, is a necessary prerequisite to our doing of good deeds, the 'fruit of the Spirit' (see Gal. 5:16–25). Christian perspectives on sin assert that both sin and sins matter; to ignore the first underestimates the depth of the corruption of our nature, while ignoring the latter avoids our need to be accountable for our actions.

Secondly, Paul places a firm stress on our solidarity in sin as human beings. We are told that 'all sinned', and that there is thus 'condemnation for all human beings' (Rom. 5:18). Further, as in 1 Corinthians 15, *henos anthrōpos* carries a corporate tinge, 'humanity as a whole', as well as a personal reference to 'Adam' or 'Jesus Christ' (Rom. 5:15, 19); *henos* is likewise used in both senses in verses 16–18. Sin affects us both as individual persons (see below, chapters 8–9), and as persons who are created to live in community (see below, chapter 4). The Jew–Gentile controversy, the background to the writing of Romans, illustrates this. Each Jew or Gentile must face his or her own sin and its consequences, yet this responsibility cannot be isolated from the sinful estrangement between Jews and Gentiles in the early church, itself a particular example of the corporate state of sinfulness in which the human race as a whole finds itself.

Paul thus presents us in Romans 5 with two inescapable facts about human nature: sin is an element introduced into human life, and we are all caught up in its thrall. The implications of this teaching have led to considerable theological reflection. Some of these will be taken up in later chapters, but one particular matter is taken up here. In the fifth century, Romans 5:12 become of crucial importance in the dispute regarding the nature of human sinfulness between Augustine and the Pelagians (a group named after the disciplined monk Pelagius, who was scandalized at the spread of immorality in the churches).[23] The Pelagians argued that there is no root of sin, or any human solidarity in sin, but only discrete sins; we sin because we copy a bad habit introduced by Adam and Eve. The Pelagians taught that this habit can be broken by human effort. Grace helps in the process, but is not essential. Augustine replied that sin was a much deeper matter, a basic flaw that corrupted human nature itself, which could be renovated only through grace. His theological reasoning was impressive, but to sustain his position from the Scriptures was no easy task. Romans 5:12 was an obvious text to discuss.

Augustine knew only Latin versions of the New Testament; in these, *eph hō* was (literalistically) rendered *in quo*. The Greek phrase carries the meaning 'because', as does the corresponding English idiom 'in that', but the Latin was taken by Augustine to mean 'in whom', namely 'in Adam'. He thus concluded that all of us sinned *en masse* in Adam's original sin, with a resultant corruption of our nature that is passed on from generation to generation physically, so that sexual intercourse is tainted with 'concupiscence'. This view certainly honours the depth and extent of sin in the human condition, but raises problems about the created goodness of human nature in its sexual aspect.[24] To this we return in later chapters; for the moment, it is important to note that a full-blown Augustinian position is not supported by the actual Greek text of Romans 5:12.

This negative picture is not Paul's final word in Romans on human nature and destiny, however. At the conclusion of this argument in Romans 1 – 8 he writes:

> [29]For those whom [God] foreknew he also
>   predestined to be conformers of the image
>   (*eikōnos*) of his Son,
> that he might be the firstborn among many brothers
>   and sisters;
> [30]those he predestined he called;
> and whom he called, these he also justified;
> those he justified, these also he glorified.

The future perspective here comes to the fore once more. Human beings are not defined solely in terms of our past or present, but in the light of what we are destined to become in Christ. This goal of our being 'glorified' (*cf.* 1 Cor. 11:7) is no accident; it has been the divine purpose in Christ from all eternity. Even so, there is a gentle indirectness here. It is *Christ* who is the image of God; those whom God calls in Christ are to come into conformity with the image of God's Son. On the one hand, this indirectness preserves the distinction between ourselves as creatures and God as our Creator: sinful creature and holy Creator are brought into communion in Christ, but not union. As Bray puts it, 'Paul's use of *eikōn tou Theou* with reference to Christ is designed to emphasize His oneness with God, not His oneness with us.'[25] On the other hand, we are pointed to the wonder of a humanity which is far more than the old one repaired: it is one re-created in Christ, predestined, called, justified and glorified. And in this state, 'nothing will be able to separate us from the love of God in Christ Jesus our Lord' (Rom. 8:38).

New humanity in Christ made visible: Ephesians and Colossians

The 'prison letters' to Ephesus and Colossae deepen this perspective of humankind as persons made for community, bound together in sin, yet renewed in Christ. They also take us a step further in the discussion, by relating humanity to the church of God as the body of Christ.

The eternal purpose of God in Christ is described in the opening chapters of Ephesians in terms reminiscent of Romans 8. 'In love [God] destined us for sonship through Jesus Christ' (Eph. 1:5), and disclosed the divine purpose 'to unite all things in Christ, things in heaven and things on earth' (Eph. 1:10). In terms of our diagram (see chapter 1), this points particularly to God's restoration of the 'downward vertical' relation: but it is inseparable from the 'upward vertical' relation, 'redemption through Christ's blood, the forgiveness of trespasses' (Eph. 1:7).

Colossians is similar, focused even more sharply on the central place of Christ,

> [15]who is the image (*eikōn*) of the invisible God,
> firstborn (*prōtotokos*) of all creation,
> [16]for in him were created all things in the heavens and
> on the earth . . .

all things were through him and for him created,
[17]and he is before all, and all things hold together in
    him,
[18]and he is the head of the body, the church,
He is [the] beginning [*archē*], firstborn [*prōtotokos*] of
    the dead,
so that he might be in all things first-placed
    [*prōteuōn*],
[19]for in him [God] pleased all the fullness to dwell,
[20]and through him to reconcile all things to himself,
making peace through the blood of his cross,
whether things on the earth or things in the heavens.

Christ is here plainly portrayed as 'image of God', who is invisible. The sense that without Christ God could not be known by us is thus strengthened. Further, a strong emphasis is placed on the significance of Christ for creation itself, and especially his key role in re-creation. He is 'firstborn' both of original life, and of life restored: the 'beginning' of both, reminiscent of Genesis 1:1 and John 1:1, though pointing forward to a vision not yet seen.[26] The re-creative work of Christ is thus described in its fullest and most comprehensive manner; reconciliation embraces everything! But, as seen earlier, the key factor is bridging the gap not between finite and infinite, but between the holy and the sinful. Such reconciliation involves costly peacemaking, the overcoming of universal estrangement, through Christ's death.

A note whose echoes have sounded faintly before in Paul is now struck loudly: Christ's reconciling work is to be seen *in the church*, his 'body', whose members he has 'reconciled in the body of his flesh though his death' (Col. 1:22). A related thought is expressed by Paul in his first letter to the Corinthians: 'you [plural] were bought at a price; so glorify God in your [plural] body' (1 Cor. 6:20). There are several senses of 'body' here: Christ's own body of flesh, our embodied state, and the church as Christ's body.[27] While distinct, they belong together, and interrelate; the church is not to be identified with Christ (Eph. 5:25–31 excludes this), but is the place where we have communion in and with Christ, through the Spirit. We have already seen that the Spirit brings the future hope of humankind in Christ into the present, as a down-payment or guarantee (*arrabōn*, Eph. 1:14) in anticipation. Where is this hope to be seen and experienced? The answer given here is 'Among God's people, in the body of Christ.' This is the force of the following parallel exhortations in Ephesians and Colossians, both constructed according to the concept of 'image of God'. In Ephesians 4 we read:

> [22]You [plural] are to put off the old humanity
> belonging to your [plural] former lifestyle, which
> is [being] corrupted through deceitful lusts,
> [23]and be renewed in the spirit of your [plural] mind,
> [24]and put on the new humanity [*ton kainon anthrōpon*],
> created according to God in righteousness and
> holiness of the truth.

The Ephesian Christians are spoken to as a *group*, having a corporate lifestyle and mind. Though they have the truth in Jesus (Eph. 4:21), their nature is nevertheless mixed; the 'old humanity' needs to be put away, and the 'new humanity' put on. Such language, close to that of 1 Corinthians 15, emphasizes that the remaking of humankind, though accomplished in Christ's death and resurrection, is no easy process. It requires a death to the old, in which sin and death 'have dominion' (*cf.* Rom. 6:9–14), in order that the new may come, not only in the future, but in an anticipatory way in a present change of lifestyle.

Colossians 3 is similar:

> [5]Kill off therefore body-members which are of the
> earth . . .
> [9]. . . having put away the old humanity [*ton palaion
> anthrōpon*] with its deeds,
> [10]and having put on the new, which is being renewed
> in knowledge after the image [*kat' eikōna*] of its
> creator.
> [11]Here there cannot be Greek or Jew, circumcised and
> uncircumcised,
> barbarian, Scythian, slave, free,
> but all [plural], and in all [plural], is Christ.

This last verse echoes Paul's earlier teaching in Galatians. It represents a strong affirmation of the renewing of the 'horizontal' relationships within the new humanity. It is the mark of 'putting on' Christ in baptism (Gal. 3:27), in which the Spirit brings us to die and be buried with Christ, so that we might be raised up with him (Rom. 6:1–14). Overcoming the division (at least in principle) between Jew and Gentile, circumcised and uncircumcised, was the great struggle of and in the early church. However, other divisions are indicated in these texts: culture, gender, and social role. New ones have appeared since: nationalism, tribalism, the generation gap, for example. Christ died and was raised so that any division in these might be removed, and the genuine diversities of creation taken up into the new and re-created humankind.

The image of God renewed in Christ

Let me bring together the argument of this chapter. The creaturely dignity of human beings, made in the image of God, was to be seen in creative relationship with God, with one another, and with the world. It was human rejection of relationship with God which brought about the corruption of the image, and so each of the relationships which flow from it. The New Testament proclaims that Christ brought, and through the Spirit continues to bring, a new reality: the reconciliation of our humanity with God, the consequent reconciliation of human beings with one another, and the expectation of the 'reconciliation of all things, whether in heaven or earth' (Col. 1:20). All of these are to be brought together in the church, Christ's body, the visible sign of the 'new humanity'. In this age these different dimensions are not fully worked out, but the Spirit brings God's ultimate plan of reconciliation into the present, a reconciliation signified in baptism into the triune God.

In terms of our chapter 1 diagram, it can be seen that Christ as *the* image of God restores all the relationships corrupted in and by sin. None of this is possible, however, unless the root of the problem is dealt with: not merely our finite nature, but our sinful state, which turns finitude into tyranny. Restoration of humankind to the divine image entailed Christ's full identification with sinners, his complete dealing with sin, and his being raised from death, as Lord of all. Fundamental to this work is the 'upward vertical' relationship in our diagram; Jesus lived out the obedience which humanity did not, as the 'second Adam', the 'new humanity'. In his death and resurrection has come about the prospect of the reconciliation of human beings – with God and each other, and of and in all things. We do not see that restoration fully yet, nor do we know what it may entail. We experience it to some degree in the church, the body of Christ, the new community of God's Spirit, who brings into the present both what Christ has accomplished and what he will accomplish, anticipating the future re-creation of humankind.[28]

A revision of our diagram is set out below. Diagram 4 needs to be read both from the top down (the divine initiative) and from the bottom up (the divine restoration). In this way the reconciling work of the triune God is seen as having a two-way direction, reaching 'down' to the corrupted creation, and also and at the same time nurturing an 'upward' response in the creatures. This work of the Spirit in the groaning creation (Rom. 8:19) enables renewed humanity to 'grow up into Christ, who is the head' (Eph. 4:15), corresponding to Christ's own 'handing up of the kingdom to God the Father' (1 Cor. 15:24), so that God shall be all in all.

It is important to stress therefore that the diagram should in no sense be taken as fully describing what we experience now. It reflects a process discerned in faith. Such faith is not sight, but neither is it scepticism or unbelief. Rather, it rests, as does the task of reconciliation, secure in the accomplished earthly work of Christ, and the hope of his return to fulfil all things. We have such faith, not as a merely human action, but as the present gift of the Spirit, who brings to life the people of God, the sign of the new humanity, and works ceaselessly to bring to full freedom the groaning creation.

In Diagram 4 we discern something of how the image of God in which we are made, and which is corrupted in sin, is reconciled, renewed and re-created in Christ, the perfect image of God. The pattern looks deceptively simple. The outworking of this perspective on the human condition involves a wide range of Christian thought and action. At its centre is the preaching of Christ crucified and risen, through the witness of God's people, focused in the ministries of Word and gospel sacraments. It is worked out in the community life of Christ's

---

God: Father, Son, Spirit

Christ's reconciliation of God and sinners	↑ The Spirit's work: gospel ministries
Christ's reconciliation of divisions (the new humanity)	The church, of all nations, classes, genders: community, pastoral ministries
Christ's reconciliation of all things	Communal life for the common good: ↓ structural, justice ministries

Creation: looking to the new heavens and earth

Diagram 4: The structure of the 'image of God' renewed in Christ

church, especially in pastoral care and household life. It spills over into commitment to taking up our stewardship of creation, both in the common life of human society and in the wider care for the created order beyond. To attempt to renew human nature using priorities that differ from these, or keeping these various aspects apart, is to distort the perspectives offered in the Scriptures. Alternatively, to refuse to be engaged in Christ's reconciling work, in all its dimensions, is to resist the Spirit. There can therefore be no complacency or exclusivity about spiritual renewal, involvement in family life, public affairs, healing ministries, community health, ecological issues, or simply issues of living. It is inevitable that churches will understand this renewal in the light of differing social, cultural and historical backgrounds, but these must be received as diverse contributions, not raised as new barriers in Christ.

Such multi-faceted renewal must be taken up, but with humility; there is a strong future (eschatological) note in the New Testament texts that places a question-mark over unrealistic enthusiasm about the possibilities of renewal now. What it means to be restored in the image of our Creator as the 'new humanity' is not fully revealed or enacted yet, but we are not without hope: 'Beloved, we are God's children now; what we will be has not yet been revealed. What we do know is this: when he [Christ] is revealed, we will be like him, for we will see him as he is. And all who have this hope in him purify themselves, just as he is pure' (1 Jn. 3:2–3, NRSV).

71

We therefore expect to see something of this hope in the present age. Yet we live in the old humanity, experienced in our mortal bodies, and therefore we need to be careful to avoid naïve utopianism. This danger is always present in Christian movements which are working for renewal; for example, in the ministry of healing, or struggles for liberation. While the quest for the restoration of the image of God in humankind necessitates concern with social justice and welfare, in this age it is a never-ending process. It is primarily God's work, centred in Christ, the one who gives his disciples the 'peace which passes all understanding'. It is seen in the shalom, the communal well-being, sharing and concern, which remains the vision and ideal for God's people to live out. It has its negative side – the struggle for freedom from sin, injustice, fragmentation, oppression – but the lifestyle of the new humanity is fundamentally positive, the communal life of God's people living in fellowship with God, each other and the whole creation. We experience these things only in part now, but look to the time when creation itself will be liberated and purged, and God's rule will extend to all the earth (Rom. 8:18–23; 2 Pet. 3:10–13).

Behind this vision lie further profound questions about human nature, both corporate and individual. Having sought to survey the testimony of the Scriptures, we now review the question of the human condition as it has engaged the Christian tradition.

3

THE IMAGE OF GOD IN CHRISTIAN THOUGHT

The Scriptures speak of what it means to be human in terms of being made 'in the image of God'. What this means precisely is nowhere told us, but it involves relationships with God, one another, and the creation; each of these relations has been inverted and distorted through sin. The New Testament speaks of the image renewed in Christ, but this is more than a past reality restored. Its fullness is known in Jesus Christ, *the* 'image of God', and, as we await his return, so we look to the full revelation of what being human entails. In short, Christian perspectives on being human centre in Christ, on what we are made to be. They have a future, expectant dimension, as well as a past and present sense of realism about mortality and sin.

Perspectives on being human cannot be understood in isolation from those who reflect upon them; the 'double focus' of theological truth and life experience cannot be avoided. Indeed, the exegesis presented in the two preceding chapters is filtered through contemporary influences. Further, wisdom about what it means to be human, even when based on scriptural testimony, is not restricted to our own age. Thus we turn to examine the way in which the notion of being made in the image of God has been conceived in Christian self-understanding. In every age such reflection involves considerable interaction with the prevailing philosophies of the day, and motives for thinking about what it means to be human vary. There is always a danger that ideas developed for one purpose and context will be misrepresented when analysed in another place and situation. On the other hand, not to attempt such an historical overview would leave us blind to our own assumptions and even prejudices.

The approach taken here is not primarily chronological, but looks at different aspects of being human.[1] The prime interest of this survey is not the story of Christian thought, but an attempt to understand the major Christian perspectives on being human. With this in mind, we look in turn at physical, intellectual and religious understandings of what it means to be made in the image of God. It will become evident that none of these testifies adequately to the fullness of the scriptural witness, but they serve to fill out the issues raised in and by historical discussion.

The image of God: physical and spiritual

Some have regarded the image as referring primarily to a physical property. Ancient texts such as the Babylonian *Epic of Gilgamesh*, and modern groups such as the Mormons, hold that humans bear a physical resemblance to the god(s), based on ideas such as our walking upright rather than moving on all fours. Some seek to define what it means to be human by way of contrast with the animals; at a popular level, reaction to Darwin's postulation of human descent from the apes revived these sorts of notions. The Scriptures, however, recognize that humankind shares a 'solidarity of the sixth day' with the animals, though being given dominion over them (see chapter 5 below). C. Ryder Smith argues that the Hebrews thought in terms of a physical resemblance between God and human beings (including in Gn. 1:26), later refined by the prophets into a less material understanding.[2] But few have followed such a bold path!

The greatest difficulty with such views is the assumption that God can be spoken of adequately in human or creaturely fashion. The Scriptures are emphatic that the Creator is distinct from creation (see for example Is. 44:9–20; Rom. 1:22ff.). It is true that human analogies are commonly used for God: arms, feet, eyes, hands, ears, nose, fingers and even loins, with actions such as seeing, grieving, loving, chastizing and speaking being ascribed to God. One cannot avoid this 'anthropomorphism' ('human formism'), since human categories are the highest we know; indeed, the fact that the supreme revelation of God, the incarnation, was in human form, gives it positive justification. Non-anthropomorphic analogies occur occasionally in the Scriptures – rock, light, power, for example – but are less than personal. There is always the danger of making God in the image of humanity. This is perhaps the most subtle idolatry – projecting our highest ideals on to God for our own purposes. It is a danger to which Freud rightly pointed, especially regarding the concept of 'father' as expressing our need for protection; though his claim that all religion is a mere matter of projection of human wishes not only contradicts the Scriptures' testimony to the reality of God, but goes beyond the evidence available to the psychological sciences.[3]

However, it is almost as dangerous to say that being made in the image of God has nothing to do with our physical nature. Christians have sometimes fallen into such a 'spiritual' view of salvation that the body, and the wider created world, have been ignored or despised. On the contrary, Christ came to redeem us not from matter, but from sin, and to restore our nature through the resurrection of the body. To be made in the image of God, and to be renewed in that image, thus involves the whole person, and the human race as a whole, as part of redeemed creation. This was a strong emphasis in the work of the first Christian theologian after the New Testament to discuss these issues, Irenaeus of Lyon (mid-second century).[4] He was faced with strongly 'spiritual' tendencies in gnostic teaching that undermined the reality of Christ's incarnation and rejected most of the teaching of the Old Testament. In response, he took up the notion of Christ as the second Adam, who 'summed up'[5] all that Israel was called to be and do, bringing about the renewal of our human nature, whose fulfilment we look for in

Christ's return. The incarnation of Christ is thus the revelation not only of the divine nature, but also of true human nature – and both in bodily form.

The importance of the inclusion of our bodily nature in salvation grew in significance beyond the immediate rejection of gnostic motifs. In the Greek Christian tradition, salvation came to be construed in terms of the bestowal on our mortal, corrupted humanity of immortality and incorruption, the gifts of Christ's great victory over death (cf. 1 Cor. 15:53–58). As time went on, it became increasingly important that this salvation should have some tangible reality in the present, and this came to be expressed in terms of our being 'participants [koinōnoi] in the divine nature' (2 Pet. 1:3–4).[6] The goal of human life comes to be described as 'divinization' (theiōsis), emphasizing the reality of our communion, through the Spirit, in Christ; as Irenaeus put it, 'the Son of God became the Son of Man, that Man might become son of God'.[7] To Protestant Christians, this sounds as if the distinction between Creator and creature is blurred, but when stated carefully it does not go beyond New Testament ideas. To many eastern Christians, however, with a more Platonic, mystical outlook, it expresses the reality of Christian salvation, the anticipation of the resurrection which we begin to experience through the Spirit even in this present age. As Lossky puts it,

> From the fall until the day of Pentecost, the divine energy, deifying and uncreated grace, was foreign to our human nature, acting on it only from outside . . . Deification, union with God by grace, had become impossible. But the plan of God was not destroyed by the sin of man: the vocation of the first Adam was fulfilled by Christ, the second Adam. God became man in order that man might become god, to use the words of Irenaeus and Athanasius. We often forget that in breaking the tyranny of sin, our Saviour opens to us anew the way of deification, which is the final end of man. The work of Christ calls out to the work of the Holy Spirit (Luke xii, 49).[8]

As a consequence of this emphasis, the eastern tradition places great emphasis on the living unity between Christ and the church, through the Spirit. It has been responsible for a fuller appreciation of the significance of the Trinity for the understanding of what it means to be human. Conversely, in the empirical ethos of the West, this emphasis on the spirituality of the physical can reinforce a false mysticism, as commonly seen in the many New Age ideas current today.[9] But whatever the dangers of its misuse, the physical aspect of being human cannot be excluded from our being made in the image of God.

To regard our physicality as fundamental is inadequate and dangerous. As noted in the previous chapter, the basic problem of the human condition is not our finitude, but our rebellion against God, with the consequent tyranny of the finite that it brings. Many people, from Confucian Chinese to modern westerners, have a strong tendency toward materialism, both in the consumer sense and also in terms of defining humanity. Australians like to think of themselves in strongly physical terms, stressing the importance of suntans, sport and physical appearance. While much of this sort of materialism needs to be challenged, the importance of physical health and well-being, and of the senses, cannot be excluded from what it means to be human (see further in chapter 10 below).

The image of God: mind and heart

The world into which the first Christians took the gospel was dominated by Hellenistic thought. Greek was the language not only of the New Testament, but also of philosophical discussion. Further, the key concepts involved in the gospel raise philosophical concerns: the nature of reality, knowledge and action. It was inevitable therefore that the church came to interact with the various strands of Greek philosophy, including its understandings of what it means to be human. The particular element which stands out in these is the importance of the mind, the intellectual dimension of being human. Sometimes this led to a despising of the body, especially when linked to spiritualized notions of salvation. It is important not to overemphasize this, as if Greek philosophers were uninterested in the realities of daily life; much of their work was concerned with ethics and politics. It was the mind, however, that was generally understood to be the faculty which distinguishes human and animal natures, and the means by which contact was made with the divine (however that was conceived).

The development of Christian understandings of God and the world came about in engagement with Hellenistic philosophy. The classical theologians, having been trained in this, utilized it skilfully, transforming it in the light of Christ, the Word (Logos) incarnate.[10] Nevertheless, these fathers, especially Gregory of Nyssa and Augustine, saw knowing God as primarily an intellectual matter. This did not mean that they were rationalists in the modern sense of dry, argumentative intellectuals. Nor did they think of reason as like a computer programme, in which outcomes are wholly determined by prescribed processes. Rather, following the Greek tradition, they saw rational knowing as contemplative and imaginative, a reflective journey in truth. Their attempts to define the image were therefore primarily intellectual.[11] Our restoration in the image or likeness of God means being 'renewed in the spirit of our minds' (Eph. 4:22–24), or being 'renewed in knowledge' (Col. 3:10).

The word 'imagination', a Latinism, reflects this intellectual, yet non-rationalistic, understanding of 'image'. 'Imagination' carries with it the connotation of creative thought, not merely the technical exercise of reason; and it is in this sense that many Christian theologians have considered humans to be made in the image of God. By 'intellectual faculties' is thus meant something far richer than mere 'head knowledge'. It is more akin to what the Scriptures term the 'heart', as understood in the philosophically religious patterns of the patristic age. This needs to be kept in mind, lest we misinterpret much of the Christian tradition. It is common to hear criticism of theologians as being too intellectual. Their work can certainly be read that way, given the intellectual games played by some who are called theologians, and the anti-intellectual ethos prevalent in much popular Christianity. But neither distortion justifies a despising of the significance of intellectual faculties to being human.[12]

In the light of emphasis on the intellect, it was not uncommon for the fathers to expound the concept of the image of God by contrasting humanity with the animal and angelic realms.[13] Like the animals, we are created beings, yet unlike them we possess imagination, the desire and capacity to grow towards or in God. Yet we are also like the angels, in that we may know God (cf. Ps.

8:5–7; Heb. 2:5–9). But unlike them we must grow in our knowing; angels are perfected already. These ideas need not be interpreted as spiritualistic: they have considerable devotional power, and those who used them looked to the resurrection of the *body* as the culmination of salvation, as has already been noted. Yet their Greek (in particular, Stoic or neo-Platonic or both, and, after the twelfth century, neo-Aristotelian) background did introduce a tendency towards an overly intellectual understanding of the image. In a culture dominated by technology, their imaginative rationalism is easily misunderstood as mere intellectualism, but in other cultural settings it still retains considerable interpretive power.

To illustrate this more fully, consider Augustine's exploration of what it means to be human.[14] He came to know God after a long search, culminating in a definite conversion experience (at least in his own perception). His Christian walk did not stop there, but continued to develop, initially through philosophical work and monastic practice, then in pastoral ministry as a bishop. This ministry saw three major crises: Donatism, Pelagianism, and the fall of Rome. In each case his responses marked a growth in understanding of God and of human nature, especially in relation to grace.

It was in his last years that Augustine penned *On the Trinity*. Despite the title assigned to this work, its subject is better understood as the Christian's journey of growth into God.[15] Two assumptions lie behind his analysis. First, given the scriptural witness that we are made in the image of God, Augustine believed that by following the Socratic dictum 'Know thyself', we may come to know God more deeply through reflection on the image within, a path possible due only to the work of Christ and the grace of the Holy Spirit. Secondly, Augustine expects to find a trinitarian image within, since the doctrine of the Trinity is the Christian response to the question, 'Who is God?'

Most interpreters of the work see the first part, chapters I–VII, as an exposition of the orthodox doctrine of the Trinity, and refutations of its opponents, clearing the ground for the second part, chapters VIII–XV.[16] In these chapters Augustine explores several possible answers to his quest for the image of God within: for example, the way we love (lover, beloved, loving), or our knowing of outward things (the thing known, the senses which know it, our knowledge of it). His final conclusion is that the image of God within us is the structure of the mind as memory, understanding, and will. The mind – or, as suggested earlier, 'imagination' in the modern sense – is creative, and in the interaction of its various aspects we grow constantly in knowing God. This knowing is not easy or obvious, however, but takes place as a gift of grace through faith, presently working 'in a glass darkly', until the day we shall see 'face to face' (*cf.* 1 Cor. 13:12, AV); in the meantime we know God chiefly in prayer.

While such an analysis conveys a sense of the main contents of *On the Trinity*, it does not do justice to its perception of what it means to be human. Augustine seems to have understood the various internal 'trinities' he proposes as more than merely a series of sharper academic examples of the image within. Rather, they describe ever deepening stages in the Christian knowing of God; beginning with acceptance of orthodox scriptural testimony, we move forwards 'into' the God in whose image we are made by way of love, sense, perception, thought, and finally vision. This interpretation sheds considerable light on the deep mystery and grand destiny of human beings. It is also patient of a corporate as well as an individual interpretation; the journey of life is taken not just by the race as a whole, or by isolated individuals, but by persons in relationship with God, in whom we live and move and have our being, even though we may be at different stages in the journey.[17]

As regards his conclusions about the image within, Augustine himself recognized that this analysis is inadequate, since memory, understanding and will do not constitute a human person, but a human mind, and the path to the knowledge of God is never fully traversed in this life. Although intellectual faculties are an indispensable element in the image of God, they cannot be the whole. Nevertheless, it is through these that the Christian grows gradually but definitely in the knowledge of God (not least through meditative study of the Scriptures), and so demonstrates the significance of the mind, imagination, and heart in being human.

The image of God: soul and grace

Perhaps the most popular understanding of the image of God is that it refers to a religious faculty within us, the 'soul'. The precise meaning of this term is difficult to specify, since it has been used in a variety of ways in both the philosophical and Christian traditions. The relation of soul and body is discussed in chapter 10; for the present, the term is used to refer to any faculty within a human being which (it is claimed) has specifically to do with relationship to the divine (however this is conceived). With regard to the image of God, 'soul' comes to be used relatively late in the development of Christian thought. The fathers spoke of the soul a great deal, since it formed a significant role in Hellenistic philosophy; but regarding relation to God they generally spoke in terms of intellect and spirit, terms which nevertheless functioned very like 'soul'. It is in the medieval, scholastic period that 'soul' comes to have a narrowly defined reference to a religious faculty over against the body, a development akin to the rise of a sharp distinction between the sacred and secular. Its importance grew with the development of purgatory, the 'place' in which the (disembodied) Christian soul was believed to be purged, until it was fit for the full presence of God. To some degree the Reformation continued to accept such terminology, although it questioned the sharp division between body and soul, and sacred and secular, which scholastic theology assumed.

The significance of the soul as identified with the image of God within came considerably to the fore in the nineteenth and early twentieth centuries, when the 'immortality of the soul' for its own sake, apart from the saving work of Christ, was stressed.[18] This has been questioned in recent decades, by biblical scholars as well as by secularists. Whatever the precise details, the idea that human beings possess a particular faculty through which they relate to God underlies much thinking about being made in the image of God. Examination of this tradition takes us from the earliest fathers to the present. What follows should be seen not only as a discussion of the image as a religious faculty, but also as an introductory survey of contemporary issues in understanding what it means to be human.

Irenaeus began an influential theological tradition concerning the image of God, which he understood as a religious faculty, even though he stressed the significance of the incarnation for understanding what it means to be human, and a 'physical' understanding of salvation, as noted above. In order to explain the evident difference between Christ's perfect, and our marred, human nature, he came to distinguish two aspects of this: 'image' (retained after the fall) and 'likeness' (which was lost).[19] His exegetical basis for so doing was the double terminology of Genesis 1:26, even though the terms are almost certainly used there interchangeably; in Genesis 1:27 both are used, while Genesis 9:6 speaks only of 'image', and Genesis 5:2 only of 'likeness'.[20] That a large gap exists between what we were made to be, and what we are now, is evidently the case, and poses many questions in trying to understand what it means to be human. The present question is whether Irenaeus's solution is adequate or helpful.

On the one hand, he argued, we all, Christians or not, possess the 'image' (*șelem, eikōn, imago*) of God which constitutes our true humanity, the essence of our rational nature. This includes human freedom, and capacity for creative thought; as noted above, it is perhaps best understood in modern terms as the imagination. Whatever the misuse made of it, this image of God remains, and is related to the body as well as to the soul, because of the incarnation.[21] On the other hand, Irenaeus held that Adam and Eve, in addition to being created in the 'image' of God, were also made in the divine 'likeness' (*d°mût, homoiōsis, similitudo*). This was possessed by them only as innocent children, as a promise beginning to be fulfilled; they were not made fully mature, but were intended to grow up into a fully mature humanity. It was the desire to accelerate this process that led to their losing this 'likeness'.[22] Its restoration is one of the gifts of the Spirit who, through regeneration, activates 'spirit' in believers, and so prepares them for full humanity in the resurrection. Put in terms of Augustine's model, for example, the grace which restores this gift to the sinner adorns memory with hope, understanding with faith, and will with love.

Irenaeus's eschatological, forward-looking emphasis is profoundly scriptural. His notion of a twofold human nature, corresponding to 'image' and 'likeness', may have rested on a distinction which is unsustainable exegetically,[23] but his usage of the distinction was understandable as he strove to preserve the universality of the image and face the consequences of sin. Nevertheless, it laid the basis for what became a cornerstone for medieval scholastic theology, the distinction between the spheres of nature and supernature, accessed through reason and faith respectively, and lived out in secular or religious lifestyles. Both spheres were understood to be the place of divine operations, through different types of grace. Yet nature, though good as created, is known to us only as affected by sin. Since our present humanity is tainted by sin, the image of God in us is less than complete; if it were wholly lost, so would our humanity be lost. Scholastic theologians such as Aquinas thus argued that at the fall an original supernatural extra gift (*donum superadditum supernaturale*) of 'original righteousness' was lost, but that the image itself remained fundamentally untouched by the ravages of sin.[24] As a consequence, human beings came to be thought of as neutral with respect to sin, and so able to prepare themselves for justification.[25]

The Reformers protested sharply at this notion that human beings could prepare themselves for justification before God. They saw the consequences of unforgiven sin and the necessity of grace as clearly as their Roman Catholic opponents, but stressed that only by God's initiative, with no sense of human co-operation or preparation, could sinners be saved.[26] This meant that they tended to regard the image of God in humanity as practically lost (Luther), or irreparably marred (Calvin) in the fall.[27] As time went on, the need to recognize that in some sense the image is still present in humanity, yet not in such a way as to displace the necessity of grace, led to sharp debates within Protestant theology. Calvin thus spoke of a 'broad' image, present in all, consisting of the soul's faculties of reason, understanding and will; and a 'narrow' image, present in the elect, the restoration of true knowledge (*cf.* Col. 3:10), righteousness and holiness (*cf.* Eph. 4:24).[28] Some spoke of 'remnants' of the image remaining, or a 'relic' of original humanity. Significant stress came to be placed on the practical experience of Christian truth, similar in kind to the fathers' emphasis, yet put in the language of action rather than contemplation.

The image of God: individual and corporate

These post-Reformation trends led in part to a growing emphasis on the individual's role in exercising faith, but the roots of individualism go back to an earlier age. From the perspective of modern western society, the Middle Ages epitomize a communal ethos, but worship had become increasingly individualistic. For example, a priest did not need a congregation to say mass, and any who were present became mere spectators, engaging in private devotions parallel to the liturgy. It would be an exaggeration to blame this on a single factor, a religious, private understanding of the image; but it was a significant influence in the growth of individualism.[29] It can be seen in the famous definition of the person by Boethius: *rationalis naturae individua substantia* – 'the undivided substance of a rational nature'. Although this definition was formulated in the context of a discussion of Christology,[30] it became widely used in scholastic theology, emphasizing the rational element of the image. However, it served to give much higher prominence to the individual person, even though *in-dividua* has the negative meaning of 'undivided', rather than the positive meaning of 'separate individual' as in Boethius. This emphasis then gained greater significance as the doctrines of purgatory and hell came to have an overwhelming place in popular piety. The classical Christian emphasis was on the destiny of the human race as a whole, in the context of the renewal of creation. This was gradually replaced by stress on the fate of each particular person before God, particularly when it came to be calculated in precise numbers of days in purgatory.[31]

The Reformation contested the nature–supernature dualistic tendency of scholastic theology, as noted above, and sought to interpret human nature in the light of the gospel of grace, received through faith. Despite this, the human person continued to be thought of in largely individual terms, especially as the central role of personal faith in salvation was emphasized. Purgatory, with its attendant trappings of indulgences, was rejected, but human destiny continued to be understood in individual terms. All sides of theological controversy in the western churches in the sixteenth century agreed on the positive aspects of what it means to be made in the image of

God. Sharp differences emerged regarding the negative side, however: to what extent are we 'capable' of knowing God in our own right, apart from divine grace?[32] Approaching the question of what it means to be human from this perspective turns the focus of attention upon the individual in isolation from humanity as a whole.

In post-Reformation thought, and especially in post-Enlightenment humanism, the corporate and communal elements present in the thought and practice of the major Reformers waned. A particular turning-point was the philosophical work of Descartes. In a situation where revelation as the basis of human self-understanding was questioned, he sought to establish it on the basis of reason alone. This entailed a dualist and individual concept of human nature: each of us is constituted as body and soul or mind, with the exercise of reason dominating other aspects (and other creatures). Although he saw himself as a Christian believer,[33] the effect of Descartes's work was to move the basis of discussion about being human away from the notion of being made in the image of God, towards humanity in its own right. This trend continued in Kant, in whose work the Cartesian dualism of body and mind was furthered in a dualism of knowledge: we can truly know only what we experience of a thing through our senses (*noumenon*), rather than the thing itself (*phenomenon*). This furthered a trend of scepticism about certainty in matters theological, including the nature of what it means to be human.[34]

In the nineteenth century, growing revolt against religion, especially in institutional form, saw the place of critical reason magnified.[35] Rationalism grew into the grand schema of idealism in Hegel, in which Christian motifs were translated into philosophical ideas, focused in the dialectical method. With regard to being human, Hegel swung away from the individual pole towards the collective (since we exist only in the dialectic of self and other) and to the spiritual (since the dialectic takes us beyond the material realm). This collectivist (and dualist) emphasis was expressed in historical materialist terms by Marx, using the method of dialectic to analyse society, rather than as a metaphysical tool, as in Hegel. Marxists approach such study with explicit commitments about the nature of human life, as do Christians. In other circles, however, sociological analysis has tended to assume that if a particular human behaviour is not uncommon, then it is permissible. Cultural anthropology has helped us to appreciate the diversity of human lifestyles, and (along with sociology) has brought a much needed critique to unquestioned assumptions about what is normal human behaviour. The description of something as a statistical norm, however, easily carries over into its being regarded as a moral standard. This misunderstanding of social research is magnified by the way it is often reported in the popular media, where the description of a common practice implies its endorsement.[36]

Psychology is the other modern science that has particularly affected our understanding of the human condition. The work of Freud and his successors focused on the individual, giving rise to concepts such as instinct, complexes, and repression, which are today part of common speech. Much of this analysis was opposed to religious perspectives, attempting to render irrelevant traditional concepts such as soul and spirit, sin and guilt, and the reality of God. Freudian psychology has also been seen as assuming the normative status of the male. Other schools, however, are open to the insights of religion and feminism, especially that of Jung, for whom both elements are essential, and for whom global as well as individual consciousness plays a major part. Along with social changes through transport and mass communications, in recent decades the psychological paradigm for understanding human beings has furthered the coming to the fore of the sexual aspect of being human. Biology has furthered this trend, particularly through the development of reliable contraception, while the social sciences have become increasingly sensitive to feminist perspectives.

Several aspects of these trends are discussed in succeeding chapters; for the moment it suffices to note that much modern reflection about being human continues to be undertaken in a 'non-transcendent mood'.[37] The rise of the empirical sciences led to the concept of the universe as a closed system, at least in the popular mind, so that what it means to be human has come to be thought of as wholly explicable by empirical investigation. But there have been contrasting voices, especially in various personalist philosophies, such as that of Buber, the psychological work of Jung, Rogers and Maslow, and the mystical elements of modern physics. Existentialism, whether in sceptical, mystical or Christian forms, focuses attention on human experience rather than general concepts as the fundamental matter of philosophical work. It has often been allied with the arts' critique of human follies, which has continued to affirm the human capacity for self-transcendence, even if the nature of visions which present an alternative to the prevailing materialism has not been clear.

A further element in modern attitudes to being human stems from a common rejection of formalism. In social and political life, this has furthered the cult of personality. One consequence of the Industrial Revolution was the division of work into public and private realms. The public world has retained a strongly corporate ethos, whether that of the trade union, the professional association, or the boardroom. In contrast, the private world has increasingly become the realm of individual relationships, and it is here that religion has been largely situated in the western world. When nineteenth-century European thinkers questioned any transcendent aspect to being human, Christian reaction was commonly to place renewed emphasis upon the soul (especially as immortal) over against the body, and upon individual religious experience, while the kingdom of God came to be interpreted in a spiritualistic, anti-material, manner. Popular exegesis of Luke 17:21, 'the kingdom of God is within [NRSV mg.] you [plural]', understood 'within you' to refer to the soul or spirit of the individual, whereas the text clearly means 'among you' (the people of God; NRSV main text). Likewise, John 4:24, 'God is spirit, and those who worship him must worship in spirit and truth', came to be understood in an idealist, anti-materialist sense.[38]

Perhaps the most basic problem with the idea of the image of God as a religious faculty in humans is the assumption that it is an individual, rather than a relational and personal, reality. Behind this is another assumption, that the image of God can be defined as an entity in itself, and so be identifiable within an individual. Again, once an individual interpretation is assumed, the question of gender arises sharply: given that women and men are different, does one possess the image more than the other? These types of questions lie behind much contemporary discussion of the image of God.

87

The image of God in contemporary discussion

In the twentieth century, being human has gradually come to be thought of in atomistic, individual, self-sufficient terms. The Christian tradition, though seeking to mitigate the worst excesses of this trend, is at least in part responsible for it. An individualistic emphasis was seen to be highly desirable and relevant in an age of exploration, pioneering and discovery. It continues to be given prominence in much modern thought, especially where the heritage of the liberal-democratic tradition is dominant. Slogans such as 'freedom of choice' and 'free market' can work only in a community where there is equality of opportunity and an ethos of co-operation, yet these are precisely the conditions which those who espouse such slogans reject as social goals. In the past, emphasis on the individual was balanced by the practical need for interdependence within the comparatively homogeneous societies which made up local communities in most parts of the world. How appropriate it is to emphasize the role of the individual in a society where community has broken down, and where there is little in common between people, even in the same town, is a moot point. Nevertheless, regard for the unique significance of each person in the sight of God remains essential to a Christian understanding of what it means to be made in the image of God, an understanding which integrates both corporate and individual perspectives.

Community and feminist perspectives on being human are key aspects of contemporary reflection. It was the theological work of Karl Barth in particular that drew attention to these questions, not only in reaction to current trends, but also anticipating them to some extent.[39] His initial work on the doctrine of humanity was done against the background of the rise of National Socialism in Germany. Barth utterly rejected its claims to divine legitimation through a nationalist understanding of divine providence. To sustain this position, he went on to reject any claim to divine truth apart from Jesus Christ, who was and is the truth about humanity. With the help and encouragement of his assistant, Charlotte von Kirschbaum, he reworked the doctrine of 'man' in the light of fresh exegesis of the 'image' texts, a Christ-centred exegesis whose influence can be readily felt in the opening chapters of this book.[40] Although elements of his work are now seen to be dated, it has brought about a paradigm shift in Christian understanding of the human condition, of increasing relevance as community and feminist perspectives continue to leaven contemporary human life.

Barth made three key contributions. His first is negative, but clears away a great deal of unhelpful ground: we are nowhere told in the Scriptures what the image of God actually *is*. Moreover, given the commandment about not making images (Ex. 20:4), we are in danger of committing idolatry if we seek to find rather than live out our status as those already made in the image of God. Secondly, Barth (following Augustine) keeps in mind at all times the truth that God is triune; the image is thus relational, involving our living as covenant partners with God and each other. In particular, as God lives in self-relationship, so do we; an analogy is drawn between the mutual life of the distinct divine Persons, and the mutual life of humankind as male and female. Thirdly, all is to be seen in and through Jesus Christ, the true covenant partner with both us and God. It is thus the community of those 'in Christ' which reveals today what it means to be made in the divine image. In this way Barth brings the doctrine of the church into close relationship with the doctrines of both God and humanity. This perspective offers an impressive account of how individual and corporate sides of being human may be integrated in a community of persons.

In recent years the need to balance individual and corporate, female and male, aspects of being human has emerged as a key element in both Christian and wider reflection. They are sometimes regarded as correlated: males are said to stress the individual (or corporate totalitarian), and females the communal, aspect of being human. As a description of historical trends (and much current practice) this contains a good deal of truth, but as a matter of definition it perpetuates the stereotypes it seeks to reject. It is in the light of such concerns that the phrase 'community of women and men' was coined by some in the World Council of Churches.[41] It indicates that the issues of gender and community cannot be separated, since both men and women are fully human, and community presupposes diversity. Later chapters will take up these issues in more detail; for the present, two examples of the issues involved will serve to bring this survey of the concept of the image of God to a conclusion.

The first is more by way of observation than argument. Many of the discussions noted thus far have assumed that by 'man' is meant 'one individual'. There are problems with this, as has been seen especially in the philosophical and work climate of this century in industrialized societies. But a vast area of reflection has been obscured by a related assumption: that the individual concerned is male. Realizing this sheds a very different light on many discussions about being human. 'Man' has functioned in English until very recently as both a generic, corporate term, 'the human race', and as a reference to a particular male person. The ambiguity raises major problems when 'man' is used by some generically, but is heard by others to refer only to males; the result is the exclusion of women. But the generic use of 'man' also allows some things to be said which are difficult to say otherwise – the line in the Christmas carol that Christ was 'pleased as man with man to dwell' for example.[42] Nevertheless, recognition of the full humanity of both women and men means that inclusive language is here to stay (see Appendix 2). In this light, reflection on being human must take as full account as possible of the distinct experiences of both women and men. What is more, since being human involves community, the different nuances of female-male, male-male and female-female relationships need consideration. Profound theological issues are raised in other areas as well: the significance of the eternal Word becoming incarnate as a male human, the use of masculine names for God, and feminine attributes for the people of God, for example. The latter issues lie beyond the scope of this book, but the question of gender and being human is taken up in chapters 7 and 8 below, though it has lain just below the surface in all that has been written thus far.[43]

The second example concerns the nature of human rights. In the West, this is generally understood to refer to the rights of each individual. In other societies, in contrast, it is understood to refer to the right of a community to preserve its own identity. The Salman Rushdie case illustrates this well. On the one hand, the vast majority of English academics and mass media insist that he should be free to write as he wishes; to allow otherwise is to infringe civil liberties, in particular the right of self-expression. Many Muslims, however, insist that his writing denies them the liberty to live as a community in submission to Allah. How can such diametrically opposed concepts of liberty exist together? In modern societies, groups such as these often live together in the one country, or even neighbourhood, rather than far separated as in times past. The earlier situation allowed stereotypes and propaganda to flourish unchecked; the present tends to question all forms of communality. The fundamental Christian perspective seeks to hold them together by emphasizing that 'personal' makes sense only in 'community', both terms finding their true meaning in the life of the triune God. In this situation it is clearly of the greatest practical importance that ways of integrating individual and corporate dimensions of being human be explored and lived. It is to this task that we now turn.

FOCUS 2A

THE HUMAN
RACE

PREAMBLE

To be human means to be made in the image of God. The exploration of this biblical motif has brought the discussion to a turning-point in the argument. Through surveying the biblical data and historical understandings of what it means to be made in the image of God, we have explored the first focus of human existence. It is now time to turn to the other focus, human life in the world as we experience it, both communal and personal. These foci are not wholly distinct, let alone opposed; the biblical data integrate them in *the* image of God, Jesus Christ, who epitomizes what it means to be human, rescues us from sin and, even more, reveals and leads us into what we are made to become, both as individuals and as a race.

The immediate question is whether to consider next the personal or the communal perspective. Ideally they belong together, and their interaction is represented in the preference for the relational term 'person' rather than 'individual' in the Christian tradition. Some would argue that the personal has priority over the corporate, especially when salvation is considered. Each human being is unique, is called to make his or her own response to God's grace, and will be brought to account individually before Christ. The present book nevertheless begins with the corporate dimension, in the light of the discussion of what it means to be made in the image of God (chapter 1), and the way this is understood in the light of Christ (chapter 2) and in Christian thought considered historically (chapter 3). The communal aspect is taken first not only on the basis of theological analysis, but also because key contexts in which we live today cannot be addressed without such an orientation, particularly human relationships in society (chapter 4), and with the natural world (chapter 5).[1] This section concludes with a discussion of human culture (chapter 6), forming a bridge to considering the personal aspect of life today.

4

HUMAN LIFE IN SOCIETY

Personal and communal humanity

The basic criterion for all Christian theology is Jesus Christ. Jesus was a particular person, who lived the life of a particular individual: a male, a Jew, an artisan, Aramaic-speaking, unmarried. Yet orthodox Christian faith asserts that in Christ the eternal Word took our human nature, not merely the life of a particular individual.[1] Further, the incarnate Christ died as both representative (on our behalf) and substitute (in our stead) both for particular persons and for the race as a whole, to redeem and so to constitute the 'new humanity'. He rose from death not only to transform dying, but to restore human nature itself, so fashioning the possibility of personal participation (*koinōnia*) in the life of God. The church, the visible expression of this participation, which the Holy Spirit brings to birth in and through Christ, is not merely a collection of individuals (though it is at least that), but is described in the New Testament using embodied, corporate terms: the 'flock', 'vine', 'bride', and especially the 'body' of Christ. It 'is not an aggregate of justified sinners or a sacramental institute or a means of private self-salvation but the avante-garde of the new creation'.[2]

The interaction of personal and communal perspectives on being human is further illuminated by considering particular people in the Scriptures. Abraham can be considered as an example of what it means to walk personally the path of faith (and doubt).[3] He is also portrayed in the Scriptures as a representative person, summing up what it means to view the human race through the eyes of faith. Both aspects are present in Romans 4; the personal is to the fore in the first dozen verses, but the representative sense is emphasized from verse 11 onwards, where Abraham is viewed as the 'ancestor of all who believe'. The same can be said of many others, such as David, Adam, Eve, Noah, Moses and especially Jacob (Israel).[4] From one point of view each is an individual, yet the Scriptures regard them more as representative persons. Such a double function also occurs in many Psalms, especially laments where the 'I' whose experience is being shared can be regarded as both an individual and a representative person (Pss. 40; 69; 73; for example). The former, personal reading is the one more familiar to those who have grown up in the individualistic ethos of the western tradition (especially Protestants). But the latter, communal reading is an indispensable element in the biblical testimony, and both senses have ongoing significance for Christians today.

The Scriptures thus provide firm support for both personal and communal approaches to the question of being human. Which of these is more appropriate to discuss first is more than a theoretical issue; it serves to indicate that the communal and personal aspects of being human are inseparable, yet distinct. Their interaction is evident in the Scriptures and Christian tradition, but needs also to be approached with current issues kept in mind.[5] The communal dimension is taken up first here, in part because it is to the fore in contemporary discussion, but chiefly because it is theologically prior to the personal, and provides indispensable background to understanding what it means to be a particular human being.[6] Humanity considered corporately, however, is seen most starkly in its negative aspect, in the corporate dimensions of sin.

Inhuman humanity

The corporate dimension of human nature should ideally be related in the first place to its grandeur as seen in creation (*cf.* Ps. 8). But sin is so prevalent that it needs immediate consideration. That each human being lives as a sinner is clearly taught in the Scriptures.[7] Sin is broader and wider than any individual's sinning, however; it is a matter not only of what is wrong with *me*, but of what is wrong with *us*. While it is possible to reform moral behaviour at the personal level, 'in every human group there is less reason to guide and check impulse, less capacity for self-transcendence, less ability to comprehend the needs of others and therefore more unrestrained egoism'.[8]

Human beings characteristically act inhumanely. The list of twentieth-century horrors is not short: Flanders, Armenia, Georgia, Changi, Warsaw, Dresden, Auschwitz, Nagasaki, Tibet, Cambodia, Ethiopia, Sudan, Chechnya, Bosnia, Rwanda . . . Few if any of those reading this book torture or maim others directly, but all of us are enmeshed in structures that keep some in affluence while others starve, offer immense opportunities to a few at the expense of the many, and place ideology ahead of human dignity. And not only humans are affected: systematic cruelty to animals is commonplace, whether in the scientific laboratory, among subsistence farmers, or in the automated production of food. 'The earth dries up and withers . . . [and] lies polluted under its habitants' (Is. 24:4–5); its resources are threatened to the point where clean air and fresh water are in danger in many places.

Christian faith in a loving God struggles in the face of such evidence that the human race as a whole is caught up in the web of sin and death. The scriptural testimony to our solidarity in sin should keep us from being surprised at such systematic evil (see the discussion of Rom. 5:12–19 in chapter 2), and its consequences (*cf.* Gn. 3:14–19; Rom. 1:24–32). It should also bring us to accept that we are accountable for this sin, not only in groups such as nations, but also as individuals (*cf.* Mt. 25:31–46). Many Christians, including myself living in an affluent Australian city, need to repent and be converted with regard to our lifestyle. This is no simple matter, since our solidarity in sin means that our status as creatures has been endemically affected, as has the whole created order within which we live. Two particular aspects of this are of critical concern today: our social life as human beings, and our relation with the world of nature, especially the animals. Those aspects correspond to the 'horizontal' and 'downward vertical' aspects of the diagram used earlier – and both 'are not what they should be'.[9]

Both the personal and the communal dimensions of human life are shaped by our historical contexts, themselves affected by sin. The rise of individualism in the West in the past two centuries undergirds the priority of the personal, but emphasizes it so greatly that human life has become fragmented.[10] It is paradoxical that the growth of technology has fostered individualism along with global problems (such as the threat of nuclear war and ecological concerns) which touch the race as a whole. This paradox illustrates further how the corporate dimension to sin transcends, but does not displace, its personal aspect. Unfortunately, the corporate dimensions of sin are not always appreciated by Christians. This has especially been the case in the last two centuries, when reaction against the intermingling of church and state led to the idea that the gospel has to do only with personal life, and so society is to be changed for the better only through change in individual lives. That change at the personal level is an indispensable and major element in social progress is true; William Temple once remarked that the greatest contribution the church can make to the social order is 'to make good Christian men and women'.[11] But personal change as the sole basis for responding to corporate sin is not the whole truth, and is itself evidence of the deceptive effect which sin can have on the thinking of even dedicated Christians. As John Gladwin puts it:

> It is not quite enough to say that it is man who is fallen and he uses or abuses a neutral environment and neutral social institutions. The world was not neutral when God created it and pronounced it good. The structures of social life are not neutral; God provided them for man's good. So also since the entrance of sin the world has not been neutral. It is under a curse, and only in Christ is it relieved of this burden. Similarly the structures of society suffer from the weakness of the

fall, with the effect that they militate against God's plan
for fully human life in the world . . .

A doctrine of sin which dwells exclusively upon
individual wrongdoing cannot cope with the need to
come to terms with the social, corporate and institutional wickedness in the world.[12]

A recent example is apartheid in South Africa. Churches
flourished among all racial groups in that country for many
years, providing support and forgiveness for both oppressor and
oppressed, and offering hope to the downtrodden. Yet the
structural sin of racism could be dealt with only at a structural
level, by changing laws and creating new political structures on a
non-racial basis. To imagine that structural change was all that
was needed swings to the other extreme, discounting the need
for personal repentance and change; but without structural
change, no amount of personal change will suffice. In Australia
a similar situation exists with attitudes to Asian immigrants;
sharing the gospel with Vietnamese young people without facing
the racism they experience in daily life inevitably reflects a
truncated understanding of sin (and of the lordship of Christ
over all of life). It needs to be remembered that South Africa was
not alone in officially restricting the opportunities for people of
a particular race to participate fully in society; Fiji is a case in
point, despite its Christian heritage. Other countries, such as
Albania and Israel, deny full participation to particular religious
traditions, including the Christian churches; working for
structural change in such cases not only promotes justice, but
facilitates the proclamation of the gospel.

In ancient Israel the corporate dimension of sin is seen
perhaps most clearly in the exile, in which all the people
suffered for the sins of the nation as a whole.[13] It was in the light
of this catastrophe that the prophets proclaimed that God deals
with people individually as well as corporately. An old proverb
had said, 'The parents have eaten sour grapes, and the
children's teeth are set on edge'; now 'it is only the person who
sins that shall die' (Ezk. 18:2–4). The same truth, of both
personal and corporate sin and accountability, is seen in Jesus'
teaching about the sheep and goats being separated at his
coming (Mt. 25:31–46). Although this passage is generally

understood to apply at the personal level, the reference in the text is to 'all the nations' (Mt. 25:32), reflecting communal responsibility for sin. It is not difficult to think of recent examples of such corporate sin: the treatment of Aborigines in post-1788 Australia, the attempt to eliminate the Jews by Nazi Germany, the deliberate genocide practised in Biafra, Cambodia and elsewhere, and, in daily life, the inability of many social systems to respond to human needs and aspirations – all of these speak of communal, structural dimensions to sin.[14]

The Marxist vision

It is at this point that the Christian estimate of human life differs from Marxist approaches. At their best, both share similar ideals about human co-operation, a common commitment to the importance of taking material reality with full seriousness, a passion for justice in human society, and a strong sense of hope in the arrival of a new future.[15] Christian faith is materialistic in the sense that it regards the created order (including nature, history and society) as real, and proclaims that salvation takes place in and through the world; it rejects a dualism between spirit and matter. It denies materialism in the Marxist sense, that no transcendent or divine reality exists. However, both Christian faith and Marxism reject the idea that 'the reality which we do perceive is in fact only matter, that is, that there is no essential difference between lifeless matter, plants, animals and man'.[16] Marx's theory of *historical* materialism asserts that material needs determine the development of society, and so human history; this is far more than a simplistic 'only matter matters' viewpoint. Marxist analysis of human society in terms of economic production has brought a significant dose of earthy realism to the understanding of history, and encouraged the telling of the human story 'from below' as well as 'from above'. As one Christian theologian puts it, 'Marxism came as a timely reminder that human beings have bodies, that they eat and work, that they live in society and history.'[17] It dissects the inhuman effects of much religious practice and ethos with a fierce precision, reminiscent of Jesus' analysis of the inhumanity of the religious authorities of his day.

Marxism has great appeal, even in a post-1989 world. It offers hope to those who long for freedom from the oppressions that characterize much human living, and a coherent, hopeful worldview, claiming to be based on empirical science, to intellectuals tired of academic game-playing. 'The great appeal of Marxism today stems from the fact that it has synthesised the discoveries of modern natural and social science into one great system.'[18] Beyond need and intellect, it offers a strong sense of solidarity among those committed to changing a corrupt system. I have seen the dedication on the faces of people singing the Internationale after a successful campaign on a social issue in which I have had a part, and felt its attraction.[19] In response, many would accuse Marxism of having failed, and of having itself become an instrument of oppression, citing as examples Soviet, eastern European and Cuban experience. Marxists might respond by arguing that the leaders of the revolutions in these societies, especially Stalin, betrayed the ideals of Marxism, or that the right conditions for the emergence of the classless society, beyond capitalism and the bourgeoisie, have not yet arrived. It is akin to a Christian responding to an attack on Christianity by saying that it has not been fully practised in any church.

Such a dialogue, however, does not face the deeper issue of the differing estimates of human nature in Marxist and Christian faith. Marxism assumes that there is nothing wrong with human beings as individuals, except that when driven by the need to protect their vested interests, they experience alienation, unless converted to a socialist view of the purpose of life. This outlook bears considerable similarity to the Christian understanding of the need for personal change, but sees the problem in the system which perpetuates vested interests, not in human beings as such.[20] Marxism, however, also assumes that human beings *as a group* are willing and able to change the world towards a 'classless society' in which divisions are removed – indeed, such change can come about only through class consciousness and action. This marks a fundamental difference with Christian faith, which has a far more sombre estimate of human sin at both communal and personal levels. These different views about the problem correlate with differences about the solution. In Marxism, hope is placed in the (revolutionary) activity of humanity itself, through class consciousness and struggle, and tends to utopian idealism. Christian hope looks to God in Christ, but nevertheless needs to be demonstrated in earthly reality, lest it fulfil the charge of 'pie in the sky when you die' which Marxist analysis so effectively and appropriately attacks.[21]

Marxist faith in human nature leads to a distinctive approach to ethics. The ultimate goal is the classless society, characterized by true humanism, in which each person will be truly free, and there will be the full and selfless participation of all. 'Freedom' is a key word in Marxist rhetoric, but, as in much secular humanism, it is overwhelmingly used in the sense of 'freedom *from*' (emancipation), with little sense of what freedom is *for*, at least before the classless society appears. Marxist language is thus highly combative, and full of military metaphors; the path to the goal of a classless society can be taken only in the midst of the realities of history, through 'class war' against the capitalist system. In the process of this conflict, all other loyalties must be sacrificed, and any means may be employed: 'all's fair in love and war' takes on a new meaning. 'This totalitarian aspect of communist ethics is the thing which has, more than anything else, shocked the conscience of the human race, and created an impression of cynical ruthlessness, which has largely overshadowed the fine humanist element.'[22]

Christian faith, in contrast, confesses that sin affects humanity at both corporate and individual levels in the present, and that its remedy applies to both. Christian ethics thus seeks to hold together means and ends, as it seeks to translate the (eschatological) ideals of the rule of God into the present. That Christians often fail in this must be admitted, and the searching analysis of human nature in its social and political dimensions offered by Marxism must be taken with full seriousness. Nevertheless, the vision of humanity that Christian faith offers – glorious in creation, enmeshed in sin and being renewed in Christ – is both more pessimistic and more optimistic than the Marxist vision. Christians may be distraught at the horror of a situation, but ought not to be surprised; they know the depth of sin's effect on every aspect of the human condition.

Conversely, Christian faith discerns the possibility of change and the hope of renewal in every situation, since it confesses as Lord Jesus Christ, through whose death and resurrection the hope of the new humanity is made real. Only as this faith and hope are practised in communities that embody reconciliation and justice, and in personal lives of dedicated commitment, will Marxists be able to see something of what it means to be human in and through Christ. This practice will never be fully realized in the present world, or in any person in this life; yet just as Christians look to the resurrection body for true freedom, and through faith in the working of the Spirit anticipate that victory here and now, so it ought to be with society. It is all too easy to be deceived about what social repentance and change mean in any particular time and place, fashioning new idols by giving our loyalty to some aspect of human creation rather than to our Creator.[23] Yet to live as if change were not possible is to deny the life-changing power of God. The Christian view of sin as affecting corporate structures means that there will never be a truly just society (or righteous person) on earth; but there can be structures that are less unjust and patterns of life that are more righteous. The task of working towards these is never-ending, and is undertaken as evidence of the ceaseless re-creative work of God in the whole of life.

Economy: wealth and money

A particular aspect of corporate life is economics. The Christian theological tradition has considered the economic-political dimensions of human society in a variety of ways, in each case related to social customs and historical situations. A full discussion is beyond the scope of this book, but some aspects of it need attention, because socio-political life is a fundamental aspect of being human. As a way in, consider how some basic terms have come to change meaning. 'Economy' today evokes exclusively commercial images, to do with statistics about interest rates, GNP, disposable income, current-account deficits, and so on. In classical philosophy, and especially in Christian theology, it had a wider reference, to the various components and interactions of a society taken as a whole. As its Greek root denotes, 'economy' (*oikonomia*) meant 'the principle or law (*nomos*) of the household (*oikos*)'.[24]

In the New Testament, *oikonomia* is often translated 'steward-ship', while an 'economist' (*oikonomos*) is described as a

105

'steward' or 'manager' (Lk. 16:2–4). This position involved responsibility for managing people or property belonging to someone else (*cf.* Lk. 16:1–8; Gal. 4:2); Erastus is described as a 'steward of the city' (Rom. 16:23, my translation). It is a title used in a striking manner of the Christian minister, who is a steward of God (Tit. 1:7), of the mysteries of God (1 Cor. 4:1–2), and of the manifold grace of God (1 Pet. 4:10). 'Economy' in scriptural terms thus brings to mind the activity of God's ministers, commissioned to manage God's resources, as people who are accountable to God. These resources include the creation itself, which humankind has been set to manage (Gn. 1:26–30: see chapter 5 below). Because of sin and its global effects, this stewardship calls us both to proclaim the gospel of sins forgiven, the good news of reconciliation and new life, and also to seek to display that new life embodied in communal life.

The narrowing of 'economy' to refer only to money arrangements has gone along with a similar narrowing in the meaning of 'wealth'. It derives from the old word 'weal' (meaning 'goodness'), the root from which terms such as 'welfare' (meaning 'well-being') derive. Wealth in this sense may be defined as the sum total of resources which enrich human living, relationships and service. Money, in turn, can be described as the 'effectual sign and symbol' of wealth. This sacramental language reflects the idea that although a banknote is in itself only a (very fancy) piece of paper, when used in exchange for goods it conveys its face value effectively; but it is not the goods themselves. Money matters, and matters considerably in contemporary human societies. Yet money is not wealth in and of itself; wealth transcends having money in the bank. In societies where the cash economy is less significant, wealth may be measured by the number of cattle one owns, the food one grows, or the degree of influence carried by one's reputation. The accumulation of capital is limited in such societies, since it requires larger barns to be built to house the crop (*cf.* Lk. 12:18); large-scale capital accumulation is possible only in a society where money functions as the effective symbol of wealth.

In modern times, with industrial development, good transport and communications, most people take for granted the existence of money and easy access to banks. It is hard to envisage a money-less society, but that was the case for several decades in post-1788 Australia, for example, where rum became a (much abused) unit of currency. The economies of many present-day societies progressed from cash to cheques, then to plastic and now to electronic transfer. Today my wages, utility and grocery bills – even many of my donations – are paid without any cash changing hands, and often with no interaction with other persons. Such changes affect the way in which communities work; some changes are beneficial, while others, such as easy credit, are highly damaging. It is said that when someone owes the bank $100,000, the debtor has a problem, but when he or she owes $100,000,000, the bank has a problem! In my own city of Melbourne, Victoria, the collapse in the mid-1980s of a large building society, and then the state bank, drastically affected the lives of many ordinary citizens, who lost their life savings. Yet several prominent businessmen have been able to escape being held accountable for huge unpaid debts, and continue to live in prosperity. In the face of such a distortion of the common life, the personal integrity of particular people may count for little, and it may cost them dearly, as was the case in the state of Victoria for several high-principled leaders. Such corruptions of the 'common wealth' come about because human life in corporate as well as personal dimensions is infected by sin.

One distortion in modern capitalist systems is the way we have come to think of money as real in and of itself, so that money has become *the* barometer of wealth. In biblical terms, however, it is the created order and the gospel of Christ which constitute the divine 'wealth' God offers us, an 'inheritance that is imperishable, undefiled, and unfading' (1 Pet. 1:4). Christian stewardship means that human beings are called to manage the wealth resulting from God's gracious activity in both creation and re-creation, so that the kingdom of this world may be transformed into the kingdom of Christ. We are to care for and promote the 'common weal', the good of the whole human community, local, regional, national and global (*cf.* Je. 29:1–7). Sharing a 'heavenly commonwealth' in the people of God, we long to see such a commonwealth on earth, but know that its full coming will be present only in the 'new heavens and earth' (2 Pet. 3:10ff.). In this light, Christians should be as committed to justice and as critical of vested interests as any Marxist, but with greater

107

realism about the difficulties involved, a more nuanced ethic, and a firmer hope. In the daily life of business, whether in the boardroom, office, factory floor or retail outlet, the pressure of the immediate easily pushes aside such considerations. Christians in government administration, farming, service industries and welfare work face similar problems, but it is the business world that is particularly affected by the confusion between money and wealth. The focus of this confusion is the stock market, which is often conducted as if only the shares themselves mattered, rather than the personal and material resources they represent.[25]

In the history of the Christian churches, it must be admitted, such ideals have not always been adhered to. In particular, gradual changes in Christian teaching about the use of money have come about, seen notably in different attitudes to concepts such as 'market price' and 'usury'. The Mosaic law places a strict prohibition on charging interest on loans to a fellow Israelite (Ex. 22:25; Lv. 25:35–37; Dt. 23:19), though it was permitted for others (Dt. 23:20).[26] The basis for this law was that in an agrarian or village society, it was only the needy who would borrow; there is no concept in the Torah of someone borrowing to start a business. By the Middle Ages, these prohibitions had been developed into a complete theology of social property, centred around the idea of the 'just price': 'the price of an article should be fixed on moral grounds with due regard to cost of material and labour and to reasonable profit; the vendor is not entitled to ask the utmost that the purchaser will pay'.[27]

With the rise of the middle classes, better transport and industry around the time of the Reformation, the ban on interest was lifted, the concept of 'market price' came to supersede that of 'just price', and much Christian theology came to support the promotion of industry. Initially this emphasis, grounded in the concept of human dominion, was formed in the light of our accountability to God, and gave considerable drive to discovery and inventiveness. The Puritan tradition, which emphasized thrift and the work of each person as a distinctive vocation, had a marked influence in the United States, bringing about a steady increase in wealth. But the Enlightenment emphasis on human reason and autonomy 'left nothing to restrain the competition for wealth', so that the *laissez-faire* economics of the eighteenth and nineteenth centuries was powerless to restrain corporate human greed.[28] At the personal level, the Puritan belief that each should do excellent work in honour of God became debased into the so-called 'Protestant work ethic', the idea that hard work was its own reward. Associated with the unrestrained use of capital (and interest) without regard for the human consequences, 'capitalism' came to have a bad name in many Christian circles. Conversely, the prohibition of private property in Marxist 'socialism' has had similar dire consequences for human society.[29]

Rebuilding a Christian theology of social relations has been a major challenge facing the churches in the last century. This task is made more difficult by a lack of awareness of the corporate dimensions of sin among many Christians, seen at its worst in the simplistic identification of personal prosperity with divine blessing, or of 'freedom of choice' consumerism with gospel values. Debates about wealth creation in modern western societies illustrate some of the issues involved.[30] Some advocate reduced government resource allocation to areas which do not 'create wealth', such as teachers, welfare workers, or arts sponsorship. But this view of wealth creation holds only when wealth is defined as raising the amount of money in circulation. The 'productivity' of a teacher may be harder to measure than that of a miner, mother or machine operator, but nonetheless contributes to the creation of wealth. According to the Christian vision, wealth creation is inseparable from the growth of people as persons in relationship.[31] Christians are to be effective contributors in manufacturing industry, on the factory floor, in the research laboratory, and as directors. Nevertheless, those so involved are called not only to ensure the quality of the product, and a fair return to all involved, but also to implement policy that is consistent with Christian ideals of what it means to be human, in social as well as personal terms. Moreover, a Christian theology of social relations entails issues of resource management: how do we assess the work of the miner and the teacher, and set these alongside the contribution of the homemaker, retired pensioner or someone with a chronic illness? On a wider front, matters such as national policy on aid and development, support of cross-cultural evangelism, or the promotion of peace and justice come into view. Christians who see their role in the divine economy as limited to immediate friends or neighbourhood fail to catch the breadth and grandeur of the divine vision for a 'commonwealth' of all races, tribes and tongues.

The 'economy of dominion'

This vision of the divine economy is more than a verbal construction; its roots lie in the very nature of God.[32] This can be seen particularly in the way in which trinitarian doctrine developed. In opposition to 'monarchian' ideas which portrayed God as a single, undifferentiated Ruler, Christians came to affirm that the 'oneness' of God was more subtle. The God revealed and known in Christ through the Spirit as our Father not only *acts*, but in some sense *is*, Triune. This is described in early Christian thought as the 'economy' of God. To explain this, let me cite what I have written elsewhere:[33]

> The 'economy' of God is the whole shape of God's work (so Eph. 1:10), the 'plan of salvation'. The Christians who opposed Monarchianism realised the dangers involved in such language. Irenaeus and Tertullian saw that the 'economy of God' had two senses. The 'plan of God' refers first to God's rule (monarchy) 'outside' God. But it can also refer to the plan of God 'inside'. In other words, the 'economy of God' points beyond what God *does*. It describes who God *is*. God *acts* as Father, Son and Spirit in history, because God *exists* as such in eternity.
>
> Tertullian boldly used the term 'Monarchy' to turn the tables on his Monarchian opponents. Someone who is truly wealthy, he argued, is a person of some 'substance', or influence, with access to considerable resources. A monarch's assets are so great that they can only be utilised and guarded through royal agents. A king thus rules his 'substance' by making use of 'agents' (*personae*). Since God is the creator of all, divine 'substance' is without limit. And since God is One, the divine character is integral to all God does. Divine power, love, mercy, justice and so on are all

110

united in God's 'substance', the divine wealth of action and character.

Thus Tertullian spoke of divine Monarchy as going beyond God's actions in creation. It reflects God's own Being. Here Tertullian brought the term 'economy' to bear. The 'plan of God' points to divine *being* as well as to divine *acts*. Likewise, the divine 'economy of monarchy' refers to God's being as well as to God's acts.[34]

The Greek term underlying our word 'monarchy' has *dominus* as its Latin equivalent. Thus 'economy of monarchy' could be rendered 'economy of *dominion*'; the whole shape of the way in which God both exists and acts as the triune Lord (*Dominus*) of all. The phrase is also applicable to human beings, in their calling to 'have dominion' as God's vice-regents over creation. In making such an application, we are pointed not only to the *reality*, but also to the *nature*, of dominion; human beings are to live and act as a community (*koinōnia*) of 'co-managers', 'fellow stewards' with God.[35] This economy of dominion is impossible to describe in the abstract, since in practice it interacts with the particular society in which it is lived out, and its full realization is possible only when human society as a whole is renewed in the new heavens and new earth. But a number of biblical perspectives are offered on what human life lived after the divine pattern of Persons in communion looks like. (Chapter 5 continues the discussion.)

First, we are to manage God's resources fairly, with means that correspond with their ends (*cf.* 2 Cor. 4:2; 6:3–10). God is a God of justice, not only with regard to atonement (just-ification) but also in calling the people of God to live justly, giving to all a 'fair share'.[36] Such matters as how honestly we fill in tax returns cannot be dissociated with concern with the justice of the tax system itself. Likewise, ensuring that those who work are treated with dignity and fairness cannot be separated from seeking the welfare of those who work without payment. Do mothers of young children (especially those without a partner) ever get a break from cooking and cleaning, for example? The way in which we manage God's resources, whether seen in personal or in material terms, is one indication of the economy of dominion.

111

Secondly, we are to be realistic about stewardship, in particular the temptations which money affords. Riches are alluring, and 'the love of money is a root of all kinds of evil' (1 Tim. 6:10). Christians are nevertheless to delight in seeing riches used well; Jesus' puzzling parable about the unjust steward means this at least (Lk. 16:1–10). It is God 'who richly provides us with everything for our enjoyment' (1 Tim. 6:17); 'everything created by God is good, and nothing is to be rejected, provided it is received with thanksgiving' (1 Tim 4:5; *cf.* Ec. 3:9–12). The resources God gives are described here not for their utilitarian purpose, but for their aesthetic one: they are to be enjoyed as instances of divine bounty rather than for their usefulness. Taking this seriously begins with personal attitudes to wealth, but moves more widely to open up perspectives on the distribution and use of communal resources, including educational resources and work opportunities – all that makes for the 'common wealth'. And, as noted above, this involves the definition of wealth which in biblical terms is broader than money, or other material realities (*cf.* Mt. 6:19–21).

Thirdly, the economy of dominion calls us to be generous stewards, as God is generous with us (2 Cor. 8:8–9).[37] Generosity involves an orientation to the welfare of the other, rather than concern in the first place for one's own. It begins with personal attitudes, but moves out into structural questions: what does it mean for a community, church or nation to be 'generous'? How do notions such as an 'adequate standard of living' measure up against this standard? It is important to note that in the Scriptures, many areas of economic life are not left to generosity. Wages, for example, are to be provided as a matter of social justice; the Scriptures stress that 'the labourer deserves to be paid' (1 Tim. 5:18; Lk. 10:7), including those who labour in Christian ministry (1 Cor. 9:13). Similarly, the poor were provided for through systematic structures such as 'gleaning' (Lv. 19:9–10; 23:22; Dt. 24:19–22; Ru. 2:2–9), and were not expected to rely on charity. In modern terms, this corresponds to structures such as the use of taxes to provide hospitals, pensions, or work programmes for the unemployed. Particular details of such structures may be negotiable, but the fundamental principles involved must cohere with the economy of dominion.[38]

A particular example of an economic structure in the Scriptures is *tithing*. To set aside a tenth of one's available resources regularly recognizes tangibly that we own property only in a derived sense, as stewards of what God gives. Tithing does not mean that the 90% remaining is ours to use at will, after a 'God tax' has been paid! Rather, it points to the human calling to be co-managers of creation as participants in the divine economy. Note that tithes were used only sparsely for relief of the poor (Dt. 14:28–29) and only in part for the support of the 'clergy' (Lv. 18:21–32); priests and Levites received their food as a right from the regular offerings made in the tabernacle or temple, not from generosity (Dt. 18:1–4). The commonest use to which tithes were put was for communal parties: normally the wheat, wine, oil, animals and so on which made up the tithe would be eaten in a slap-up party 'at the place that the LORD your God will choose' (*cf.* Dt. 12:15–18). But if this place was too far away, the goods were to be sold, and the money used to pay for a party in the right place. The Israelites were commanded to 'spend the money for whatever you wish – oxen, sheep, wine, strong drink or whatever you desire. And you shall eat there in the presence of the LORD your God, you and your household rejoicing together' (Dt. 14:26).

The tithe feast was open to all – Levites, widows, aliens, orphans (Dt. 14:28–29). The faithful bringing in of the tithes would see God join the party, as it were: 'see if I will not open the windows of heaven for you and pour down for you an overflowing blessing' (Mal. 3:10). Communal meals such as those envisaged here say a great deal about the economy of dominion: anyone who spends a significant amount of income on open-house parties where the Lord is the primary guest is not going to be penny-pinching in daily life! The tithe is a measure of the light-hearted seriousness of stewardship, a corporate, structured recognition of our dependence on divine generosity, rather than on human manipulation of resources. Tithing means far more than giving a precise percentage of 'our' wealth (*cf.* Mt. 23:23). It is a structure that calls us to see all 'our' resources as God's, on whom we depend for our welfare, and for whom we act as accountable stewards. But tithing does get us down to the actual issue of what we do with money and other resources that are 'ours'.

113

Each Christian household has many opportunities to consider how it exercises the economy of dominion through its allocation of the resources God has entrusted to it. For a typical middle-class Australian inner-urban family such as my own, this includes being care-full yet care-free in budgeting; weekly support of the local church, in time and involvement as well as money; monthly giving to the wider church in its evangelistic, caring and justice ministries (using direct bank transfers where possible); and regular personal and monetary support of people and causes beyond the church, including political parties and particular social campaigns from time to time. Some families with children at home allocate to them a percentage of the household income to take care of their school and other needs, so that they learn to be resource co-managers. Above all, everyone is called to be hospitable of table and board, not thinking too hard about how much it costs; God's party matters more!

The ideas which lie behind the tithe go far beyond the level of the household. They pose questions to churches who would deny resources to the wider mission of Christ, to communities who earmark wealth for local use only, or to nations who perpetuate unfair trade practices, refuse to grant overseas aid, or offer it with dependence-creating strings attached. Such practices render the celebration of God's generosity impossible, because they presuppose that it is *our* wealth we are protecting, rather than divine resources given for the common good and common joy. In short, fun-raising belongs together with fund-raising! The tithe represents a tangible illustration, a generous glimpse of what human life is headed towards in the economy of dominion.[39] Human society, in its structural and politico-economic aspects, is meant to be characterized by generosity in celebrating God's gift of the task to be co-managers with God of all that is.

In the process of responding to such a calling, the wider context of the environment in which we live must be considered. What does it mean to be human as creature? The next chapter thus moves from the social aspect of being human to our relationship with other creatures.

5

HUMAN LIFE IN CREATION

Humankind and otherkind

It is not easy to be precise about where a boundary is to be drawn between humankind and otherkind.[1] The Scriptures closely associate them as fellow creatures, distinguishing them only in their differing capacities for relationship with God. Human beings are first described in the Scriptures as 'earthlings' taken from 'earth', *hā'āḏām* from *hā'āḏāmâ* (Gn. 2:7–9).[2] With all creatures, we exist in the first place as material beings. God gives us the gifts of work, hearing and speech (Gn. 2:15–20), shared to some degree with other creatures, but received by humans with an awareness of our ability and accountability in their use. Associated with these is the gift of partnership as male and female (Gn. 2:23–24), a sexual nature shared with other creatures, but exercised distinctively by human beings as those creatures made to live as persons in communion with God and one another. What does it mean, however, to live in interrelationship with other creatures?

The Mosaic law seeks to shape the lifestyle of the people of God, and has a good deal to teach about human duties to the earth and its non-human inhabitants. The land itself belongs to God, who allocates various portions for the tribes to tend, saying, 'The land shall not be sold in perpetuity, for the land is mine; with me you are but aliens and tenants' (Lv. 25:23).[3] Land is not 'owned' by Israel, but is to revert back to the original 'tenants' in the Jubilee, the fiftieth year, the sabbath of sabbaths (Lv. 25:25–34; *cf.* 1 Ki. 21:1–4). Further, the land is affected by human actions, to the extent that it is used as shorthand for the nation as a whole. When Israel was rescued from its enemies, 'the *land* had rest' (Jdg. 3:11, 30; 5:31; 8:28); when Israel sins, 'the *land* commits great whoredom' (Ho. 1:2). After Israel had neglected the sabbath provisions for centuries, the Chronicler depicts the exile as giving the land its overdue sabbath rest, to enable it to recover from its abuse (2 Ch. 36:21; cf. Lv. 26:34–35).

Land, people and all living things are thus bound together, especially under judgment: 'the land mourns, and all who live in it languish, together with the wild animals and the birds of the air, even the fish of the sea are perishing' (Ho. 4:3). This was so from the very beginning; the first human sin led to a divine curse on the ground, so that work became toil, undertaken in hard struggle rather than with creative energy (Gn. 3:17–19). The nexus between human life and land is seen in the first homicide; when Cain murders Abel, Abel's blood 'is crying out . . . from the ground', which is cursed once more to impede human use of it (Gn. 4:11–12). The law exudes concern for the interrelationship between human beings and nature beyond occasions of judgment, however. This concern is seen not only in abnormal life situations such as war, in which fruit trees were to be spared (Dt. 20:19), but also in regular life, through the sabbath rest. It is this divine 'rest', rather than the creation of humanity, that is the actual climax of the creation account,[4] and that expresses God's own pleasure in the finished creation (Gn. 1:31 – 2:3), extending beyond men and women to animals (Ex. 23:12), and the land itself (Lv. 25:5).

The close link between all creatures is especially evident in the Psalter. Psalm 104 celebrates our kinship with all creatures, all of whom depend on the work of God: the heavens and earth, winds and waters, wild animals and birds, grass and plants, seasons and times. It is acknowledged that God 'brings forth food from the earth, wine to gladden the human heart, oil to make the face shine, and bread to strengthen the human heart' (Ps. 104:14–15). These gifts, however, are not seen as given to humankind only; rather, 'all look to you to give them their food in due season' (Ps. 104:27). The Lord's generosity extends to all creatures, among whom human beings are here distinguished only by their distinctive capacity for sin (Ps. 104:35). The songs of Israel never tire of celebrating the truth that 'the earth is the Lord's and all that is in it' (Ps. 24:1; *cf.* 19:1–6; 29; 136:1–9; 148; Jb. 38 – 41).

The universe as we know it, however, experiences frustration and brokenness: 'the fate of humans and the fate of animals is the same; as one dies, so dies the other. They all have the same breath [or, spirit], and humans have no advantage over the animals; for all is vanity' (Ec. 3:19). Yet in describing creation the Scriptures testify of realities beyond past and present. Not only human beings, but the whole oppressed creation looks eagerly for the time when God's saving work will bring to birth the new heavens and new earth (Is. 55:11–12; 66:22–23; *cf.* Rom. 8:21), in which there will be cosmic harmony, and no more killing (Is. 11:6–9). This hope is then expressed in terms of the reconciliation of all things in Christ (Col. 1:15–20; *cf.* 2 Pet. 3:11–13). In sum, whether seen from the point of view of creation or of redemption, of past, present or future, otherkind 'has intrinsic worth before God apart from relationship to the human'.[5]

Dominion and service

The biblical teaching that humans exercise dominion in creation has been discussed in the previous chapter with reference to humanity in society. We now consider the implications of the economy of dominion for otherkind. Psalm 8, along with Genesis 1, acknowledges that God has assigned to the human race a place over the rest of creation:

> You have given them dominion over the works of your
> hands; you have put all things under their feet,
> all sheep and oxen,

and also the beasts of the field,
the birds of the air, and the fish of the sea,
    whatever passes along the paths of the seas.
                                            (Ps. 8:6–8)

Be fruitful and multiply, and fill the earth and subdue
it; and have dominion over the fish of the sea and over
the birds of the air and over every living thing that
moves upon the earth (Gn. 1:28).

Dominion is given a great deal of attention in Christian
thought and practice, but only these two texts teach this creation
mandate (as it is often called). The latter text not only ascribes
to humanity a place of dominion over the animals, but places
both over plant life: 'to . . . everything that has the breath of life,
I have given every green plant for food' (Gn. 1:30). Again, the
Mosaic law distinguishes clean and unclean animals, only the
former being allowed for human food (Lv. 11; Dt. 14:3–20).
There are thus multiple hierarchies implicit in the structure of
creation, warning us against simplistic understandings of the
relative place of different life forms. Some of these distinctions
appear to be already in view in the original 'very good' status of
creation, but others would seem to be accommodations to its
fallen state. An example of the latter is the food laws, which were
apparently of temporary duration, as shown by the lifting of the
distinction between clean and unclean in the early church (Acts
10:9–16).

Before too much is made of the paucity of explicit references
to human dominion in creation, it needs to be acknowledged
that the biblical story is overwhelmingly anthropocentric, that is,
it focuses on humankind. Indeed, the story's turning-point is
anthropocentric, in the life and work of Christ, God enfleshed
in human form. In the face of the enormous abuse of the
creation mandate by human beings, to assert an anthropocentric claim today is not easy, particularly since it has largely
been societies regarded as 'Christian' which have polluted the
earth's air and water, which control its resources for their own
good, and which seem incapable of changing the way in which
resources are used. Such corporate sin presents a major
challenge to Christian faith, both in itself and for its accept-

118

ability to non-Christians. As Hall puts it, 'It remains indelibly fixed in the minds of our critics that the world of the people who "have" on this planet is historically and avowedly a Christian world . . . the epicentre of this "Christian" First World, the United States, is at the same time the most devotedly "Christian" nation.'[6]

In reaction to human abuse of the earth, some seek to deny that humans have a distinctive status or role in the scheme of things.[7] Yet to ignore or deny the unique status of humans among the creatures is as dangerous to nature as abusing it. It is simply the case that we do have power to change nature. Only when this is recognized can strategies and criteria for its exercise be formed; the sole response open to us is not *whether* we utilize the resources of the earth, but *how* we do so. This power is not given without responsibility; in both Psalm 8 and Genesis 1 humans are held accountable to God, for whom we are to act as 'under-managers'. All who take this scriptural teaching seriously are called to recognize our culpability, both personal and corporate, for misusing God's creation, and our responsibility to live as creatures given dominion over it.

Human beings thus exercise a management role in creation on behalf of God, and are to follow the divine example of creative care. Since we are made in the image of God, how we live will be greatly influenced by the manner in which we think of God. A concept of God as authoritarian monarch will reinforce a domineering attitude to creation by humans, as they forget the *economy* of monarchy (see the previous chapter). The emergence of deism in the Enlightenment, for example, encouraged the rise of 'a technocratic attitude to the world about us, encouraging attitudes of dominance'.[8] If God is thought of as over and against nature in a deistical sense, then nature is conceived as over and against those made in the image of God, who consequently see their role as subduing nature in the sense of dominating rather than managing or keeping it (*cf.* Gn. 2:15). At another extreme, pantheism identifies the divine and the natural, with the result that humans come to worship nature, and act without criteria towards it. A modern worldview which comes close to this is Lovelock's Gaia hypothesis, which holds that living organisms and the environment evolve together as a single, planetary organism. One consequence of

119

this is a lifting of a sense of responsibility in human behaviour towards the planet, in favour of a more 'fateful and fearful' attitude towards nature.[9] On the other hand, the Christian concept of God as Trinity, Persons in relationship, in whom all things live and move and have their being (Acts 17:28), undergirds a more participatory, 'partnership' view of the relationship betwen humankind and otherkind.[10] As I have written elsewhere:

> It is monism and deism, 'plain oneness' views of God, which are linked with 'feminine' and 'masculine' power respectively. The doctrine of the Trinity rejects 'female' imaging of God in 'mother Earth' terms. Such imaging is not that of gentle caring, but carries with it notions of dark powers and fickle fate. The doctrine of the Trinity also rejects 'male' imaging of God in the deistic terms of an autocratic dictator.[11]

In trinitarian terms, the economy of dominion is expressed by God's life-giving, sustaining presence in and through all things, calling them not only from nothing to being, but also, when sin had entered, raising human beings from death to life. The universal dominion of God has now been disclosed to us in Jesus, revealed and named as 'Lord' (Phil. 2:11; 1 Cor. 12:3), and 'head over all things' (Eph. 1:22), in whom the whole divine economy is summed up (Eph. 1:10).

The Christian tradition, however, does not appear to have seriously applied the manner in which Jesus displayed the economy of dominion, through 'taking the form of a slave' (Phil. 2:7), to the human exercise of dominion. The famous statement of Pilate, '*Ecce homo!*' – 'Behold, *the* Man!' – identifies Jesus as the typical human being (Jn. 19:5, my translation). Yet the person set before us in this episode is no great hero, or someone of great beauty and appeal, but the One who gave up all 'rights' so that others might receive life through the sacrificial service of the cross.[12] Likewise, the letter to the Hebrews describes Jesus as the summary of all that is human in the terms of Psalm 8, but relates this to his redemptive suffering: 'As it is, we do not yet see everything in subjection to [human beings], but we do see Jesus, who for a little while was made lower than the angels, now crowned with glory and honour because of the suffering of death' (Heb. 2:8–9).

It is frequently affirmed that Christians, in following the Way of Christ, are called to live sacrificially, giving themselves to Christ's service. Such a perspective is not easy to practise, but no Christian would deny its challenge in the area of interpersonal and social relations, the 'horizontal' aspect of our 'image' diagram. In the New Testament it is also brought to bear on our relationship with otherkind (the 'downward vertical' aspect). Our status as human beings who have dominion must be interpreted in the light of the dominion which Christ exercises; displayed in compassionate, sacrificial, costly service for the sake of others. Of primary significance in this divine service is Christ's restoration of our relationship with God (the 'upward vertical' aspect, our 'being-with-God', in Hall's terms); but it cannot be dissociated from the restoration of humans one with another (the 'horizontal' aspect, our 'being-with-others'), and neither can be abstracted from the reconciliation of all creation in and through Christ (our 'being-with-nature'). Hall thus writes of 'the sacrificial element in the stewardship of nature', and asks, 'Can we be content with a social system that expects sacrifice only on the part of non-human species?'[13]

Christian discipleship therefore needs to take with full seriousness our responsibility to live for Christ in relationship with the creation of which we are a part. As argued in earlier chapters, such a responsibility is inseparably related to our status as made in the image of God. This not only relates to our created nature, but is now revealed through Christ in terms of the new self we are called to be, 'renewed in knowledge according to the image of its creator' (Col. 3:10).

Sixth-day solidarity

How then do we relate to otherkind? The most obvious corporate aspect of human existence is that we are living beings, sharing life with all organic creatures. The same term, *nepeš*, is used in Genesis 1:20–24 of all creatures, and in Genesis 2:7 of humans: both share what Anderson calls ' "the solidarity of the sixth day", the inescapable bond which we as humans share with other creatures'.[14] In the past a distinction between human and other organic life (especially the animals) was often taken for granted. In pioneer environments it was often asserted strongly, to undergird the need to 'conquer nature'. This kind of ethos was prominent in nineteenth-century Australia, Canada and the United States, as native forests and animals – not to mention indigenous peoples – were exploited; it continues today in Brazil, Thailand – and Australia. The waves of European exploration and colonial expansion in the nineteenth century were undergirded by the belief that humans are infinitely above the 'brute beasts', who needed to be tamed. Hall argues that Darwin's hypothesis, in which humanity has its ancestry in the animal world, 'shocked so many good Christians not because it challenged their belief in Scripture . . . but because it made them embarrassingly conscious of the very thing their whole social apparatus was constructed over against: their obvious physical relatedness to the so-called higher mammals'.[15]

In popular speech, to say that someone acts 'like an animal' is highly insulting. The assumption behind it is that human beings and animals are fundamentally different. In theological terms, the distinction between humans and animals has often been associated with the notion that human beings possessed souls, while other forms of life did not.[16] In many fields, when the notion of 'soul' was discarded, what was considered essential to being human has not uncommonly been defined in terms of what we can do that animals cannot: speak, reason, build, use tools, form cultural artefacts, for example. The Scriptures recognize that such differences exist, but say little about their significance, preferring to express human distinctiveness in terms of our being made in the divine image.[17] Animals are acknowledged to have value in and of themselves apart from their usefulness to human beings. As a result, they are to be shown kindness, and treated justly. The Torah taught, for example, that 'You shall not muzzle an ox while it is treading out the grain' (Dt. 25:4), a text used by Paul to support justice between human beings (1 Tim. 5:18)! Jesus' references to creatures are also significant: the birds of the air, and the grass of the field, are fed and clothed by God without human intervention, while the beauty of lilies exceeds the greatest glory human beings can fashion (Mt. 6:26–29; Lk. 12:24–28).

The world of the first Christians was largely rural, and

humankind and otherkind lived in constant contact and interdependence. In city or industrial contexts the distinction between human and animal is generally felt more keenly, since contact with non-human forms of life is infrequent, and food is bought rather than grown or killed. Contact with the beasts takes place largely through domestic animals, or an animal-related leisure interest such as horse-racing or pigeon-fancying. In this context, where animals other than pets are rarely in contact with humans, and especially where meat is prepared at some remove from its consumers, animal rights have become a significant issue. This cause has been furthered by concern about animal experimentation that involves cruelty, and the threat of the extinction of many species.[18] In the countryside, the difference between human and other organic life is felt as far less marked, since daily life is spent in living contact with animals, plants and nature, and the differences and mutual dependences that do exist are appreciated.

The sense that humankind and otherkind are markedly distinct has grown apace in the time since the Enlightenment and the Industrial Revolution. The widespread acceptance of an evolutionary view of human origins would seem to question this, since it emphasizes that we are part of the animal world. However, that view became closely associated with the idea that human beings are the most evolved, and so the 'highest', form of life on earth, with full rights to use 'lower' beings as they wish. Darwin's theory of evolution emerged in a time of optimism, and gave credence to the notion of 'progress'. 'Humankind believed that it could extend its realm of power over nature', and 'the myth that our future was best secured through Christianity was gradually replaced by faith in scientific progress'.[19] Such ideas remain fixed in much popular consciousness, reinforced by the affluence which technological advances have brought; but they have long been displaced in the academic world. More significantly, they have been rejected outright by those who question the dominance of technology in modern societies, seen archetypally in the threat of nuclear and ecological disaster. Ideas such as these, whether derived from Christian faith, evolutionary scientism, Marxism, or human commitment to survival in the face of disaster, are seen by many today as an anthropocentric view of life. Any human dominion over other creatures is rejected as a belief which justifies systematic cruelty to animals, threatens the diversity of species on earth, and fails to regard anything other than human life as having ultimate value in and of itself, even to God.

A great deal of enmity has been shown towards nature by many industrialized societies, epitomized in the frequent language of 'control',[20] not only in capitalist societies, but also in socialist ones: 'towards the different political systems, the ecological crisis is apparently neutral'.[21] Considerable resources exist in the Christian tradition to shape a more positive understanding of the interaction between humankind and otherkind, for example in Franciscan spirituality. Yet ideas which denigrate otherkind in relation to humankind have been challenged in official Christian teaching only in very recent times. As recently as 1953, the (US) National Council of Catholic Bishops could say, 'Every man knows instinctively that he is, somehow, a superior being. He is superior to the land he tills, the machine he operates or the animals which are at his service.'[22] Growth in awareness of environmental issues since the 1960s has made people more sensitive to the heritage we share with other living creatures, an understanding enabled by the development of global communications.[23] The emergence of ecological concerns, repudiating the dominance of a techno-logical approach to life, and sometimes questioning Christian understandings of the place of humanity in the scheme of things, has spurred deeper reflection on the relation of humankind and otherkind. The United Nations published a 'World Charter for Nature' (1982), and convened the 'Earth Summit' at Rio de Janeiro, while considerable theological work has been undertaken in this area.[24]

Anthropocentrism or biocentrism?

Anthropocentrism assumes that human beings are the centre of all things. Christian faith rejects blatant forms of this as idolatrous and selfish. Less immediately selfish forms, such as conservation justified for the sake of future human generations, are still anthropocentric, however. Christian faith affirms the unique place which humankind has been given in relation to otherkind, and so, it must be admitted, is anthropocentric in some sense. Today Christian faith sorely needs to adopt a 'chastened, sober anthropocentrism'[25] which recognizes the unique place of human beings *among* the creatures. This is especially the case in contexts where any idea of anthropocentrism is displaced by a 'biocentric' view, which regards 'life' (*bios* in Greek) as of higher significance than any particular form of it.[26] In a previous generation Albert Schweitzer urged a philosophy of 'reverence for life', rejecting distinctions of higher and lower life forms. Given the history of modern societies, such ideals are both understandable and laudable, but they need to be set in a wider framework of creation as under the ongoing care of God.[27] In recent decades there has come about a greater appreciation of the insights offered by indigenous peoples, many of whom have lived in harmony with the land and its resources for centuries. For example, aboriginal Australians, of whatever tribal or cultural heritage, evince a sense of mystical bond with their environment that both challenges the exploitative attitudes of many immigrants and offers hope for human adaptation to an inhospitable continent.[28] As in ancient Israel, land is thought of as a heritage held in trust, for which human beings are accountable, rather than as a neutral object which can be owned.

The human race thus shares life with the animal kingdom, and with all organic or living matter. Life, however, is no abstract reality, existing independently, but is always found in the concrete existence of a particular being; it needs an adjective to make sense; for example, 'human life', or 'floral life'. It is easier to use the participle 'living' to qualify another word than to speak of 'life'; 'living being' or 'living flower', for example. In Christian thought, only God is life in and of itself, the 'I AM WHO I AM' (Ex. 3:14). The value of life is to be determined not by human estimation, but by divine. Perhaps the most striking example in the Scriptures is Job 38 – 41, where the long discussion about crocodiles, ostriches and other animal life has no point other than that these creatures matter to God!

The profound significance of 'blood' in the Scriptures is noteworthy here.[29] The covenant with Noah, which reiterates our status as made in the image of God, includes the divine requirement that there will be reckoning for all blood-shedding, especially of human beings (Gn. 9:4–6; *cf.* Lv. 17:10–16). It is thus recognized that 'life is, in a special manner, God's property, and as a sign of this man is to keep his hands off the blood'.[30] Life is seen most fully in Christ (cf. Jn. 14:6), who laid down his own life, shedding his blood, so that the broken, sin-dominated life of others might be made new (cf. Jn. 10:11–18; 2 Cor. 5:19–21). Jesus was raised to life, not from nothingness, but from its corruption and opposite, death. This new life is now made available through the Holy Spirit (Rom. 8:1–11), not only in believers, but also in the whole groaning creation (Rom. 8:18–23). On the one hand, this line of thought points to human beings participating in a process wider than human history; anthropocentrism involves elements of biocentrism. On the other hand, it emphasizes that God is the only source of life, as Creator and Redeemer; the truest perspective on human life is 'theocentric'. The theocentric perspective centres on Jesus Christ as Lord (Dominus), through whose life, teaching, death and resurrection has been disclosed the immeasurable treasure that is God's work in creation and salvation, and for whose return we long.

Being at home

The relationship between humankind and otherkind can be further focused in considering where it is that we feel truly 'at home'. From one point of view, all creatures are made to live on this earth as our home, sharing the same space, time and environment; this is the 'solidarity of the sixth day'. All of us continually search for a true 'home', where we can find security, meaning, and familiar comfort: what sociologists have called 'the sacred canopy'.[31] Since sin entered in, this search has taken on tragic dimensions, because all of us experience 'home-lessness', not being accepted or valued in our social context.[32] In Christendom, people 'had a place in the cosmic order of things and were at home in the universe',[33] even if the way in which they conceived that place gave too much importance to the church and its institutions. In the past two centuries, however, with the rejection of God in many industrial societies, this sense of place has diminished, and has come to be replaced by a restless search for a 'home' we must build for ourselves.

In the process of trying to build such a home, the unbridled use of the earth's resources, and the unchecked utilization of science and technology, have brought about a different kind of a search for home, through ecology. Nature, and natural things, have come to be regarded as 'home' for many, as they reject the manufactured worlds of science, technology and industry. 'Feeling·somewhat homeless and ill at ease in the world man has created, many people are turning to the world of nature,' as Walter puts it.[34] As has been argued above, deepened awareness of human solidarity with the animal and plant worlds is vital for contemporary Christian faith and life; but nature is as fallen as we are. An appeal to 'doing what comes naturally' as justification for behaviour is no guarantee of goodness! From a Christian perspective, any search for a definitive home here on earth, even that of the family, is fruitless and even dangerous, without the recognition that our true place is in God, in whom 'we live and move and have our being' (Acts 17:28). Creation as we experience it is fallen, and with us groans because of both the oppression of futility and the expectation of release (Rom. 8:18–23). Isaiah portrays this hope in terms of unnatural peace among all creatures: 'the wolf shall live with the lamb, the leopard shall lie down with the kid, the calf and the lion and the fatling together, and a little child shall lead them' (Is. 11:6).

In the light of this, and especially in apparently hopeless situations, Christians can come to the conclusion that 'this world is not our home, we're just a-passing through', as the Negro spiritual put it. Such a view carries some truth, but easily leads to a strict separation of earth and heaven, and tends to contrast the physical and the spiritual. Taken to an extreme, Christians who espouse attitudes like these can come to despise their creaturely status, in no sense feeling at home in this age. Refusal to act with regard to ecological concern leads to the fallen *status quo* prevailing, and the opportunity for a Christian perspective and contribution, including the prophetic act of denouncing the idolatry of nature, is denied. This passivity is as disobedient to the divine command to have dominion as using that command to justify unrestricted misuse of the earth's resources.

In sum, both anthropocentrism and biocentrism find their true meaning only in relation to God, in theocentrism. Likewise, our true place in relation to other people and to the natural world is found only as we, in partnership with otherkind and other people, live in relationship with God, our life-giver, Creator, sustainer, and true home.[35] There is a sense in which humankind and otherkind share this earth as 'home', but we do so as co-participants in a fallen creation, in which human sin has the deceptive capacity to convince us that we can make our final home here. It is to the future restoration of all things in Christ that all are called to look, and in the light of this vision to practise the beauty, peace and justice of the 'new heaven and earth' in this present fallen universe.

The concept of home, however, does point us to the close interactions between human society and the environment(s) in which we live as a race – to human culture.

6

HUMAN CULTURE

Every human society is remarkably complex and delicate. The myriad ways in which human beings relate to one another in kinship groups across differences of age, gender and language, pass on customs and lore to the next generation, conduct their political affairs, despise, ignore, honour and betray one another, make war, peace and love, develop classical, popular and folk traditions in the fine and performing arts – the list could go on and on – evoke a response of wonder.

Culture and cultures

By 'culture' here is meant the sum total of all these interactions in a particular setting. It is a term incapable of precise definition, since any definition will itself be affected by cultural assumptions. In British English, to describe people as 'cultured' carries connotations of their being well educated, knowing their social manners, and speaking in a particular way. That is not the idea of 'culture' discussed here. Culture is a facet of human life, touching its every aspect, and every human being, not a special interest for a few dilettantes. Culture is like the air we breathe. Unless we are ill, or are making a deliberate attempt to concentrate on it, breathing is something we take for granted. So it is with culture; unless we deliberately focus upon it, or move to live in another culture, we are largely unaware that we are 'cultured'. A shift of cultural context is obvious enough when we travel to another country, especially if we do not understand the language. But it also takes place in daily life. Each of us knows occasions when we have felt 'out of place'. A party may feature music we cannot stand or sexual behaviour that contradicts our values, or we may have dressed inappropriately. If asked to 'bring a plate', we may have literally done so, as some English friends did once – unaware that for Australians the request means bringing food to share. In cases like this, although we are part of the larger culture in which the party takes place, it is clear that we are not at home in a particular 'sub-culture'.

In the two previous chapters, the 'horizontal' and 'downward vertical' elements of being made in the image of God have been considered. Human culture involves their interaction and combination, and is such a distinct aspect of being human that it deserves discussion in its own right. As an example of this interaction, consider the role of weather in human life. The English friends mentioned above had come to live in Australia for a year. Early in their stay they remarked on the prominence of weather forecasts on Australian television; several heatwaves later they knew why! The cycle of the seasons, or lack of it, and the need to adapt to extremes of heat and cold, affect matters as diverse as clothing, farming, social life, economic welfare, and whether Easter is a spring or an autumn rite. The way in which a particular society celebrates New Year is dependent on the calendar used, the weather cycle at the beginning of the year, and religious beliefs about time. Things get a little confusing when, as is the case in Melbourne, the western, Jewish, Islamic and Chinese New Years occur at different times of a particular year, with different meanings and varying degrees of importance to those involved.

The Scriptures themselves reflect the variety of human

cultures. They are a culturally diverse collection of writings, gathered over a period of at least 1,500 years by people from a wide range of social backgrounds. Customs are recorded from a diversity of middle-eastern, Judaic and Hellenistic cultures, though some are condemned, and none is regarded as ultimate. The lifestyles of nomads such as Abraham, Sarah, Rebekah, Jacob and Esau differed markedly from those of the 'cultured' Moses, settled village life as depicted in the book of Ruth, the international world of a Solomon, the city life of the kings, or the various Jewish communities of Egypt, Babylon and Persia. People such as Ruth, Samuel, Joab, Hezekiah, Amos and Huldah all assumed that the culture in which they lived was continuous with their relationship with God, whereas Esther, Ezekiel, Daniel and his friends had a conscious realization that their lives were lived over and against the dominant culture. These attitudes were strongly shaped by the physical environments in which their lives were set. Again, what it meant to be 'at home' in Israel could vary in meaning; tabernacle, temple and synagogue respectively suited tribal, national and dispersed political structures.

In the New Testament churches, no culture is identified as either wholly home for, or wholly inimical to, the gospel. Paul can affirm both his Roman citizenship and his Jewish heritage as significant, though not ultimate (Acts 16:37; 22:3; Phil. 3:4–8), while the Roman imperial system can be both tolerated (Rom. 13:1–7; 1 Pet. 2:17) and viewed as detestable Babylon (Rev. 18). In the early churches, which formed the tangible sign of the new humanity in Christ, the variety of human cultures began to be encompassed, though not without difficulty. A central issue in their life was the question of Jew–Gentile relationships, a cultural difference with deep theological roots. Although the Torah unambiguously required circumcision for all members of the people of God (Gn. 17:9–14), in the light of Christ this requirement was lifted for non-Jewish (Gentile) Christians, though not prohibited (Acts 15:15–21; cf. 16:3). This major change took place only after much wrestling with the issues involved, and with particular divine guidance (cf. Acts 11:1–18; Gal. 1:16–17).

At the end of his ministry, Jesus had commanded the apostles to make disciples of all the *ethnē* (Mt. 28:19), a word usually translated 'Gentiles' elsewhere in the New Testament, rather than 'nations', as in most English versions of Matthew 28. In today's terms, in which 'nation' has a particular, socio-political meaning, it might be better rendered 'cultures', or 'peoples', all of whom are to hear and respond to the gospel (*cf.* 1 Cor. 9:22). In this age, in which sin and death continue to corrupt human life and culture, there is always ambiguity about culture. The church, as the sign of renewed humanity, is to be the place where human culture begins to be cleansed and renewed, in anticipation of the Christian hope.[1] The vision of a fully restored, purified humanity in the new creation pictures a multitude of believers from every *ethnē*, all tribes and peoples and languages (Rev. 7:9). Further, 'the glory and the honour' of the *ethnē* are brought into the heavenly city, though 'nothing unclean will enter it, nor anyone who practises abomination or falsehood' (Rev. 21:23–27).

The variety of human cultures and sub-cultures is thus acknowledged in the Scriptures. Nevertheless, they are regarded with considerable ambiguity, to be resolved only at the End, and which goes back to the very beginning of human history. The development of human culture derives from obedience to the divine command to be fruitful and multiply, and to till and keep the earth, and is seen in the growth of human culture in the pre-flood narrative: agriculture, city-founding, tent-dwelling, music and smelting (Gn. 4:2, 17, 20, 21, 22).[2] The gaining of such skills is nevertheless closely associated with murder, suggesting that with growing variety came rivalry (Gn. 4:8, 23–24). It was the spread of human evil that brought the great flood (Gn. 6:11–13), but the flood concludes with God's promise to restrain the curse on the earth (Gn. 8:21–22), and pour renewed blessing on the surviving humans and 'every living creature that is with you', in the form of a covenant (Gn. 9:1–17). Further, the expansion of the human race in the table of the nations in Genesis 10 is recorded without critical comment, as a divinely sanctioned development in the variety of human cultures (*cf.* Gn. 10:32).

There are thus features of every culture that bear some correspondence to the divine intention in creation; the wide range of matters given comment in Proverbs and Ecclesiastes bears this out. Other aspects of culture reflect sinful distortions of human living, and particular cultures can become so depraved that they merit divine condemnation. Sodom and Gomorrah are examples which have become legendary (Gn. 18:16 – 19:29; 2 Pet. 2:6; Jude 7), but a similar fate is promised to an idolatrous Israelite city (Dt. 13:12–18) and an even worse one to towns which would not receive Jesus' disciples (Mt. 10:15), and where there were active congregations of God's people (cf. Lk. 10:13–15). No human culture or sub-culture can be self-satisfied, or closed to the insights and challenges offered by others, even when it has been shaped and influenced by Christian faith (cf. Rev. 2:4–5, 16; 3:3, 15–19).

Cultural plurality

Many societies are made up of a wide range of cultural groups, with varying relationships between them. Most commonly, there is a dominant culture reflected especially in language, and a number of minority cultures. Sometimes the latter groups are effectively distinct enclaves within the dominant culture; the typical case is a tribe, as in several African nations, or a linguistic group within a nation, as in Wales or Canada. At other times attempts are made to suppress or exclude non-dominant cultures, resulting in structured racism, civil war or even genocide, as has been seen in Cambodia, Rwanda and the former Yugoslavia. In some parts of the world, cultures have lived side by side for centuries, but major cultural shifts have taken place in many places since the end of the Second World War due to immigration and the emergence of a global consciousness through rapid growth in communications and travel.

In my own country, Australia, the national government promoted a vigorous programme of immigration after 1945, and generally maintained since then, of both refugees and migrants. This has resulted in a series of policy changes in the decades since then, changes in which the Christian churches have been significantly involved.[3] Initially everyone was expected to assimilate into the dominant Anglo-Celtic culture (including aboriginal Australians), and many refugees were keen to do so. As time went on, however, it became clear that both dominant and minority cultures were themselves under-going change and creating change in one another, resulting in a policy of integration (similar to the concept of the melting-pot in the United States). With the emergence of a second and third generation of NESB (non-English-speaking background) Australians, larger issues began to emerge in the 1970s, and a policy of multiculturalism was adopted. This attempts to acknowledge the ongoing presence and interweaving of many cultures within the overall framework of one nation. Although supported by all major political parties, it is a policy over which continuing debate takes place. Some see multiculturalism as an impossibly romantic and even dangerous ideal, because it could be taken to imply not only a relativism of cultures, but also of truth – and some indeed support the policy because of its relativizing possibilities. Others, in the light of their concerns to oppose racism and set forward justice, regard multiculturalism as the only possible way forward.[4]

Modern industrial societies have seen rapid growth in communication and travel. Even if we rarely encounter someone of a different religion at home, we shall almost certainly do so via television, a holiday, or study at school or university. A further consequence of social mobility and affluence in many societies has been the proliferation of sub-cultures. The word 'teenager', for example, was coined only this century, but today it represents a whole world of values, interests, music, dress, customs – and potential for profits.[5] This teenage world generally contains sub-sub-cultures of varied and often competing musical tastes, sporting interests, and options regarding study, employment and unemployment. Similar comments could be made about the sub-cultures associated with differing geographical or work settings. In Australia, there are significant differences between the inner city, the country town, the outback and the suburbs, with further variations between inner, eastern, western, outlying, garden, and bay-side or seaside suburbs in Sydney and Melbourne. When we look at paid work, the sub-cultures of a farm, factory, office, shop or hospital are markedly different, with differing modes of behaviour, speech, relationships and manners. In a typical week, most of us will move between a number of sub-cultures, mostly adjusting as we go, causing embarrassment, laughter or offence if we transgress customary codes of conduct. Such an apparently simple matter as when to call a friend 'Mr Smith', 'Mr Chairman', or 'Fred' illustrates this. Many Anglo-Celtic Australians would resent there being any difference of address, while those of Asian background would consider it quite rude not to make such distinctions.

Pluralism or relativism?

For the most part, cultural pluralism forms part of the spice of life. The sheer variety of human interests, artistic expressions, kinship and social patterns, languages, idioms and customs is simply amazing. Yet this stimulating variety can have the effect of relativizing values; if something is good enough for one cultural or sub-cultural group, why is there not acceptance for every custom?[6] A particular feature of the post-1945 pattern of immigration, not only in Australia but throughout the western world, has been the much greater visible presence of non-Christian religious groups. In Australia, it has in part brought religion to the official attention of a highly secular society, and in part furthered the tendency to pluralism. When a different way of life seems as valid and effective as our own, it can be highly threatening, in particular for Christians, if it appears to call into question central beliefs such as the sovereignty of God or the uniqueness of Christ. This is a significant example of the difficulty of distinguishing cultural pluralism from theological relativism. It is one thing to affirm enthusiastically that human cultures are varied, and another to say that any cultural practice is as good as any other. This idea is prevalent in western societies, and at an extreme says that no belief can be held as true (not even the conviction that this is the case!).[7]

How should we respond to cultural pluralism? In the first place, any idea that a particular culture, especially our own, embodies the Christian faith, must be put aside. This identification is usually made in a search for security, or the desire to be comfortable in life. Walter points out the dangers of such attitudes. Theologically, our 'security is not to be found in this world or in ourselves but in an all-loving, almighty God'.[8] Culturally, 'what is noticeable, especially within Protestantism, is that Christians in different socio-economic groups tend to belong not only to different churches but also to different kinds of churches'.[9] In my own city of Melbourne, founded in 1835, the first fifty years saw the Church of England, the Church of Scotland (Presbyterian), and the Roman Catholic Church (strongly Irish) take root in the emerging colony. Whatever their strengths, each felt itself to be *the* church, responsible for all the souls in a particular area; and each sought to influence government policies, with little awareness of other churches except as competitors. The laudable ideal of comprehensiveness presupposed a broad identification between a particular church and a particular culture: English citizens were Anglican, Scots were Presbyterian and the Irish Roman Catholic.[10] Although this form of 'culture religion' has largely died away, it has been to some extent replaced by new forms, in which Anglicans are still rather English, Greeks are definitely Orthodox, Italians and Spanish are Roman Catholic, Turks are Islamic, Pentecostals are heavily influenced by American cultures, and many ordinary Australians are secular in religion. When my sons were attending their local primary school, in which not only English but also Italian, Greek, Arabic, and Turkish were used in the classroom, the only event of the week which divided students ethnically was Religious Education!

A better approach to cultural pluralism is to take the opportunity for reflection upon one's own cultural outlook; the old adage, 'Travel broadens the mind', remains true. My first stint of living overseas was in South-East Asia, learning Chinese. I returned to Australia far more aware of my instinctive attitudes about life, including prejudices, because of the experience of a very different linguistic and social environment. A year in the US, in a cultural context similar to my own, helped me appreciate the effect of the natural environment on culture, through the way in which four definite seasons affect living. Exposure to other cultures offers the opportunity not only for critical perception and the exposure of prejudice, but also the chance to learn different ways of doing things. This learning comes not only from experts, but from spending time among peoples who have developed ways of living in particular environments. Immigrant Australians, for example, have only recently begun to appreciate the achievement of aboriginal Australians in developing intricate cultures in a harsh natural environment, so as to be able to live within it in a sustainable manner; while the coming of people from all over the world in the last fifty years has enriched Australian lifestyles immeasurably. The plurality of cultures thus offers the possibility of critical reflection and learning, and can be a sharpening agent in avoiding the idolatrous confusion of the particularities of a culture with universal loyalties.

These initial approaches help us to face both fear of the different and the romantic tendency to admire it uncritically, and to learn about ourselves and others; but they do not provide a positive response to the challenge of relativism. Ultimately it is a question of identity: are we essentially defined through relationship to God, or through relationship to a particular culture? The answer may appear to be obvious, but relationship with God is known only in and through a particular time, place and environment, and is itself based on the particularity of God's relationship to creation in and through Jesus Christ. Tradition, the way in which the message of Christ is handed on to us, cannot but influence our perception of what that message is, and the manner in which we 'tradition' it to others (*cf.* 1 Cor. 11:2 with 15:1–5). It is only as our relationship with God deepens, through and with the people of God in the world, that our security grows, so that we are enabled to face new challenges in an open, critically sensitive way, rather than by dismissive reaction.

In the midst of this issue we encounter the effects of sin on human cultures. No society, or aspect of any society, is free from the outworkings of human pride, self-centredness and the desire to be in control: these are signs of the corruption of our God-given dominion. Customs such as human sacrifice, female circumcision, widow-burning, foot-binding, prostitution, slavery and torture are clearly opposed to God's will for human life. Others are less obviously wrong, but reinforce sinful attitudes such as selfishness, greed or lust; television commercials provide plenty of evidence of the highly ambiguous culture of consumerism. Even in those aspects of a culture which embody the highest ideals to which human beings aspire, or which celebrate the goodness of God that pervades everyday life, sin is present. Consider birth, retirement, setting up a new home, or beginning a meal: a child can be seen only as evidence of a parent's achievement, whether in fertility or child-rearing; retirement as boasting or escaping to laziness; a new home can provide the chance for ostentatious display; and even grace at the table can be a means of controlling behaviour. Indeed, the worst idols are precisely the best things set in the place of God, and it is their God-given goodness which makes them attractive.[11]

Christ and culture

Christian response to any issue centres around Christ. The manner in which culture interacts with Christ is delicate. On the one hand, Christ is 'the true light, which enlightens everyone' (Jn. 1:9), and came into the world to bring fulfilment to human life (Jn. 10:10). On the other hand, 'the light has come into the world, and people loved darkness rather than light' (Jn. 3:19). Human beings have found an apparently endless succession of ways to corrupt the good gifts of God, whether in the pettiness of daily life, the settled sins of envy and sloth, or the evil enormities of systematic cruelty. No culture is exempt from the effects of sin, yet none is beyond the renewing work of Christ; Christian responses to cultural pluralism and relativism therefore require a nuanced approach. In his classic study *Christ and Culture*,[12] Richard Niebuhr describes five typical ways in which Christians relate the two.

1. *Fundamental opposition* ('Christ against culture'): Christ has nothing to do with human culture, but is indeed entirely opposed to it. Christians have a clear choice to make between God and Mammon, Christ and Caesar, the Spirit and Satan.

2. *Fundamental agreement* ('the Christ of culture'): Christ is part of human culture, albeit its high point, to be identified with the best in each. Christians are to be indistinguishable from their cultural background.

3. *Synthesis* ('Christ above culture'): Christ is both continuous and discontinuous with human culture. Christians have been led part of the way to Christ through culture, but a further step of faith beyond culture is required.

4. *Tension* ('Christ and culture in paradox'): the tension between Christ and culture remains unresolved in this life. Christians live in two worlds, subject to two authorities, Christ's and the state's, and must seek to honour both commitments though aware of the paradoxes involved.

5. *Conversion* ('Christ transforms culture'): Christ converts people within their cultures, and in so doing transforms their cultures towards the priorities of the kingdom of God. Christians are called to be transformed themselves, and to be instruments of cultural transformation in and through Christ.

Niebuhr denies that any one of these is *the* Christian answer, though the last position is the one he regards as the best starting-point in formulating a response to culture. Rather, each of the above responses is needed in different situations; absolutizing any of them distorts the delicate balance between the work of God in creation, providence, redemption, and re-creation. As an example, let me apply this structure to some aspects of the dominant Anglo-Celtic culture in Australia.[13] *Fundamental opposition* needs to be shown to some elements of this culture; for example, the widespread assumption of white supremacy: here Christians have a clear choice to make between Christ and racism. *Fundamental agreement* can be affirmed, however, with regard to the egalitarian values of Australian society; Christians should be indistinguishable from others in their concerns for equality of opportunity. *Synthesis* is needed in the same area, however; Christians need to go beyond egalitarianism expressed in merely negative terms (what Australians call the 'tall poppy syndrome'), to a positive appreciation of the varied contributions which different people offer. *Tension* remains over nationalism; Christians are expected to commit themselves, as Australians, to a tolerance that can easily become a denial of the claims of Christ, not only regarding other faiths, but in relation to neighbouring nations and lifestyles. *Conversion* is needed with regard to the fatalism in much of the male Anglo-Celtic Australian outlook, summed up in slogans like 'She'll be right, mate', 'Your number's up', or 'Cop it sweet'; Christians are called to ensure that their own view of God's work is based on a personal, gracious, Christ-centred, doctrine of God, and to seek to be agents of transforming the impersonal, reward-based and distant concept of God typical of the Australian cultural mainstream.

There are many aspects of culture which could be considered in the light of this analysis, especially the arts. The fine arts, such as painting and sculpture, have been viewed with both suspicion and enthusiasm in the Christian tradition. Some, fathers of the church as well as Puritans, have seen them as little more than opportunities for idolatry and breaches of the second commandment. Others have gladly welcomed their use for the glory of God, though with varying perspectives: the Orthodox permit only the use of two-dimensional art, in icons, while Roman Catholics allow for statues as well. The way in which cultural trends interact with Christian faith is also multiform; whether a 'Christ against culture' or 'Christ of culture' position is appropriate entails consideration of a particular cultural context. Architecture is a case in point here; should a church building look distinctive, or blend with its environment? In an Islamic culture, unsympathetic to Christian faith, a building resembling classical Christian models would emphasize this contrast, but a less visible one may be wiser. House design is another case in point; double garages may be a cultural norm in new Australian suburbs, but should Christians assume that owning two cars is a lifestyle standard?

The performing arts are another vital aspect of cultural expression. To what extent should Christians adopt cultural forms to express the faith? In England, for example, firecrackers are seen as celebrating the defeat of the enemies of Protestantism on Guy Fawkes' Night, whereas the Presbyterian Church in Taiwan refuses to use fireworks, given their association in Chinese cultures with scaring away spirits. Drama and music, like the fine arts, have had a chequered career in Christian tradition. Acting, for example, was so closely associated with Graeco-Roman legends of the gods that in the third-century church, actors were not allowed to become Christians unless they renounced their profession. In the Middle Ages, however, it was the church which preserved and developed the dramatic arts, to teach the faith to non-literates. Music was viewed with suspicion in the churches until the last few centuries; it was seen as stirring up the passions, and detracting from the words sung to it. Another issue is the style of music allowed; in different times and places polyphonic, baroque, accompanied, romantic, vaudeville, jazz, rock or heavy metal have all been proscribed, though today all but the last are generally acceptable.[14] In each case, a whole welter of cultural associations is involved; an Afro-American singer or trumpeter had to choose between 'devil's music' (such as jazz or the blues), and gospel music. The two musical styles represented two lifestyles which were regarded as having little overlap.

Space forbids fuller treatment of these invigorating aspects of human culture. Three particular examples will suffice to illustrate the issues involved in the interaction of social and environmental facets of human life in culture: marriage, language and humour. Marriage is considered as a 'rite of passage', one of the turning-points in human life, such as birth, puberty and death, which are surrounded by customs. Language forms the basis of human cultures, since it uniquely embodies our capacity not only to communicate but also to reflect. Humour concludes the discussion because it discloses many cultural nuances in human language, but mostly because it is fun to be human.

Culture, weddings and marriage

Kinship and family relationships lie at the heart of concepts of marriage.[15] Many English-speaking Christians regard a church wedding as the only way in which a marriage should begin. Given the absence of any details about weddings in the Scriptures, and the variety of custom in Christian history, however, are we to view *de facto* relationships as wrong, unfortunate, or a legitimate way of being married? Again, in contemporary western societies, marriage takes place at the initiative of a couple who are 'in love', sometimes without other family members' permission or even knowledge. Yet in many other cultures marriages are arranged by the families concerned. To a westerner, this looks like manipulation of someone's personal life, but the strength of the extended family in cultures where marriages are arranged, and the high failure rate of marriages in cultures where the couple initiates the marriage, raise questions about making the latter a universal norm. Whatever the manner in which a marriage begins, it can easily become an instrument of oppression, to the point at which many question its validity· or usefulness as an institution, and look to more communal arrangements for child-rearing, and to personal fulfilment as the major criterion for sexual relationships. How do Christians understand what it means to be married in such a climate?

Concepts of marriage have also been affected by lengthened life expectancy.[16] Until early this century, the promise to be true 'till death us do part' meant on average a period of about twenty-five years, long enough to raise one generation of children, and perhaps to see the third generation. A marriage promise today is likely to need to last well over fifty years, so that many marriages will see more years without children than with them. Moreover, many couples today try not to interrupt a career during child-rearing; this is a symptom of the reality that their separate lives are expected to continue to develop independently. In the light of these sorts of factors, the person someone married in 1970 is not going to be the same ten or twenty years later, let alone forty. Celebrating a fiftieth (golden) wedding anniversary is likely to remain a rare event, but the rarity is now largely due to marriage breakdown rather than to mortality. Do these changes in culture change the *kind* of promise that is made at a wedding? At the least, this observation underlines how important it is that any couple entering marriage should do so realistically, ready to grow, adapt and change. Many, however, have come to the conclusion that marriage is a temporary partnership, entered into with the expectation that it is likely to last only a decade or so. This is evident in the growing number of 'trial' marriages, *de facto* partnerships, and, even where there is a wedding, the practice of arranging a contract covering the disposal of assets if the marriage should end.

Views such as these regard marriage as solely a matter of contract between two individuals, with little if any communal aspect. Other societies, however, have seen marriage itself as communal, in polygamy (more than one woman being married to the same man).[17] Given its prominence in traditional African cultures, Christian leaders in that continent have put considerable effort into formulating policies towards it. Polygamy is more difficult to exclude than one at first sight might think; after all, it was practised by Abraham, Jacob, David and Solomon.[18] Faced with objections from western Christians, some African Christians respond by asking about the extent to which serial monogamy, a succession of spouses, is morally superior to polygamy.

In the light of this cultural plurality regarding the nature and practice of marriage, how do we avoid a relativist approach which sees any structured relationship between men and women as possible, depending on the cultural context? All Christians support the ideal that Jesus teaches, namely that marriage is to be between one man and one woman in an exclusive, life-long commitment (Mt. 19:3–12). The details of how a particular marriage begins, is lived out and ends, however, remain open. Moral theology in the western church has developed criteria for a valid marriage (such as loyalty, free commitment, and fruitfulness), defined the 'goods' which marriage offers (procreation, companionship, and sexual intimacy), and explored its meaning, signifying the union between Christ and the church (Eph. 5:32).[19]

All these concepts take a variety of cultural expressions, many features of which may qualify or challenge Christian ideals. For example, in a traditional church wedding, what importance is to be placed on the manner in which bride and groom enter? Should the bride process on her father's arm, or should the couple walk in together? How does the cost of a wedding, involving long-term debt in some Asian contexts, relate to Christian perspectives on stewardship? Does video-filming reduce the couple's role from being the 'ministers' who enact the marriage, to being mere actors in a family soap opera? What relationship does the wedding have to the engagement or betrothal which precedes it? How does what happens at the reception or wedding breakfast which commonly follows, interpret what is happening? In Australia, it has not been possible to send telegrams for years, but at many receptions the best man still reads out ribald 'telegrams' concocted by the guests after a well-lubricated meal![20]

Questions like these illustrate the fascinating and disturbing complexities involved in responding to cultural pluralism, and the way in which enduring Christian ideals can be transmitted in a variety of ways.

Culture and language

Language is perhaps the most fundamental aspect of human culture; by it we are able not only to communicate, but to reflect upon our living.[21] Animals can communicate, and so in some sense can be said to possess language skills (*cf.* Gn. 3:1–5; Nu. 23:28–30). It is humanity, however, to whom God brings the animals so that they may be named (Gn. 2:19). The divine gift of speech is first used to express the recognition that man and woman are made for a distinctive partnership, involving creative communication with one another (Gn. 2:23), in obedience to God (Gn. 3:2–3). Its next use by the first humans, however, is to acknowledge their fear of God, to pass blame – and for one partner to 'name' the other, just as the animals had been defined (Gn. 3:10–13, 20). Language is thus a basic facet of human existence, especially suited to hear and reflect on the Word of God, but also distorted by, and the instrument of, sin. As James puts it, the tongue might be small in size, but like a rudder it guides the whole ship, and like a fire or wild animal it cannot be tamed. It has enormous potential for both good and ill: 'With it we bless the Lord and Father, and with it we curse those who are made in the likeness of God' (Jas. 3:9).

Language is depicted in Genesis as being originally a means of universal communication: 'the whole earth had one language and the same words' (Gn. 11:1). Under sin, this human unity becomes the fuel of proud ambition which sets itself up to displace God, whose condemnation of such treason leads to the multiplication of tongues at Babel (Gn. 11:3–9). This is not the end of the story; the coming of the Spirit on the day of Pentecost reverses the Babel tragedy, not by creating a single language and culture, but by enabling every nation to hear in its own language the mighty acts of God (Acts 2:5–11). Human beings are made of one race (Acts 17:26), yet there is no return to the past, but rather the transformation of the present. The variety of human languages may be due to sin, but in God's good grace it also serves to express the wonderful variety of both human and divine creative ability. God's use of the variety of human tongues is seen in the multilingual character of the Scriptures, written in two major languages, Hebrew and Greek, with parts in Aramaic, and phrases from Persian and Latin. Even the title on Christ's cross is multilingual, representing the Jewish, Greek and Roman heritages, which covered the known earth. The earliest church found it quite a challenge to incorporate Hebrew and Greek-speaking Jewish Christians in the one body, and managed to do so not by suppressing diversity, but by formulating structures which were able to embrace it (cf. Acts 6:1–7; 21:37 – 22:2).

Language is a subtle thing. A word or phrase in one language rarely if ever conveys exactly the same nuance in another. The terms 'father' and 'mother', for example, signify 'biological parent' in every language, but this by no means exhausts their fields of meaning. What each conveys in Chinese, English and French, for example, is inseparably related to family patterns in the cultures from which the languages come. Further, within each culture there are many sub-cultural variations. In Anglican circles, for example, to address a priest as 'Father Chris' is natural to some, but unthinkable for others. If Chris is a woman, very few will call her 'Father', and I have never heard a woman priest addressed as 'Mother'; these terms are distinct not only in their biological meanings, but in the way in which they work metaphorically.[22] Beyond these wider fields of reference, 'father' or 'mother' used of my own parents has a unique meaning for me, one which mixes biological, cultural and Christian concepts with my own experience.

In the light of this, classical Christian theology speaks of language in terms of 'analogy'.[23] From one point of view, every word has a particular, 'univocal' (single-voiced) meaning, or it has no content. On the other hand, if it is to be understood by others, and used to explain other words, it must have an ambiguous, 'equivocal' (equal-voiced) meaning. If this were pressed, however, every word would carry such a broad reference as to mean nothing. The concept of analogy holds these paradoxical extremes together. How do I know what a word which is new to me means? A known word which is close to the meaning of the new word is taken, and then qualified to give an idea of what the new word means; a base concept is modified. In practice, this is often repeated several times, using a variety of modifiers and bases, usually with little awareness of the process which is taking place. We learn meanings largely through picking up cross-references and allusions in everyday life, through conversation, reading, film and television, for example, as well as by deliberate study. It would perhaps be convenient if words worked in a precise way, but life would be much the poorer; poetry, rhetoric, pun and slang would be lost.[24]

Language can usefully be described as the 'sacrament of

meaning'.[25] A sacrament, according to the Catechism in the *Book of Common Prayer*, is 'an outward and visible sign of an inward and spiritual grace,' and 'a means whereby we receive the same, and a pledge to assure us thereof'. Two errors are avoided here. On the one hand, identifying the sign with the thing signified destroys the distinction between the outward and the inward. This approach tends to idolatry, since God's grace becomes literalized; transubstantiation, at least as popularly understood, is the classic example. On the other hand, wholly to separate the sign and the thing signified leaves no connection between the outward and the inward. This approach undermines our reception and assurance of the reality of God's grace; Zwinglianism, again as popularly understood, is the classic example. A sacramental approach to language is best illustrated by considering the relation between the words of the Scriptures and the Word of God.[26] Strictly to identify the words with God's own self-expression may render the text itself an object of worship, so that merely hearing or reading it, even in a language not understood, comes to be what matters; this is the tendency of fundamentalist approaches, whether medieval or modern. On the other hand, to say that there is no relationship between the Word of God and the words of Scripture denies hearers any possibility of knowing God through them; this is the tendency of liberal approaches. Most Christians approach the Scriptures respectfully, expecting to hear God's Word in and through them, but refusing to worship the text. The indirect yet effective relation between Word and words is acknowledged by the common custom of praying for the Holy Spirit, who inspired the Scriptures, to illumine the hearers. As with the gospel sacraments, faith does not *make* the outward sign to be the grace signified, but *receives* the outward sign as an effectual means of grace.

This kind of analysis can be applied to language itself. Identifying words with the meaning they signify is the temptation of ultra-empirical approaches to human life, characteristic of pragmatism (whether economic, materialistic or religious). This reduces meaning to formulae, making it apparently easy to define what is right and wrong, and rejecting the whole range of poetry and the arts. On the other hand, partly in reaction to the totalitarian ethos of the first approach, others deny that any connection can be made between meaning and language: 'the very idea of meaning smacks of fascism'.[27] In this extreme postmodernist view, words are mere self-expression, only incidentally giving access to meaning (if any exists). To say that 'language is the sacrament of meaning' avoids both extremes. It recognizes the subtleties entailed in language; whether in prose, story, conversation or poetry, it includes such features as metaphor, simile, allegory and allusion. But it refuses to dissolve away meaning, recognizing that precise definition is not the only way by which cognitive content is conveyed.

Consider the key role that words play in Christian life. We use them to pray, to preach, and to confess both sins and faith, and we often set them to music. We even use them by *not* using them, in times of quiet and silence. Words can inspire, express, encourage – and hurt, mystify, or exclude.[28] *How* we speak goes beyond the meaning of words, however, and reflects cultural assumptions. Accent is an indicator of the variety of linguistic and social sub-cultures which exist even within a particular language. One factor in Australian life is the relative uniformity of accent across the vast country. The accent range is not wholly uniform, but nowhere near the accent variations in the USA or Britain.[29] Accent often functions as a social marker, as *My Fair Lady* sought to demonstrate; in many societies, opening your mouth immediately classifies you sharply. I remember with some passion a well-educated minister friend being asked to take English lessons because he spoke with a slight middle-eastern accent. Parsonic tones in the pulpit still abound, and I have heard the Australian accent criticized as 'not suitable for church'! On the other hand, some Australian Protestants take on an American-tinged accent when praying, especially for key theological terms containing an 'r' sound, such as 'God', 'Lord' and 'word' ('Gar-rd', 'Law-rrd' and 'wir-rrd'). Such changes of accent between speech in daily life and public worship indicate a lack of integration between the sub-cultures involved. (A useful test is to check whether we sound reasonably the same when giving out notices in church as when praying or preaching.)

Language and culture thus interact in a myriad of ways. One particular aspect of human culture in which language plays a central role is humour. The following conversation between Humpty Dumpty and Alice offers a delightful transition.[30]

147

The animal that laughs[31]

> 'When *I* use a word,' Humpty Dumpty said, in rather a
> scornful tone, 'it means just what I choose it to mean –
> neither more nor less.'
> 'The question is,' said Alice, 'whether you can *make*
> words mean so many different things.'
> 'The question is,' said Humpty Dumpty, 'which is to
> be master – that's all.'

The last comment discloses the masculine bias of Humpty
Dumpty, even if his approach to language seems at first sight to
owe a good deal to de Saussure! A little later the scales are
balanced:

> 'That's a great deal to make one word mean', Alice
> said in a thoughtful tone.
> 'When I make a word do a lot of work like that,' said
> Humpty Dumpty, 'I always pay it extra.'
> 'Oh!' said Alice. She was much too puzzled to make
> any other remark.

The discussion then moves to the famous poem constructed
largely of words newly coined, which English listeners still
somehow understand and enjoy.

> 'Twas brillig, and the slithy toves
> Did gyre and gymble in the wabe;
> All mimsy were the borogroves,
> And the mome raths outgrabe.

> 'That's enough to begin with,' Humpty Dumpty inter-
> rupted: 'there are plenty of hard words there.'

Why do many find such a conversation amusing as well as full
of insight? Humour is a funny thing: it is almost impossible to
understand why we laugh. To begin, note that 'human' and
'humour' share a common root, the Latin *humus*, 'earth';
laughter is an earthy phenomenon. As Kuschel puts it, 'Laughter knows no limits, no tabu, no respect, and there is as much

laughter at the holiest as at the most banal. Thus laughter embraces the whole spectrum of life and morality: from goodness to meanness, from humanity to barbarism.'[32]

Humour, whatever its nature, has many functions. In the face of oppression it can be a means to cope with life; this is especially evident in the Jewish tradition of humour. When used to laugh *at* others, it can be without ethics, cruel; for this reason it was suspect to Plato, and carefully regulated by Aristotle. In daily life this can cause problems; it is very difficult not to laugh at a genuinely funny joke, even though it may be demeaning to others – but the laughter may stick in our throat. Humour thus has a subversive quality, getting behind our accepted ideas, even when we regard them as worthy, true and to be maintained. Yet the ridiculous needs to be seen as such; here the subversive quality of laughter takes up a prophetic role, and can be a means of change. Newspaper cartoonists are a good example of this double possibility; an effective cartoon can play a significant role in exposing hypocrisy, or it can undermine a person's humanity in public. As with all aspects of culture, humour discloses not only the joy and wonder of being human, but also the dire effects of sin, distorting relationships and perceptions.

Can humour exist apart from sin, however? John Cleese was a member of the Monty Python team which made (among many other things) *The Life of Brian*, a film based around the life of Jesus.[33] Commenting on its preparation, he said: 'The moment you got really near the figure of Christ, it just wasn't really funny because Christ was wise and flexible and intelligent and he didn't have any of the things that comedy is about – envy, greed, malice, avarice, lust, stupidity.'[34] If this is the case, should humour be regarded as inconsistent with truth? Is there no laughter in heaven, even over a lost sinner who repents (*cf.* Lk. 15:7, 10)? Or is it that we can know laughter only in and through our sinful condition, which God accepts and redeems into a new creation?

There appears to be little explicit humour in the Scriptures, but this may be because the texts are so familar that the element of surprise, so central to humour, is excluded. Again, without access to a full understanding of the cultural and sub-cultural norms behind the original languages, many humorous allusions are missed. This is made the more difficult because most people have access to the Scriptures only in translation; explaining a pun (*cf.* Am. 8:1–2) or an amusing story (*cf.* Lk. 16:1–9) is about as entertaining as explaining a joke! Even so, the amount of direct evidence is not great, and most conveys a negative tone. Perhaps the most famous is the first recorded laughter, by Abraham (Gn. 17:17) and especially Sarah (Gn. 18:12–15), at the prospect of her bearing a son in old age. This is laughter at the ridiculous, laughter born out of fear, but it eventually issues in the laughter of joy, so that the child is named Isaac, 'laughing boy' (Gn. 21:6–7). It cannot be said that laughter begins in innocence in this tale, but it certainly ends there.

In the Psalter, divine laughter is heard, but it is the laughter of derision at enemies (Ps. 2:4; 37:13; 59:6), echoed by the righteous about the wicked (Ps. 52:6; Jb. 22:19), or by Israel's enemies against them (Ps. 80:6). Only once in the Psalms is laughter spoken of in positive terms: 'When the LORD restored the fortunes of Zion . . . Then our mouth was filled with laughter, and our tongue with shouts of joy' (Ps. 126:1–2). The Preacher may say that 'there is a time to laugh' (Ec. 3:4), but he speaks elsewhere of laughter as 'mad' (Ec. 2:2), bettered by sorrow (Ec. 7:3), a stupid act of fools (Ec. 7:6), and a cynical pleasure at feasts (Ec. 10:19). Proverbs is nearly as gloomy; there is mocking laughter (Pr. 1:26), 'Even in laughter the heart is sad' (Pr. 14:13), and even the 'capable wife' who laughs does so 'at the time to come' (Pr. 31:25), not with pleasure in the present. God's final address to Job refers to laughter three times, to express the absence of fear in the ostrich (Jb. 39:18), horse (Jb. 39:22) and crocodile (Jb. 41:29). Bildad may assure Job that God 'will yet fill your mouth with laughter' (Jb. 8:21), but it is a false word. Humour appears from time to time in war, but as mocking laughter, with no element of sympathy (2 Ch. 30:10; 2 Sa. 10:4–5).

The New Testament adds only a little more: Jesus was laughed at for his naïvety concerning the dead daughter of Jairus (Mt. 9:24), but he promises laughter for those who weep – and mourning for those who laugh now (Lk. 6:21, 25), advice similar to that given by James to sinners (Jas. 4:8–9).[35] On the other hand, Paul calls Christians to be 'fools for Christ', open to being misunderstood in order that the joy and blessing of the paradoxical foolishness of the cross might be shared (1 Cor.

1:21–31; *cf.* 2 Cor. 11:1, 16–21; 12:11), but it is a costly foolishness. In the light of our common assumption that living as the people of God is full of joy, this picture is unexpected. Laughter is almost always portrayed in negative terms, a prime means to flaunt superiority, mock or express embarrassment. The positive side is recognized to exist, but its expression is rare. Part of the difficulty is that 'laughter' appears to be distinguished from 'blessing' and 'joy' in scriptural vocabulary, and seems to be reserved for the destructive, vindictive side of humour. Blessing is a frequent concept, meaning both 'well-being' (*eulogeō*) and 'happiness' (*makarios*); it is characteristic of God to be 'blessed', and thanksgiving consists of 'blessing God' for the thing concerned. Joy is far more common than laughter, and is often unrestrained in its expression; it seems to be the characteristic activity of angels!

Good humour is thus by no means absent from the Scriptures, but the reality of the effects of sin is taken seriously; the general view of laughter in the Scriptures is thus best described as worldly wise. The wry wisdom of Jewish humour derives, not from a few cheap chuckles, but from a profound sense of irony, providing resources to survive and cope with the tragedies and foibles of life. Humour provides a way of laughing in the face of adversity, of mocking those who think they can oppress, and so subverting their power. This is not just an activity for gloating humans: it is one in which God joins, delighting to vaunt over petty foes.

Humour can do more than face adversity, however. A shared joke presupposes a commonality of culture, and fosters community. It builds bridges between people, as every after-dinner speaker knows, and can put things in perspective, abolish anger and demolish conceit. More significantly, humour can shift the imagination, forcing us to see things from someone else's perspective.[36] In this way, humour both presupposes a shared cultural matrix, and offers a way by which it can be transcended, or its sinful aspects challenged. Such a function is close to Jesus' use of parables; listeners are drawn into a story and eased into taking sides, and then suddenly find that they have switched allegiance – or that they have to protest at the story's being told at all (the characteristic reaction of the Pharisees).[37]

It is quite an art to be able to shift the cultural assumptions behind a conversation, so that the priorities of Christ are maintained. Being able to use humour is a big help. Such an act of subverting assumptions takes place at the personal level, but it proceeds from, and itself affects, the ongoing movements which shape human life that we call culture. As Frost puts it, 'In every relationship, every conversation, every thought, every act, we contribute to culture.'[38] We need to accept the reality of the fact that we see life only through eyes distorted by sin, but also know the possibility of release from its binding. 'Now we see in a mirror, dimly, but then we will see face to face', and reach our true end, the joyous good humour of God's love (1 Cor. 13:12).

And so we reach the point where it is appropriate to turn from the perspective of the race as a whole to consider the human person.

FOCUS 2B

THE HUMAN
PERSON

PREAMBLE

Melbourne trams are made to carry as many people as possible. Tram travel means being close to many other human beings, of various ages, kinds of dress, ethnic backgrounds and languages. I never cease to wonder at the stories, background, resources and potential represented in each. Whether withdrawn, talkative, smelly, pushy, appreciative, happy or worried, every single one is a person made in the image of God, someone for whom Christ laid down his life and took it up again, someone in whom the Holy Spirit seeks to awaken the life of the new heaven and new earth. Each one needs to be seen, not only in the light of past or present, but through the eyes of faith and hope, in terms of the person God intends him or her to become. I realize that some know little or nothing of the love and truth of God in Christ, and that each of us falls short of the glory of God. Nevertheless this does not detract from the enormous privilege and responsibility that attend each human life. Human beings are fascinatingly varied and interesting, both heartbreaking and annoying, inspiring and creative.

The aim of this Focus is to explore what it means to be human at the personal level. As you read these chapters, three aspects of being human need to be kept in mind. First, your own life is unique; each person has a slightly different reading of this book. I say this not to diminish or relativize its content, but to encourage you to reflect on your unique identity, expressed and grounded in your distinctive relationship with God, other humans and creation. Secondly, whatever the varieties of culture, language or age, each of us is either a woman or a man, and approaches reflection on human life from the distinct perspective of either. Chapters 7 (on human uniqueness), 8 (on being a woman) and 9 (on being a man) focus in turn on these two aspects. Chapter 10 concludes this Focus by discussing each human being as an embodied and sensual person. None of these topics exists in isolation, but is experienced only in distinctive interaction through the particular, unique life experience that is yours.

Thirdly, every human being lives as a sinner. This is by no means the first or last word on the human condition, but it colours all we think, feel and do, especially when we try to understand our own selves. As in Focus 2a, sin is not given its own chapter, since it is not a separate feature of human life but affects every aspect of being human. Sin is not the first thing to be said about being a human person, though we forget it at our peril. What God made and remakes us to be is 'very good'; that is the foundation of both memory and hope.

7

THE UNIQUE
PERSON

Human societies often assume that the life experience of each person is to be subsumed under that of the wider community, and that individual needs and hopes are to be shaped and disciplined by the goals and ideals of the group: the nation, ethnic culture or political ideology, for example. At best, this represents a resistance to self-centred living, and a recognition that as human beings we are made for community. All too often, however, it has resulted in oppressive submission to the requirements of the state, or of custom and convention. The assertion of the importance of the individual in western society may have been considerably overdone, as noted in earlier chapters. Nevertheless, behind this stands a great truth: the distinctive significance of each person in the sight of God. Today this notion is assumed to be obviously true, but it is all too easily and quickly set aside when divine revelation about human nature is ignored or repudiated.

Human dignity

The Judeo-Christian source of the notion that each person is unique and precious is the law revealed by God to ancient Israel. This law is itself grounded in the concept of humanity's being made in the image of God (see chapter 1): 'Whoever sheds the blood of a human, by a human shall that person's blood be shed; for in his own image God made humankind' (Gn. 9:6). To modern ears this may sound repellent, but it represents in the strongest possible terms the divine significance of human life, both of the race as a whole and also of each person. No distinction is made regarding gender, social position or class, as was common among other ancient peoples.[1] The Mosaic law spells out this divine command in greater detail and with wider application, especially in the Decalogue, the 'ten words' (Ex. 20:1–17; Dt. 5:6–21). The only distinction mentioned in these commandments comes in the one about the sabbath, and that is to insist on the application of the law of rest to all, regardless of gender, family place or social class. On the seventh day 'you shall not do any work – you, your son or your daughter, your male or female slave, your livestock, or the alien resident in your towns' (Ex. 20:10). As noted in chapter 5, the sabbath points to a lifestyle that integrates human, animal and plant life, and which, while assuming the dignity of labour, avoids the graceless idolatry of human effort.

Regard for each human being as unique and precious finds detailed expression in a number of provisions. The life of a parent (Ex. 21:15), slave (Ex. 21:20–21), foetus (Ex. 21:22–24), and anyone else (Ex. 21:12) is protected, yet not blindly; the penalties for taking life vary, and allowance is made for accidental or consequential death (Ex. 21:13, 21; Dt. 4:41–43; Dt. 19:2–13). A further example is slavery, which lay at the heart of ancient social economies, but ultimately proved to be inconsistent with the ideals of the Torah. Among the Hebrews its existence is recognized, yet hedged about with restrictions that emphasize the full dignity of the slave, both male and female, in effect transforming slavery into time-limited employment (Ex. 21:2–11; Lv. 25:35–43; Dt. 15:12–18). This example is significant in that it shows that a person is to be valued not only for his or her life in itself but also for the contribution he or she is able to make to society. Capacity to contribute is not the only criterion by which someone is to be valued, however. Parents, as those through whom God had given life, are to receive particular respect (Ex. 20:12; 21:17; Lv. 19:3), as are the aged (Lv. 19:32), even though they may be apparently unable to contribute anything.

No distinction is to be made between persons in the practice of justice, since each is made in the divine image, and is the object of divine concern. Justice is to be enacted following the divine example: 'The LORD your God is God of gods and Lord of lords, the great God, mighty and awesome, who is not partial and takes no bribe, who executes justice for the orphan and the widow, and who loves the strangers, providing them food and clothing' (Dt. 10:17–18).

Respect for human life and dignity is displayed at its deepest level in the Torah in the laws about aliens, who would normally have had no rights. They are to join in the sabbath rest (Ex. 20:10; 23:12), must not be wronged or oppressed (Ex. 21:21; 23:9), and are to be allowed to glean (Lv. 19:10; cf. Ru. 2). This respect for the full dignity of even the foreigner is summed up in the following remarkable words, which come soon after the more familiar command to 'love your neighbour as yourself' (Lv. 19:18): 'The alien who resides with you shall be to you as the citizen among you; you shall love the alien as yourself, for you were aliens in the land of Egypt' (Lv. 19:34).

Teaching such as this continues in the prophets (cf. Am. 5:24 – 6:7; Mi. 2:1–10). It is strengthened in Christ's interpretation of the law, especially in the Sermon on the Mount, where action towards others is inseparably related to attitudes towards them (Mt. 5:21–48). Jesus thus takes Israel's perspective on human dignity further, notably in the parable of the good Samaritan (Lk. 10:29–37). The question 'Who is my neighbour?' here receives what seems to me its most profound and subtle answer. According to the parable, my neighbour is not in the first place the needy person whom I help, but the one, perhaps a stranger or alien, who helps me, unwilling though I may be to accept aid. At its deepest level, it is Christ who is my neighbour, the one who meets me in my need, and calls me to be a neighbour to others. As Barth puts it, in this parable, ' "Go and do thou likewise" means "Come, follow me." '[2] Conversely, as Jesus teaches in

159

Matthew 25, in welcoming the stranger, dressing the naked, caring for the sick or visiting the prisoner, we act as neighbours to Christ. 'As you did it to one of the least of these . . . you did it to me' (Mt. 25:34–40); and as we fail to do so, we fail to minister to Christ, and suffer eternal consequences (Mt. 25:41–46). In this teaching lies the rejection of both do-gooder charity and an individualistic interpretation of human life. The affirmation of personal human dignity is understandable only in the light of my relation to others, and both they and I are embraced in, through and by Christ.

Both Old and New Testaments thus emphasize the uniqueness of each person, made in the image of God, whose fullness is seen in Christ, to whom we look for what we are to become. The dignity of each person is grounded in both creation and re-creation. Each and every human being is made in the image of God, and is someone whom Christ came to redeem and fashion into a member of the new humanity (1 Tim. 2:3–6, and see chapter 2 above). T. R. Glover tells the story of the sixteenth-century scholar Muretus, on whom, since he was near death, some doctors were about to operate. They regarded him as of interest only for his experimental value; one doctor said (in Latin) to the other, 'Let the experiment be tried on this worthless body.' Muretus, being conscious and knowing Latin, responded, 'Do you call that worthless, for which Christ was content to die?'[3] Christian belief acknowledges the mortality of human beings, but we were not made for mortality, and it is not the destiny which God intends for us. Each person is to be seen as a creature made in the image of God, a sinner for whom Christ laid down his life, and for whose re-creation he rose again. Further, the unique distinctiveness of each person is seen at its fullest in the church as the body of Christ, where the Holy Spirit activates and distributes ministries 'to each one individually just as [he] chooses' (1 Cor. 12:11). Each member of Christ is the object of the sanctifying work of the Spirit, who leads us towards the consummation of all things in Christ. A creature whom the Spirit brings to new life, reshapes in growing holiness and goodness, equips for God's service, and prepares for his or her place in the new creation, is of eternal worth to God, and carries profound dignity (cf. Rom. 8:1–27).

In sum, human life is to be regarded with awesome solemnity, embodying the distinctive work of God our Creator and Re-creator, into whose image we are being made. In the light of modern patterns of thought and practice about human living, several implications of this claim need to be spelled out.

Human freedom

What it means to be human must be seen in the light of the persons we are to become, rather than what we once were. Likewise, freedom has two main sides: what it is *from*, and what it is *for*, and the latter is of primary importance. For many today in western societies, however, there is almost no conception of 'freedom for': 'freedom' means merely autonomy, being able to do what I like. This concept of freedom has no positive content, existing in a vacuum rather than in an interactive environment.[4] Similarly, a fish is able to swim only in water, and a bird to fly only in air; reversing these contexts would be fatal for both species.[5] According to Christian faith, human being and human freedom are primarily determined by the purpose for which we are made, to live in the image of God; living otherwise is as lethal as a bird's attempt to fly in water, or as a fish's to swim in air. As regards 'freedom *from*', oppressive economic systems, manipulative families, disabling personal backgrounds and psychological problems are typical contemporary prisons from which we seek release. Systems and people are indeed part of the presenting problems in the search for freedom, but Christian faith sees the source of our captivity as deeper, grounded in the sinful condition of humanity at both corporate and personal levels. Freedom from sin may not be the primary focus of freedom in Christian perspective. Yet until its bondage is loosed, we cannot be free from its deadly effects, and so liberated for the inconceivable life prepared for those who love God (*cf.* 1 Cor. 2:9–10).

Jesus taught, 'If you continue in my word, you are truly my disciples; and you will know the truth, and the truth will make you free' (Jn. 8:32, a verse often truncated when cited). When pressed about this he responds, 'Everyone who commits sin is a slave to sin . . . if the Son makes you free, you will be free indeed' (Jn. 8:34, 36). As argued above, it is the law which underpins human dignity; but under sin, we turn the law, given by God for our well-being, into a set of rules and regulations by which we attempt to control our own destiny and the lives of others. Sin, typified by rebellion against God and apathy towards him, is the root of human evil, and uses the law to oppress us; transgressing God's law draws down a curse on our relationship with God (Gal. 3:10–12), brings death (Rom. 5:13–14; Eph. 2:1, 5) which rules us through sin (Rom. 5:17), and gives the satanic accuser power over us (Rev. 12:10). Above all, sin brings divine wrath on rebellious sinners (Jn. 3:36; Rom. 1:18; Eph. 5:6), the settled opposition of God to all that is evil.[6] In terms of the diagram used in chapters 1 and 2, as the 'upward vertical' relationship with God is corrupted from freedom into estrangement, freedom in our relations with one another and with the created order is likewise turned into oppression.

Redemption is a metaphor which speaks powerfully about freedom; a redeemer sets the oppressed free, transferring them from captivity and slavery to an owner who has both the right and desire to embrace them.[7] The New Testament writers present Jesus as the one who 'redeems' us from the shackles of sin and death, the curse of the law, the devil, and the wrath of God (Tit. 2:14; Gal. 3:13; Heb. 2:14–15; Jn. 3:36). Christ's redeeming work is not merely a rescue; if it were only that, his victory would consist of sheer force, and might be shown to be right.[8] The redemption he won is all of a piece with divine justice, obtaining full forgiveness for us at the immense cost of his own life-blood given up in the sacrificial service of others (Mk. 10:42–45; Rom. 3:24), and so being eternally effective (Heb. 9:15). Everyone redeemed in and by Christ is to esteem this newfound freedom as of supreme value, in the light of the promised 'freedom of the glory of the children of God' (Rom. 8:21), and live knowing that he or she was 'bought with a price', so as to 'glorify God in [the] body' (1 Cor. 6:20) while waiting for 'the redemption of our bodies' (Rom. 8:23).

The shape of human freedom in Christian perspective thus centres on Christ, who both sets us free from sin and ushers us into a new hope of freedom. Although we do not experience this freedom fully now, we anticipate our 'inheritance towards redemption' through the Holy Spirit (Eph. 1:14). As Paul puts it, 'where the Spirit of the Lord is, there is freedom' (2 Cor. 3:17), because the Spirit is the one who gives life, both in creation and re-creation. Christians in every age know the frustration of living in the tension between hope and present reality, but have also seen men and women freed from many tyrannies into transformed living. For example, the New Testament church gave to the ancient world a new virtue, chastity; to those addicted to sex, the gospel brought new freedom to live in committed, loyal relationships. Likewise, countless men and women have been set free from slavery to drugs, demonic oppression, guilt, destructive relationships, and the petty distortions of everyday peccadillos, into lives of self-control. The New Testament does not promise total freedom in this life, however, not even from sin (1 Jn. 1:6 – 2:11), but the promise and hope of full freedom are so real as to be spoken of as effective now (*cf.* 1 Jn. 3:2–10).[9]

Human freedom in Christian terms is paradoxical; the paradox is due to human sin, not to the nature of divine freedom.[10] Christian freedom means living not as slaves to sin, but in slavery to God our redeemer (Rom. 6:17–22), as sons and daughters, rather than slaves, in the household of Christ (Gal. 4:1–7).[11] As Paul wrote to the Galatians: 'For freedom Christ has set us free. Stand firm, therefore, and do not submit again to a yoke of slavery' (Gal. 5:1). The paradoxical nature of freedom is due not to any defect in the notion itself, but to the effects upon it of sin. A person who has done no wrong has a fully free choice between right and wrong. Once wrong is done, this freedom of choice disappears, since subsequent choices can only be between degrees of wrong; the option of doing what is wholly right no longer remains. As this tainted freedom continues to be exercised, its range is constantly narrowed into fewer and fewer right choices, so that the nature of the freedom is seen to have changed. It was this type of argument that Augustine used against Pelagius, who held that each person had a clean slate of ongoing choice. Only the first humans had real freedom, Augustine argued; once tainted, the human will continues to be able to choose (*arbitrium* in his terms), but has no power to choose what is wholly good (*voluntas*). As Kelsey summarizes it:

> Basically we all will to be happy. Augustine contends that our decision about what makes for happiness is a

special kind of act of will (call it *voluntas*). To pick something as the basis of our happiness is to love it. As created, Adam exercised will as *voluntas* in freely loving God. He was related to himself in the way that images God. That provided the basis on which he exercised will as *arbitrium*. Every choice among alternatives was made in service of God. Then Adam chose (*voluntas*) a creature (himself!) instead of God as the basis of his happiness. Thereby he constituted himself in a new way. He retained the capacity for free choice among alternatives, but the chooser was now defined by a new way of relating to himself. He was constituted as a non-God-lover, a self-lover. He chose freely, but every free choice was chosen in service to himself. And that is a situation one is not free to change . . . The dynamics of the *imago dei* are such that if the image is distorted, the person is radically deformed and in bondage.[12]

The notion of free will is thus somewhat misleading; will is an essential aspect of being human, yet the will is not free but enslaved. The grace of God is indispensable in order for the will to be freed from its bondage, and is sustained in the freedom of obedience (*cf.* Article X).[13] What matters for our purposes is the recognition that human freedom is not something we can know or understand fully in our present experience. Freedom is an indispensable element in human life, but is clouded through sin. It breaks in through the saving work of Christ, though even our freedom in Christ continues to be distorted by sin, and it looks to its full freedom in the new creation. Jesus' first recorded sermon holds together these truths:

> The Spirit of the Lord is upon me,
>   because he has anointed me
>   to bring good news to the poor.
> He has sent me to proclaim release to the captives
>   and recovery of sight to the blind,
>   to let the oppressed go free,
> to proclaim the year of the Lord's favour.
>   (Lk. 4:18–19)

The Spirit who anointed Jesus as the Christ was the Lord's means of sending him to bring freedom to the poor, the captive and the oppressed. This freedom is inseparable from the coming of the Jubilee, the 'year of the Lord's favour' (*cf.* Lv. 25:8–17), when everything was to be set free. With all creation we await the fullness of that freedom still (*cf.* Rom. 8:21); in the life and ministry of Christ, and through the Spirit sent at Pentecost, this freedom breaks into the present experience of every person in Christ.

Human indignity

Human life as we know it, as noted in every chapter of this book, falls far short of the glory which God intends. Indignity seems to characterize the way life is actually experienced. There have been a number of explanations for this, some of them already discussed. At the social level a wide range of factors comes into play, yet at the personal level sin is understandable as the core of the problem. According to the Scriptures, sin is not a merely surface matter, but a fundamental corruption of the very essence of what it means to be human. It is a radical distortion at the very root of human existence (see chapter 2). Many would disagree, holding that human beings are basically good, sometimes in reaction to what they perceive to be a wholesale denigration of the human in traditional Christian doctrines of sin. It is vital that the essential goodness in all creatures is affirmed, lest the creative goodness of God is denied; but since the entry of sin this goodness feeds our self-centred pride, so that human life as we know it is sinful in every aspect.

The technical term used to describe the human condition of sin is 'total depravity', which sounds to modern English-speakers as if we are hopelessly evil, and never do anything good. This is not its original Latin sense, which was quite precise.[14] 'Total' is used in a positive sense to refer to all the various dimensions of human life, and so to deny that there is any aspect (such as reason) which is unaffected by sin. It is not a negative term, meaning that there is no good in human life. Rather, its undoubted good is precisely the problem, since when that good is directed towards self-love rather than the love of God, its very goodness powers the reality of evil. 'Depraved' is used in contrast to 'deprived': sin is not only the loss of an original righteousness (it is at least that), but the corruption of our being, so that we cannot of ourselves turn to love God, apart from God's grace enabling us.[15] A tree is still a tree, even when it has degenerated into being a corrupt tree, but it produces only corrupt fruit; regeneration is essential for new life to take place. This analysis requires a subtle response to sin; any direct attack upon it, as if it were a reality in and of itself, will also be an attack on the good which is its material cause, and runs the risk of widening rather than shrinking the circle of sin. In contrast, Christ undertook his atoning work by turning the other cheek to evil, absorbing the full consequences of sin on the cross, and through resurrection renewing human life.[16]

Sin is a desperately real factor in the life of each human; a head-on approach, however, may do more harm than good. The good which lies at the core of sin needs to be regenerated, and set free to live for the love of God. A particular example may make this argument clearer. A campaign against pornography runs the risk of attacking sex itself, so increasing the sinful distortion of human sexuality. It cannot be said that Christians have a particularly strong track record when it comes to dealing with sexual sins, especially in the last century or so. The Scriptures are quite realistic about sex; stories such as those of Judah, Amnon and Tamar (Gn. 38; cf. Mt. 1:3), and David, Bathsheba, Amnon and another Tamar (2 Sa. 11 – 13), disclose its terrible power when abused, while the sexual love seen in Isaac and Rebekah, Jacob and Rachel, and the Song of Songs embodies its profound depths when expressive of committed relationships. Jesus lived a single life, but was no stranger to sexuality, gaining a reputation for associating with sexual sinners (Lk. 7:34–35; Jn. 8:1–11) and other socially unacceptable people. Paul is quite explicit about sexual relations (see 1 Cor. 7), and the early Christians found no embarrassment with the Scriptures' realism. As noted above, the one new virtue they gave to the ancient world was chastity.

As the gospel was taken into the wider world, the great contrast between Christian and Graeco-Roman lifestyles became a major emphasis, in both apologetic and catechetical writing; the attractive *Letter of Diognetus* is a good example. World-denying ideas slowly entered into Christian thought and practice in these centuries, however, as the gift of a disciplined lifestyle came to be understood in narrow terms. Clergy were forbidden to marry more than once ('digamy') and then not at all. The 'order' of virgins developed into a spiritually revered group. All of this came to a head in Augustine's notion, based on a misreading of Romans 5:12, that the root of sin, 'concupiscence', was transmitted in sexual intercourse (see chapter 2). Hence virginity came to be seen as a way of life spiritually superior to marriage, and sex in marriage was viewed as good only for the purpose of procreation. The Christian tradition thus came to have an ambiguous attitude to sex, affecting English-speaking Christians especially through the negative aspects of Puritanism in the USA, and the prudery and double standards which came to characterize Victorian England. In Australia, the wowser streak of much Protestantism has reinforced a false asceticism until quite recently,[17] but that is now replaced by a 'me-generation', feeling-oriented view of Christian life.

The work of Sigmund Freud began a major reappraisal of the place of sin, especially in relation to sexuality. Freud's work is often depicted as opposed to Christian faith but, as McDonald notes, 'there is nothing inherently antagonistic to the Christian faith in the psycho-analytic methodology devised by' Freud.[18] He certainly rejected the concept of the gods, seeing them as no more than projections of the human need for security from the powers of nature, for meaning in the face of death, and for moral guardians. These are not our present concerns, but two particular points of Freud's work are relevant here. First, he rejected the concept of sin, in its place putting the various instincts and complexes of the human unconscious, especially the libido (sexual urge) and aggression (death wish). Any morality external to the individual is also rejected, as no more than the internalizing of the customs and attitudes of a person's community. In the light of the weight of moralism in the Europe of his time, and the new awareness of the variety of human cultures, the latter conclusion is understandable. Yet in the light of the scriptural revelation of both the law of Moses and the teaching of Christ, it is much too sweeping. Further, it fails to account either for the grandeur of humankind, or for the sheer volume of human sin; we are much more than 'a blown-up ape, or sex-obsessed biped'.[19] Secondly, Freud interpreted religion and its concomitant elements (such as guilt) as neuroses, illnesses of the psyche resulting from the thwarting of instincts by the prohibitions of morality. In Berkouwer's words, Freud held that 'religion answers to no other reality than the psychic creation of man in distress'.[20] The mechanism of unconscious repression is employed to explain the dis-ease of a person's internal conflict, interpreted as guilt feelings.

The notion that guilt is primarily a feeling is perhaps the enduring legacy of Freud regarding Christian perspectives on being human. Many people, at least in western societies, today think of guilt as an unpleasant, even disabling, sense of remorse, which needs to be dealt with if they are to function fully as human beings. The idea that guilt is ever legitimate is contested, because it is assumed that feelings that cripple human well-being are always regrettable: it is the feelings that need to be dealt with, not any lifestyle or action which may have provoked them. The language of right and wrong is often avoided in public discourse today; people speak of (in)appropriate beha-viour, or of someone's being sick, thus replacing the idea of a moral standard with a situational or medical model for sin. In such a context, 'guilt' carries little if any objective meaning. Only in the courtroom does 'guilty' have a sense apart from feelings, and even there resistance is shown to the idea that the convicted person bears guilt. It seems that the 'guilty' plea has come to have a technical meaning, isolated from the idea of guilt in common parlance, which generally understands it as a feeling.

Even so, sometimes a more objective approach to guilt surfaces. In Australia, especially in the years leading up to the bicentenary of European settlement in 1988, the guilt felt by present-day non-aboriginal Australians was discussed a great deal in public, to the point where some spoke of the development of a 'guilt industry'. Although most reactions focused on guilt as a feeling – 'Why should I feel guilty for what I did not do?' – the present plight of black Australians could not be denied. Their suffering had evidently come about as the product of wrong actions, and could not be explained away as due to any inherent defect in the oppressed (which would be racism), or to the environment (in which they had flourished long before Europeans arrived). The only way forward was the acknowledgment that aboriginal Australians have been sinned against, and that unless other Australians turn away from prejudice to respect, listen at length, and make tangible efforts to change, no reconciliation was possible. In this context guilt came to be discussed as having to do with more than feelings.

In the light of the psychologizing of guilt, it may be better to use the term 'contrition' to describe the feelings associated with doing wrong.[21] It will not help those who reject any notion of right or wrong, but it offers a way of speaking that avoids confusion about what guilt means. Conversely, it is undoubtedly true that Christians have sometimes been more concerned with the importance of their sins than with the grace of their Saviour.[22] It is also true that the power of the church to forgive sins has sometimes been abused to become a means of controlling people's innermost lives. The insights brought by the psychological sciences offer significant resources in exposing such sins, and in assisting people to live lives free from their consequences. It is important in this context to recognize that the interpretation of feelings is closely related to cultural expressions of responses to suffering or wrong (gender differences are considered in the following chapters). A westerner may speak of guilt feelings, a highly individualistic approach; Chinese have a more social perspective, seeking to deal with the embarrassment of a loss of face; while Koreans portray the situation in terms of *han*, a pervasive community mood of despairing oppression. The manner in which psychology is employed in various cultures thus entails cultural sensitivity.

In the Christian tradition guilt is not regarded as a feeling, embarrassment or mood, but is the status of being in the wrong, whether before God or before other human beings. It is relieved, even to the most undeserving of sinners, by the confession of sin in and through Christ (*cf.* Jas. 5:16–20; 1 Jn. 1:8–10). The forgiveness of sins can be a powerful instrument in healing a person broken by sin, and in freeing the penitent to love God, neighbours, and his or her own self in obeying the two great commandments. In this way, self-love undergirds rather than corrupts healthy self-esteem. In 1988, many white Australians, especially Christians, were unsure how to integrate their guilt feelings with a proper self-love. One of the most positive aspects of that year was the publication by Sally Morgan, a young black Australian, of her autobiography, *My Place*.[23] Although it spoke of many grievous sins done against her forebears and herself, the response it triggered was not guilt feelings, but a sense of pride. Non-aboriginal readers finish this story uplifted by a renewed awareness of the privilege of living in a land they share with people of such dignity as Sally and those about whom she writes. When whites come to recognize worthy self-esteem in aboriginal Australians, they see them in a new light, as partners rather than guilt-producers, and are enabled to live with a new sense of self-esteem themselves.

Human indignity in Christian perspective focuses on the reality of sin, and its dire consequences of corrupted relationships with God, one another, creation, and one's own personal self. The modern approach to guilt as merely a feeling to be dealt with is entirely inadequate as a response to wrongdoing, but the effect of sin on feelings must not be discounted either. The forgiveness of sins, and the rebuilding of sin-spoilt lives, make up the wonderful remedy offered by and in Christ. In saying this, recall to whom it is that the call to repentance is made; Jesus and the apostles demand repentance from the stiff-necked or self-focused devout, exemplified in the Pharisees. Helpless sinners have forgiveness announced to them before any mention of repentance (*cf.* Mk. 2:5–17; 11:27 – 12:44). Sin, guilt, contrition, repentance and confession are not in the first place matters to be demanded of others, but they are taken on by the devout disciple (*cf.* Lk. 18:10–17).

Human rights and the sanctity of life

The language of rights dominates much modern thought. The Scriptures do not use this terminology, but it is nevertheless a significant concept, not least because of its use in the Constitution of the United States, and in a number of United Nations declarations. 'Rights' is a term which is easily misused; in particular, to assert one's own rights without regard for others is sheer self-centredness. At a philosophical level, stress on human rights can mask the assumption that each individual is an isolated, autonomous, independent entity, coming into contact with others only when necessary. Each of us is thought to be like a shiny billiard ball, independent and self-contained, bouncing off others rather than interacting with them. Sometimes the language of equality implies this kind of view of human life, and fails to recognize different levels of culture, interest, opportunity, or ability. Such a billiard-table understanding of human existence contrasts strongly with the Christian ideal of the person in community as the foundational reality of human life.

No individual man or woman should be isolated from the human race as a whole. The distinctive dignity and worth of each person, and the consequent practice of justice, can be known only through living in community. The integration of personal and communal levels of human rights is complex, being marred by the ravages of sin, but it is made possible in Christ (see chapters 4 and 5). This integration is all too easily denied in human living, at every stage of life; a child can be effectively orphaned at home or school, a young person isolated through lack of friends or skills, a middle-aged man trapped in hope-destroying work, an older woman denied honour and community through an ungrateful family. Such isolation can happen even in Christian circles, which are not exempt from selfish attitudes and behaviour. It can be reinforced through an overemphasis on the need for personal response to Christ, wrongly understood in exclusively individualistic terms. The embodiment of this response in baptism, a community-forming act, points to the fulfilment of personal identity and rights in serving Christ, in and through the community of faith, in and for God's world. Personal integration remains partial in this life, however. We know ourselves in faith and hope, but not in sight: 'now we see in a mirror dimly, but then we will see face to face' (1 Cor. 13:12).

Human rights and dignity will never be recognized or practised as fully as they ought to be in this life. Full personal identity and integration are present, if partial, realities, whose fullness is something towards which human life, under the influence and creative work of the Spirit, is moving. In the present we are called to defend the rights of others, especially of those whose rights are threatened or denied. This concern for others represents the epitome of obedience to the law and the prophets (*cf.* Mi. 6:8). It is in this sense that the phrase 'human rights' supports and expresses Christian insights on human life, especially at the personal level. It has particular relevance to the unborn, who have no possibility of asserting their own rights, and so need others to assert them. Even in this case, however, the phrase 'right to life' can come to be used as if life were a human property, rather than the gift of God our creator.

Closely associated with the language of rights is the concept of the sanctity of human life. In the strict sense, only God is sacred. If application of the term to human beings implies that human life has an unqualified, absolute value, then we have made ourselves the centre of the universe. In Paul's terms, such a use serves 'the creature rather than the Creator' (Rom. 1:25), and implies an idolatry of the human race. The truth behind the sanctity of human life derives from our being made in the image of God, who is wholly sacred. It affirms the scriptural recognition that human beings are set in the highest place by God, having dominion over all things (Gn. 1:26–28; Ps. 8:4–8). Further, Christ came in human form, sharing our flesh and blood, rather than in the form of an angel or other creature (Heb. 1:2 – 2:18). When human life is discounted or diminished, speaking of its sanctity offers a useful slogan to focus opposition. Nevertheless, the phrase needs to be used with care, lest support is given (whether unintentionally or otherwise) to individualism or pride.

The particular issue of abortion has already been mentioned; as with euthanasia, it relates to what might be called the *quantitative* aspect of the sanctity of life. If life is sacred, its existence under any conditions comes to be regarded as an absolute value.[24] There are other factors, however, which could be said to embody its *qualitative* aspect. In recent years attention in this area has focused around the 'handicapped', 'disabled', or 'differently abled'. The terminology illuminates some of the issues: 'handicapped' and 'disabled' are taken to imply that there is a definable standard of what is 'normal', which some do not meet.[25] Those so regarded can be treated as less than fully human, whether explicitly (when viewed as less valuable to society) or implicitly (through being patronized). Both valuations are challenged by the concept of the sanctity of human life; God values each and every human life, not merely for its usefulness but for itself, and works in and through each person to equip him or her for service to others. None of us is 'normal' or fully abled, but is affected by limitations and by the corruption of sin. The gospel of grace announces acceptance and healing for all in Christ, and their enabling by the Spirit to offer their lives in service to God. These realities are present now, in faith and hope, though never fully realized. We look to a new creation where this faith and hope will be realized fully – and it is love that builds bridges between the new and old (*cf.* 1 Cor. 13:13).

The terminology 'differently abled' raises other issues. The impairment of one sense often reinforces and sensitizes other abilities; perhaps the clearest example is the blind, whose sense of hearing and touch is acute. It needs to be recognized that visually impaired people face particular dangers, especially in the age of the car. To speak of some as 'differently abled' can reflect refusal to recognize the reality of limitations, and the need for particular assistance to be offered, and for allowances to be made. Here the danger is that rejection of patronizing attitudes can undermine the sanctity of life by refusal to accept the distinct quality of life that each person lives. People who cannot walk lack an ability which most people have; both denying or denigrating their full humanity, and pretending that they can do things which require walking, undermine the sanctity of their quality of life. It is important to note that these are rarely issues for those who lack a particular ability; the problems lie in the attitudes and actions of others towards them.

The need to encourage and enable all to participate as fully as possible in contributing to human communities undergirds the terminology about being 'challenged'. It shifts the emphasis away from the disabled person to everyone; each one of us faces challenges, whatever our abilities, prejudices, gifts, limitations or talents. At its best, the terminology fosters the recognition both of the full humanity for which we have been made, and of God's respect and enabling of all human life; and it avoids undermining the quality of that life by paternalism or unreality. At its worst, it can become a way for the more articulate to insist on politically correct language, assuming that a change of speech patterns alone will change attitudes and social policies. To ask that someone be called not 'deaf' but 'aurally challenged' does make a point. The complexity of the issues involved in communication can be worsened by the complexity of the words used, and the energy and humour needed for practical action diverted into politically correct discussion.[26]

Whatever the terminology, the concept of sanctity of life points us to the recognition that human life depends wholly upon the creative generosity and re-creative love of God. The life of Jesus is characterized by his delight in enabling the disabled, and in challenging the self-satisfied (see *e.g.* Mt. 11:2–24). Rather than being treated as a member of an abstract class of persons, each one of us longs to be regarded as a person with particular hopes and dreams, abilities and needs, and to be enabled to live in relationship with others. Each of us needs the challenge both to receive and to repent, to give and to forgive, living out a quality of life that is characterized by practical love.

Such theological perspectives thus question some modern trends, while supporting others. They led Christians in the past to reject infanticide and wilful abortion, to seek to bring healing and rehabilitation, to qualify strongly any participation in war, and to work to abolish slavery. In recent years Christian witness related to human life has emphasized the significance of work, the rejection of racism, and the full dignity of women.[27] It has not always been a united witness, and involves constant struggle. It can become captive to the latest fad, or wrongly resist what is true in human experience according to divine revelation. Nevertheless it remains a witness to a vital aspect of biblical truth: the unique dignity of each human being, of whatever age, society, ability, language, culture or gender.

Male and female

At the corporate level, to be made in the image of God entails being made as male *and* female, created for interactive partnership. At the personal level, it means being made as male *or* female. What does it mean to live as a particular woman or man? Men and women differ in their roles in conception and childbirth. Beyond these obvious differences, however, attempts at precise definition of being male or female are fraught with difficulty. It is useful to distinguish sex from gender: the former represents the range of biological distinctions between male and female, the latter the roles adopted by or ascribed to men and women. Gender is a complex matter; it can refer to gender *identity* (attempts to describe the differences between men and women), gender *relations* (the patterns of power, norms, customs and roles which govern women and men's lives), or gender *representations* (the ways in which gender concepts help to organize ideas about culture, nature, knowledge and social perspectives).[28] All gender roles are socially constructed, according to the prevailing consensus of studies in areas as diverse as biology, anthropology, social history and literature. As Simone de Beauvoir put it, 'one is not born a woman, one becomes one'.[29] It is widely accepted today (at least in the West) that there is a gender duality in each person, all of us possessing masculine and feminine aspects in varying ratios, and that what these terms mean is culturally determined through the varied experiences of child-rearing.[30] In popular thought the feminine is associated with creativity, and with being soft, receptive, and pretty; while the masculine is linked with hardness, power, initiative, and looking rugged. Though such generalizations express common ideas, and are given theological justification in much of the Christian tradition,[31] they are of little help in understanding what it means to be a woman or man, and are themselves stereotypes which undermine the positive and distinctive aspects of both genders. They are especially danger-ous when the male gender is constructed in such a way that men can embrace both masculine and feminine qualities, but women can embrace only selected aspects of both. Here 'men, despite their maleness, have symbolic versatility, and women, because of their femaleness, do not'.[32]

Socially, every culture raises boys and girls with varying expectations and assumptions about life roles. Some of these attitudes and customs are highly oppressive, while others seek to protect the distinctives entailed in being male or female. In recent decades a great deal of effort has been invested in seeking to remove injustice and oppression between the sexes, both in society generally (especially, though not only, in the West) and in the churches. Many modern efforts to minimize or eradicate gender differences show the difficulty of overcoming them, and demonstrate the close interaction of biological, environmental and cultural factors.[33] At the personal level, it is profoundly difficult to explore being female or male, since each of us experiences life from one or other perspective. Each life involves both a particular embodying, upbringing, life experience and consequent self-understanding, itself affected by the act of trying to distinguish gender distinctiveness. It is nevertheless important for our understanding of what it means to be human to reflect on the significance of being a woman or a man.

Peta (my wife) and I have several times conducted sessions for young people on being male and female, beginning with the following exercise to open up some of the issues. The women are asked to talk among themselves about what they would dislike and enjoy about life if they were men, and the men are asked to think similarly about life as women. Each group then listens to what the other group has said. The men and women then meet separately once more, this time for the men to think about living as men, and the women as women. The outcomes of these discussions are always fascinating, breaking down many misconceptions. It is often the first time those present have thought about what it means to live as a woman or a man, rather than as an individual person of indeterminate gender. Insights emerge about Christian life, too, especially about how easy it is to misunderstand the ministry of others due to failure to see it through the eyes of their being men or women.

A good deal of the material in this section derives from workshops such as these. Reflection about life as a woman or as a man is a relatively recent phenomenon among academics, although it has been a perpetual topic of human thought. Until relatively recently, however, it has focused largely on explicitly sexual differences, even though there are far-reaching social distinctions involved. In these approaches, much of life was regarded as gender-neutral, disguising the reality that our gender interacts with every aspect of living. Feminism has given rise to much deeper awareness of the distinct lifestyles of women and men, and contends that women's lives have been understood in terms of men's. Daphne Hampson writes of her experience in the church: 'To be forced to argue that one is a full human being of equal dignity (for that is what it felt like) is quite extraordinarily undermining.'[34] Conversely, some Christian responses to feminism are unsympathetic, defending separate spheres of life for men and women, with woman's sphere being subordinated to man's, and at deeper levels submerging feminine imagery in masculine.[35] More positive Christian responses to feminism can emphasize the difference, equality and interdependence of men and women, yet still assume that each person can be largely understood apart from his or her being either male or female.[36] Further, only in recent years has exploration begun of what is distinctive about being a male human; in particular, while 'man' can refer either to humans generally, or to men only, distinctive vocabulary to speak about men is lacking (see further Appendix 2 below).

Life has traditionally been divided into several stages: childhood, youth, adulthood and old age. These 'four ages of man' at first sight may seem to be unrelated to gender; but it takes only a little reflection to see that this is not the case. The transitions from child to youth are different for women and for men, as have been the occupations of adulthood until quite recent times. Life expectancy for women and for men was generally similar in most societies, though for very different reasons: women died young in childbirth, men in war. In modern western societies, however, women generally outlive men, with both commonly surviving beyond the traditional 'threescore years and ten' (Ps. 90:10, AV). Today we tend to sub-divide the 'four ages' further: childhood becomes infancy, early childhood, childhood and pre-pubescence, for example. The concept of the teenager has emerged in the affluence of the post-1945 western world, with its own distinctive sub-culture, while adulthood has had ideas such as 'mid-life crisis' and 'retirement lifestyle' added. The marked growth in life expectancy in the West has led to a rapid growth in the number of older people, sadly seen more as a problem than as a source of wisdom. All these changes are related to economic and social developments, the trend to the specialization of knowledge, and the compartmentalizing of life, which are in turn related to gender differences.[37] They have resulted in the emergence of a bewilderingly wide range of sub-cultures in modern societies, whose influence is disguised because they operate within a common language, and under the dominance of mass media.

177

Woman and man today

Three particular developments that have shaped life stages in the past century or so are noted here. In each case the more negative aspects come to the fore because they have affected the roles of women and men in negative ways, but enormous benefits for human life generally have also followed from these developments.

First, the Industrial Revolution led to the separation of the worlds of home and work into private and public realms. Instead of labouring together with women on a farm, albeit with many role divisions in their work, men came to work away from home, in factories or offices. The home then became the place of women, often entailing considerable responsibility when households were large; though, as suburbs began to develop, many women became increasingly isolated in small family units. Conversely, many men came to define themselves in terms of paid work and productivity, with consequent loss of the opportunity and ability to express intimacy.

Secondly, the growth of industry led to the need for universal education, initially for men, and then for women and men alike. This introduced two boundaries in early life, going to and leaving school, each with its own social consequences. As public health has improved during this century, the age of puberty has dropped from around fifteen or older to about twelve, with young women maturing on average a year or more earlier than young men. Yet since the 1950s the average number of years spent in school has increased markedly in most societies. The combination of these social changes has meant that sexually mature young people face a decade or more with no possibility of marriage; the teenage cultures are one outcome. These cultures (the plural is deliberate) have generally been marked by stereotyping of differences in sex roles, oppressive for both women and men alike. For example, consider the issue of women's appearance. It has formed a significant part of female identity since time immemorial (*cf.* 1 Pet. 3:3–4). Yet the availability of inexpensive cosmetics and clothing, the growth of peer-group pressures, and the emphasis on the importance of good looks that comes through today's visual media, have reinforced the idea that women are defined in terms of appearance.[38] Conversely, men have been encouraged even more – particularly through advertising – to see women as made for their enjoyment and use. The need for sexual control on the part of men has long been an issue for their living (note the male-specific teaching of 1 Cor. 6:13–18; 1 Thes. 4:3–4; and especially Mt. 5:27–28). The conjunction of the trends noted above has placed extremely strong pressures on young men to perform sexually, without regard to the relationships involved.

Thirdly, the availability of reliable and inexpensive methods of controlling conception has reinforced and further developed these trends. It has liberated many marriages into a new enjoyment of sexual union, as planned parenthood has removed the fear of pregnancy, and so has strengthened the welcome into this life which each new child should receive.[39] It has enabled many women to participate in the public world of work, and to have far greater control over their living. Correspondingly, it has meant that many men have been freed to live and work with women rather than against or separate from them, in both the home and the wider world. Effective conception control has also strengthened the negative sides of the trends noted above, and brought a new factor into play: the 'contraceptive mentality'. This term points to a shift towards excluding the responsibility of child-rearing from marriage, and the focusing of male–female relationships exclusively upon sexual gratification, especially when that has become the dominant motif of the teenage years. Paradoxically, the technology which, probably more than anything else, led to the flowering of feminism has also led to a greater emphasis on men's domination of women through defining them as sexual objects.

It is the constellation of insights resulting from reflection on trends such as these which has come together in the movement known as feminism. It has brought new awareness of the way in which human life in every aspect has (until recently) been interpreted largely from male perspectives, not least in Christian theology. It is in the light of this realization that the next two chapters seek to explore being human from the perspectives of being female and male separately. After not a little thought, I have chosen to begin with woman's life because it has been given more attention in recent decades, while the exploration of what it means to be a man has only just begun.

179

8

BEING
A WOMAN

What does it mean to be a woman? It is said that women are a
mystery to men. Much better would be the recognition that
every woman and man is a true mystery, reflecting the wonder
of being made in the image of God in distinctive ways. It is
impossible for a male such as myself to discuss what it means to
be a woman based on direct experience, but an approach can be
made, since we are all made in God's image. In doing so, I
gratefully acknowledge the help of women friends who have
been willing to speak about themselves in very personal ways.

To begin, let me return to the group workshops mentioned
above. No doubt the comments made say a lot about the social
role in which participants have grown up and now live, but they
are representative observations in contemporary western
society. The men generally saw the most positive thing about
being a woman to be the sense of being close to one's body, a
sense which they observed in most women, but struggled with in
themselves. These comments drew very positive responses from

the women, who identified 'connectedness' as a most significant aspect of being female. The commonest response of the men's groups to what they would *not* like about being women, however, was menstruating. The choice of this aspect caused amazement among most of the women, but it broke the taboo on speaking about periods.[1] Blood is a central factor in human existence, a vital symbol of life and death. All humans bleed, but the menstrual cycle is distinctive to women, who thus experience blood as a regular part of life. For the vast majority of men, by contrast, bleeding is an abnormal experience, encountered only in places such as abattoirs or the battlefield, or in events such as brawls or road trauma. Whatever our gender perceptions, however, blood remains a key aspect of Christian faith, especially because of the central place given to the life-giving blood of Christ.[2]

The blood of life

In the group discussion, some (both women and men) argued that the only real differences between men and women were related to childbirth. Most of the women strongly resisted this idea, seeing their lives as having greater significance than being mothers only. To be a mother, one who bears and gives life, is a great privilege. To affirm a woman in these terms only, mother or not, however, is to define her in terms of functional (re)productivity, rather than as a person made in the image of God.

Fertility nevertheless seems to lie at the centre of many women's life perspective. Whatever her relationships with men, for half her lifespan or more a woman's body prepares each month to conceive and bear a child. The menstrual period is a constant reminder to each woman that she is embodied, a person who must deal monthly with 'bloody reality', 'the curse'. The consequences are many. Erin White writes, 'Whether I am fifteen or fifty, everybody and everything can be affected because my body does this strange thing every month, thwarting my desires, and upsetting my relationships. I am no longer in control.'[3] Yet this experience is also to be celebrated. Noting that the menstrual and lunar cycles are similar, White goes on to say, 'I feel linked with the moon and the tides . . . my body

181

pulses in rhythm with nature.' Periods can 'often engender intimacy between women, between women and men, women and nature'. The monthly flow of blood would appear to affect women's thought patterns, especially when associated with premenstrual tension (the 'PMT blues') or pain, orienting them to a cyclical more than to a linear approach to life. In theology, this may imply that women are oriented more to the sustaining work of God as creator, while men may be more oriented towards the historical work of God as redeemer, though neither emphasis excludes the other (cf. Is. 42:5–6; 43:1; 45:9–13; 54:5). Such ideas must be seen as tentative at this stage of understanding of the interaction between our bodily natures and relationship with God, but are suggestive nonetheless.

Some feminists see menstrual periods as denied or even ridiculed in the Christian tradition. Blood in the Christian tradition, it is argued, is linked symbolically with the forgiveness of sins through the bloody death of a male, and with the blood of the martyrs (whether men or women). Both these links come together powerfully in the two major Christian rites, baptism and holy communion, which symbolically represent being 'washed in the blood' and drinking 'the blood of Christ'. Women in the Christian tradition lose out, it is contended, either by their needing a male saviour, or by there being little or no symbolic recognition of the celebration of life which it is the privilege of women to bear and nurture. When the administration of these sacraments of the gospel is restricted to men, women are further suppressed, to the point where, for some, Christian faith itself is felt to deny woman's real humanity – and is rejected as immoral.[4] A more sympathetic analysis points to the close relationship in folk religion between blood, baptism and birth. This is often questioned today, since baptism is a 'new-birth rite', not a 'birthright' (as I myself would put it). Yet, especially in the many centuries before birth was relatively safe, the bloody dangers of passing through the waters of birth are undoubtedly felt by many women to be symbolically interrelated with the death to sin represented in baptism, even if this association is not rationally realized or expressed. Folk religion here points to a profound truth, that creation and redemption are connected, not isolated.[5] Women's life experience faces the realities of birth and death embodied by blood, as contrasted with that of many men, who experience these realities through such unnatural activities as road crashes or war. It is the death of Jesus, rather than his birth, which is the means of our 'redemption through his blood' (Eph. 1:7; cf. Rom. 3:23–26). Even so, as the church sings God's praise in the 'Song of the Church' (*Te Deum*), it acknowledges that Christ did 'not abhor the virgin's womb'.[6]

Menstruation may be a taboo topic in polite society, but it is discussed realistically in the Scriptures. There is no hint of the subject being taboo, and it is never spoken of lightly or flippantly. Leviticus 15:19–24 provides for the purification of a woman for the seven days following the onset of her menstrual period. She herself, along with anything on which she lies or sits, anyone who touches these, and any man who has intercourse with her, is 'unclean'. Apart from the regulations of Leviticus, the story of David and Bathsheba is realistic and sensitive (2 Sa. 11:2–4). David not only stole Uriah's wife; he breached the Levitical law against a man having intercourse with a woman during menstruation (Lv. 18:19), and rendered himself unclean (Lv. 15:24).[7] The length of time for which a woman was unclean, seven days, is also realistic, as typical of the length of a menstrual period. That a man who has an emission of semen is unclean for one day is sometimes seen as deprecatory to women, but this also corresponds to practical realities. Nevertheless, the idea that a menstruating woman is unclean seems to imply that something is wrong with being a woman. Several responses need to be made to this. First, it is not the only regulation about uncleanness. Chapters 13 and 14 of Leviticus concern leprosy, while chapter 15 begins and closes with regulations about continuous bodily discharges (Lv. 15:1–15, 25–30). Immediately preceding the menstruation regulations, similar regulations are made for men who have an (involuntary) emission of semen (Lv. 15:16–18). In each case the length of time for uncleanness relates to the particular case; no punitive element is involved, but a realistic approach is taken.

In English the word 'unclean' carries the connotation of moral or social disgrace, but in ancient Israel this was not the case. The distinction between clean and unclean was more akin to what might be termed 'regular' and 'less regular' states of life.

Language again raises problems: 'less regular' may sound like a value-judgment, but is used instead of 'non-normal', the term employed by Douglas.[8] Menstruation, however, is a normal part of a woman's life, but different from the times when she is not menstruating. To speak of it as 'abnormal' carries pejorative connotations in English which 'unclean' in Hebrew does not. It is true that by the time of Jesus, the category 'unclean' carried strong connotations of being a social outcast, with an implied sense of excommunication and so of unholiness. But the pairing of clean and unclean is distinguished from the contrast between holy and profane, which has to do with positive or negative relationship with God. In Israelite society things were normally or regularly clean, and could be set aside as holy by the process of sanctification. Similarly, something or someone unclean could be cleansed so as to be returned to the regular state. To be unclean was not the same as being profane, though what was unclean was not to come into contact with the holy, nor was the profane to come in contact with the clean (*cf.* Lv. 18; Nu. 4).[9] Menstruating women were thus normal, but not regarded as in their regular state. No religious sanction is involved, however; a woman unclean due to menstruation was cleansed merely by washing.

The whole structure of the division between clean and unclean, holy and profane, is removed with the coming of Jesus. His work of atonement covered not only the reality and consequences of sin, but also brought an end to all such regulations. The letter to the Hebrews argues towards this conclusion, but rejects any idea that as a result holy living does not matter.[10] Rather, holiness is now to be seen in unrestricted relationship with God, and with the saints of God, and is to be expressed in daily living freed from the burden of sin, looking continually to Jesus (Heb. 12:1–2). Luke notes that the first community in Jerusalem, as a consequence of the coming of the Spirit, held all things as common, *koinos* (Acts 2:44). This commonality was expressed in sharing goods, but entails a deeper level of fellowship, *koinōnia*, unrestricted by the laws of uncleanness.[11] The rejection of the clean/unclean distinction did not come about easily: it resulted in much internal conflict, reflected vividly in Peter's twice-told vision about clean and unclean foods (Acts 10:9–16; 11:5–10). The admission of women as full members of Christ was one clear corollary of this removal of cleanliness regulations, even though it would seem that adjustments were made to male–female relationships in Christ for the sake of commending the gospel in a patriarchal world (*e.g.* 1 Cor. 11:2–16).[12]

The affirmation that in Christ 'there is no longer male and female' (Gal. 3:28) removes entirely any denigration of woman due to (mis)application of the Mosaic laws touching uncleanness. It is embodied in Jesus' healing of the woman with a discharge of blood (Lk. 8:43–49 is the fullest account). Her touching his garments technically rendered them, and so Jesus, unclean, but he shows no concern at this. Rather, he affirms her faith, which reached beyond the regulations of uncleanness to touch him. Her faith was rewarded not only in her healing, but also in her own internal awareness of healing – and it was possibly her bold act which prompted Jesus to take the initiative only minutes later in touching the dead daughter of Jairus (Lk. 8:54).[13] As Erin White writes, 'this girl was ritually unclean on two counts, being dead and being of such an age that she had just begun or was just about to begin menstruating . . . Jesus' touch is therefore highly significant'.[14] It embodies God's reaching out to woman in all of her life.

Childbirth and mothering

Menstruation is the experience of all women who reach puberty; giving birth is not. Yet menstruation prepares the way for conception and childbirth, and the regulations in relation to these are similar to those for menstruation (Lv. 12:2–5). A woman is 'unclean' for a longer period after the birth of a female child than after the birth of a male. By contrast with the regulations about menstruation, more than washing is needed for her return to regular life; religious ritual is required to bring about the status of being clean. No difference is made at this point between male or female children: in all cases an offering is to be made to the Lord, to make atonement for the woman (Lv. 12:7). The offering varies, depending on the woman's economic standing, but not on the sex of the child born to her. The need for 'atonement' here does not mean that the woman had sinned in conceiving or giving birth, or that the child was sinful; the term is a technical one, with a range of meanings in the Hebrew

Scriptures. This ritual was undertaken on behalf of Mary (Lk. 2:22–24), without implying that either she or Jesus was sinful.[15]

Modern medicine has perhaps led to the loss of the sense of trepidation with which most human societies have approached childbirth. The numbers of women dying miserably in childbirth, and the rates of infant mortality, have declined significantly in most societies, while understanding and technology associated with conception and childbirth have grown remarkably. These factors mean that the profound mysteries of birth and life do not seem to be appreciated as widely today as in previous ages. Giving birth can be a deadly serious matter, fraught with great danger even now. In anthropological terms, birth is a 'boundary' or 'liminal' experience, removed from 'regular' life, though being one of its most significant moments. Birth is marked by serious ritual in all human societies. The Levitical rite involved a burnt offering, symbolizing full dedication to God, and a sin offering, which dealt with unintended sin in the ritual itself; neither of these categories is to do with deliberate sin.[16] Augustine's teaching on original sin carried with it the notion that sexual activity – and thus conception – derived from 'concupiscence', and so is sinful, or at best second-rate. This is a distortion of scriptural teaching, which affirms the wonder and mystery of sexual relations (Eph. 5:31), and states that children are 'a heritage from the LORD' (Ps. 127:4). The birth of a child is too significant for it not to be marked by deeply meaningful rituals. It is a time for great rejoicing, both for the arrival of a new human being, and for the safe passage of a woman through the life-threatening act of giving birth, which can never be taken for granted.[17]

Childbirth is not the experience of every woman, and for many its impossibility brings great grief. In many societies, loss of fertility entails loss of meaning in life (cf. Gn. 29 – 30; 1 Sa. 1 – 2). Many women continue to feel this, as evident today in the vast resources devoted to fertility research and techniques.[18] From what has been argued thus far, it is clear that to define a woman's life in terms of giving birth is false, and undermines the full dignity of what it means to be made in the image of God. For women who are mothers, childbirth and child-rearing can take up perhaps twenty-five years, or about a third of a lifespan: this leaves two-thirds of their life not directly involved in mothering. Many women are able to blend child-bearing with a career, and others do not become mothers, whether by choice or involuntarily. Nevertheless, the particular embodiment of women revolves around fertility. A man may yearn to have children, but cannot bear them; the most loved child has never been part of a man's own body. If the classic male temptation concerning children is to regard them as possessions, the classic female one is to see them as extensions of the self.[19]

Sin in women's experience

'All have sinned and fall short of the glory of God', teaches Paul (Rom. 3:23), women and men alike. In earlier chapters the concept of sin in the Scriptures was analysed, and was seen as having both corporate and individual aspects. Sin is serious, and has damaging and eternal consequences, yet Christians have sometimes overemphasized its significance, especially in relation to sex. Although the notion that sex is sinful has many times been shown to be unbiblical and un-Christian, at a popular level it still persists, and feeds the opposite idea that any restrictions on sexual activity are wrong.

The discussion about sin is today taken beyond sex to issues of gender. Some would see the concept of sin as itself a masculine construct, designed to give religious legitimacy to forms of social and gender control. It is frequently asserted that the Scriptures place the blame for sin on women.[20] Paul comments twice on Genesis 3 in such a way as to give credence to this claim. He writes that 'the serpent deceived Eve by its cunning' (2 Cor. 11:3), and more directly, that 'Adam was formed first, then Eve; and Adam was not deceived, but the woman was deceived and became a transgressor' (1 Tim. 2:13–14). Yet to read these texts as if men played no part in sin is misleading – and for men to do so is itself sinful, since this interpretation refuses to acknowledge responsibility for wrong-doing. Paul wrote of the sin of Adam in terms which spoke of the first man, as well as of representative humanity. In the New Testament, sin is ascribed to human disobedience by both the human race as a whole, and men and women individually, particularly in the full discussion in Romans 5 – 7 (see chapter 2 above). In Romans 7, Paul's own confession of personal sin, it is

187

evident that he as a male sees himself and his own inmost self as the source of his own disobedience.

At the corporate level, sin affects women in a number of ways. An important distinction in feminist theology is that between 'women's sin' and 'women's sins'. The latter refers to the sins which women commit; the former, however, refers to the (supposed) inherent defectiveness entailed in being woman, responsible for sin. This view is disturbingly common in many understandings of the Scriptures, particularly regarding the place of Eve, in the Christian tradition.[21] Christ did away with exploitative relationships between women and men, as is evident both in his own lifestyle and in the full participation of women and men alike in the early Christian communities (cf. Acts 16:14–15; 18:2–4, 18; Rom. 16:1–3). Appreciation of this has led many churches to open all ministry positions to men and women alike, while those that do not do so nevertheless recognize the equal standing of women and men in God's sight.[22] Yet women do not live as people who are freed from the interlocking structures of the distinctive effects of sin on their lives as women. For example, the tendency to define women as sex objects, or in terms of their ability to produce children (especially sons), is deeper than can be eradicated by education or social behavioural change alone. Christian women need liberation from seeing their ministry as second-rate servility, restricted to the flower and cleaning rosters in church. Every Christian has the privilege and freedom of living as the servant of Christ, possibly including flowers and cleaning. The issues here are many: mothering, domestic work, career issues, women's groups, gynaecology, women in local and elected political life, and so on.[23] Given the effects of sin in human beings, whether women or men, Christians do not expect to see full liberation in this world. Nevertheless God calls both men and women to live in the hope of such liberation, demonstrating in our own living the rule of Christ and his power to reconcile male and female.

At this corporate level the response to sin is similar for men and women, even if we bear differing levels of responsibility for it, and derive different benefits from it. At the personal level, however, many women regard some sins differently from the way men regard them. Sins are traditionally classified into sins of commission, doing what we ought not to have done, and sins of omission, not doing what we ought to have done.[24] According to the Scriptures, men and women alike commit both types of sin, but as a generality it could be said that men are more prone to sin in terms of commission, and women in terms of omission.[25] The basis for this assertion relates to the argument that women have traditionally been those who follow or support, and have been deeply socialized towards a receptive and passive lifestyle, rather than one which takes initiative. That there are many exceptions to this generalization is true, but it needs to be taken seriously, especially regarding the way in which women are asked to confess their sins in church. Thus a downtrodden woman may have had little opportunity to do anything actively at all in life. For her, to confess sins in terms of what she has *done* wrong can produce a false guilt, or distorting introversion, that is far from the grace of Christ.[26] Conversely, there are many ways by which a submissive woman can actively sin, for example through manipulative use of her appearance, or by gossip and feminine wiles. To deny that women sin would be to place women on a pedestal of false purity, which denies their full humanity just as much as portraying them as the source of all temptation and evil (the classic stereotypes). But women do have their distinctive ways of relating to sin.

Connectedness and sisterhood

The most positive factor in being a woman (according to the discussion group noted earlier, in much literature I have read, and through my conversations with women) is embodiment sensed as 'connectedness'. The traditions which reflect on experiences such as monthly bleeding, carrying a child and breast-feeding involve a distinctive sense of being embodied. This carries notions of being 'whole', not in isolation from others, but as part of the web of life itself. At the personal level, body, spirit, mind, psyche, soul, self – whatever particular subdivisions of human nature are named – are seen and felt to be closely interrelated. The use of reason is affirmed, but never in the modernist, post-Enlightenment sense of technical reason isolated from the imagination, intuition or bodily experience. Knowledge includes 'listening to one's body', and trusting that physical reactions to situations are vehicles of discernment, in unity with more cognitively or externally received perspectives.[27] Much of this approach is possible for men, but there is something about the constitution and distinctive life experiences of women which illuminates the processes of knowing.

Embodiment is highly valued in feminism, but an overemphasis on the importance of the body can also be destructive. Being embodied and shapely, in much of contemporary society a woman is constantly assessed – by men, women and herself – by the standards of what is attractive to men. The trends noted in the previous section are relevant to this, but the growth in visual media reinforces it. Photography, the cinema and especially television have heightened our awareness of the visual in human relationships.[28] This has many good aspects, but its very goodness entails the possibility of deep corruption. At one extreme, visual pornography has reached altogether new depths. A rude sketch is quite different in its effects from a (touched-up) photograph of an impossibly even-skinned woman, or a video of (artificially enhanced) sexual activity. In Australia today, the average newsagent has rows of magazines full of sexually explicit photographs, defining women in terms of depersonalized bodies made available for male usage. Television news, sports, drama and comedy rarely present women who are not perceived as attractive to men. Advertising mostly uses women for visual effect rather than for what they may know, say or do, and diet and fashion ads overwhelmingly target women, especially those who are young. All of this visual stimulation has the effect of reinforcing the idea that woman is defined by her body, whose attractiveness to men is what really counts. Young women may become so concerned with their looks that they become ill, and anorexia and bulimia flourish today on an alarming scale. Thus, in a paradoxical way again, focus on the significance of the body (a focus strengthened by some aspects of feminism) can lead to the dehumanizing of women. As noted before, the most powerful idol is the corruption of the greatest good, here the beauty of the human body. Responding to the 'beauty myth' needs to go beyond criticizing it, to enabling women to affirm and delight in the wonder of their distinctively embodied humanity.

'Sisterhood' is a term which has come into common use with

feminism. It conveys the sense that being a woman means more than living as an individual female human being. Sisterhood entails a sense of solidarity with other women, even those with whom little else seems to be in common. It carries strongly relational connotations, of women relating as diverse equals, as sisters who live their own full humanity. In contrast to this is 'womanhood', a term understood to define women in terms of men, women's humanity existing as a special case of 'manhood'. In some radical feminist circles 'sisterhood' is used to exclude men from full humanity, finding its extreme form in lesbian separatism. Both these positions deny the concept that women and men, living in mutual relationship, display what it means to be made in the image of God. They are therefore rejected by Christians, but this should not prevent our using the terms in ways that are consistent with this truth. Even so, it needs to be recognized that while living in mutual relationship, integrating nature and culture, is 'undoubtedly the most satisfactory position, it is almost impossible to live out in the context of prevailing dualistic structures'.[29]

Connectedness and sisterhood are often consciously set over and against 'dualism', seen as a key aspect of a male-dominated understanding of reality.[30] Many feminists would view Christian faith as contributing to dualism at the personal level, rooted in a split between the inner and outer self, and so between the spiritual and the physical (see the next chapter). This split is then related to the division between the private and public realms, leading to patterns of domination and subordination in human relationships, specifically between men and women. This dualism is seen as the foundation of patriarchy, the arrangement of society as a gendered hierarchy in which women are regarded as secondary to men. This type of view is indeed present in much of the Christian tradition, but orthodox Christian faith rejects all dualisms except the fundamental distinction between Creator and creation, with the consequent dynamic dualism of obedience and rebellion.[31] Some feminists would regard the retention of this distinction as itself patriarchal, rejecting it in favour of a monistic cosmology, namely that all that exists shares in a single reality; this is a worldview sharply contrasted with Christian belief. Nevertheless, emphasis on a connectedness which corrects false dualisms is a major positive contribution of feminist theological perspectives. The experience and tradition of connectedness make up the everyday mystery experienced by many women, whether they have heard of feminism or not, but it is feminism that has focused the appreciation of both women and men on this aspect of living.

The sense that being a woman entails sisterhood with other women is reflected in many places in the Scriptures. The well was a place for women's work and gathering (*cf.* Gn. 24:13; Ex. 2:16; Jn. 4:7ff.), and it was women who sang the songs of victory (Ex. 15; Jdg. 5; 1 Sa. 18:6–7). Midwives had their own community of work (to which Ex. 1:15–21 is a glowing tribute), and women friends shared struggles and joys (for example Naomi and Ruth, Elizabeth and Mary). None of these sisterhoods should be romanticized; rivalry, jealousy, betrayal and hatred were present, along with bravery, laughter and joy (*cf.* Lk. 1:39–56; Phil. 4:2–3). Sinful attitudes and behaviour were present particularly among wives in polygamous households, a situation exacerbated by male structuring of human relationships (*cf.* Sarah and Hagar, Rachel and Leah, Hannah and Peninnah: Gn. 21:9–21; 30:1–24; 1 Sa. 1:1–8). A profound sisterhood is depicted in the Scriptures among the woman disciples of Jesus; they provided for his needs (Lk. 8:2–3), stood with him in death, and were the first witnesses of his resurrection (Jn. 19:25–27; 20:1–18; Lk. 24:1–11). Such patterns of solidarity continue, not only in 'liberated' societies, but often even more strongly in traditional cultures where women and men remain largely segregated. Sisterhood belongs to all women, not only to feminists.[32]

As a man, I cannot describe this sisterhood from the inside. But it is vitally important that its reality be acknowledged as part of the doctrine of humanity. Otherwise being a woman will be understood only in individual terms, or only in relationship to men. It is for this reason that it is important for men reading this book to try and sense something of what sisterhod means. Large areas of life, both beyond and within the church, remain the province of women, and it is here that the instinctive bonds of sisterhood are built up. My experience of these is necessarily very limited, but I have sometimes been the only man in a group of women, especially in Christian feminist circles, and become aware that I am a spectator of a definite though indefinable corporate ethos in which I do not share.[33] Perhaps the most accessible way in which men may sense something of what sisterhood means is through singing. I have found it illuminating to be part of a tiny minority of men in a group singing hymns; not only are the register and tone of the voices different from men's or from mixed voices, but the metaphors in the words take on different hues. Several women have told me that they find singing (and reading aloud) with women much easier than with men, because in their experience women tend to listen to one another rather than trying to lead others. In part this is due to the greater volume of men's voices, but it also reflects common male assumptions about the relative roles of women and men in the church, and the over-confident sense in many men that they are masters of the truth rather than needing to listen and discern. That some groups of women have accepted me has been humbling, and led me to appreciate more deeply the privilege of being a member of this human race in which women and men participate, alike yet distinctive.

It may be difficult for a man to understand what it means to be a woman. What, however, does it mean to be a man? To that question we now turn.

9

BEING A
MAN

Let me recall the group workshops mentioned previously. When asked what they thought was the best thing about being a man, the women's groups spoke of men being independent. The men, however, were mostly tongue-tied. Some spoke only in negative terms – of not having menstrual periods, for example, or never having to face the prospect of childbirth. When pushed, these men realized that the only good thing they could say about being a man was that they were not women – a terrifying position for both the men themselves and the women they knew. And I admit that when I wrote the initial drafts of this chapter, I found that I had said nothing actually positive about being a man! Many of the men in the group workshop spoke of the embarrassment they felt as Christians about what society expected of them as men: loutish, drunken or rude behaviour, aggressive ambition and sexual conquest. A few regretted the lack of recognition for their interest in the arts or personal relationships, expressing the fear that such interests would be interpreted as casting doubt on their manliness. If men historically have assumed too easily that it was good to be a man, and that male perspectives were the norm, today many men, including Christian men, are in danger of false guilt about being a man. This chapter thus seeks to make some explorations, albeit very tentative ones, into this area. We begin by asking what it means to be 'manly'.

Being manly

The phrase 'play the man' carries contrasting, yet illuminating meanings. On the one hand, it indicates sacrificial bravery, especially in the face of danger. The college where I teach is named after Nicholas Ridley, who, when about to be burnt at the stake, was encouraged by his fellow martyr, Hugh Latimer, with the words: 'Be of good comfort, Master Ridley, and play the man.' On the other hand, someone who engages in rough-house sporting tactics is said to 'play the man rather than the ball'. The ambiguity of the phrase indicates the dilemma many men find in being manly, to the point where some regard the whole concept as merely a social construct, and a dangerous one at that.

Most men do not realize they are men. When he looks in a mirror, many a man sees a human being, not someone thought of as a man; his gender is invisible to him.[1] Many men think that being a man is the norm, while being a woman is a special variety of human being. As noted in an earlier chapter, some books on being human have a special chapter on 'woman', implying that the rest of the book is actually about men; women may have special and distinctive experiences, but men do not. More broadly, much history and culture is thought of as if it could be equated with male experience. Gendered language is a case in point; in English, the word 'man' has traditionally done double duty, to refer to the human species generically, and also to the male gender in particular. The assumption behind this use of male language generically is that male experience and insight can represent those of women as well, encouraging men to continue to presume that they are the norm of being human – the 'generic fallacy'. It also means, however, that men lack the vocabulary to describe their distinctive experience as male human beings.[2]

195

What then can be said about being a man? If it was difficult for me as a man to speak about being a woman, it is also difficult to answer this question, since I cannot help interpreting my own experience as if it applied to other men. It is not easy to sort out what is man-distinctive to my human experience as a male; each person is both limited and equipped by his or her own unique genetic make-up, background and experience. Further, what we mean by gender roles is itself a constructed reality, learned from many subtle interactions between biological, psychological, social and cultural factors.[3] But an approach needs to be made, and in doing so, I gratefully acknowledge the men who have been willing to speak about themselves in personal ways. Many women have moved beyond writing and working about women-distinctive experiences, and have developed women's perspectives on everything under the sun. Men, however, have only recently begun to interpret what is distinctive to male living, learning to approach life aware of the distinctive perspective brought by seeing it through male eyes.[4]

It is good to be a human being, whether a woman or a man. The opening chapter of the Scriptures concludes with the statement, 'God saw everything that he had made, and indeed, it was very good' (Gn. 1:31). As well as this general perspective, there is particular affirmation that it is good to be a man, in Jesus. Jesus was a man 'without sin' (Heb. 4:15); all other men share the corruption entailed in sin, yet still share the image of God. True manhood is revealed in Jesus, and all men are made for the renewal of their nature in and through him. Thus it is good to be a man not only in relation to the past; it continues to be good in the present, even while we look for men's full maturity in Christ.

What then is distinctive about being a man? The most obvious factor is male physique. Men are on average taller, heavier, and stronger than women in many tasks. Men have traditionally engaged in work which involves a high degree of physical labour: hunting, farming, mining, wharf labouring, factory and road work, for example. Many men enjoy such work, even though for many others it can mean soul-destroying toil. The heritage of sweat is appealed to vigorously in Australian beer advertisements, despite the fact that machinery has replaced much of the sheer effort involved in physical work. In western societies the labouring aspect of being manly has thus declined in significance, though it remains strong in the prominence given to sport and sporting heroes, and the (proper) pride many men feel in physical well-being. Men's physical strength can also be used in nurturing ways, through self-sacrifice. Gilmore examined the concept of nurture among males, and came to this conclusion: 'Men nurture their society by shedding their blood, their sweat, and their semen, by bringing home food for the child and mother, by producing children, and by dying if necessary in far away places to provide a safe haven for their people.'[5] There is some truth in this, but the idea of nurture through sacrifice can disguise male oppression of women. From a woman's perspective, such 'dying in far away places' often meant leaving her isolated and vulnerable. Closer to home, why do men so often use physical strength to dominate others, whether through actual violence, or as a lifestyle which is grounded in violence? Does it have any direct relationship with male embodiment?

If 'connectedness' describes woman's experience of embodiment, then 'externally focused' is the way I would describe the equivalent male experience. In the Scriptures the first words of the male, on seeing the female, are ones of fulfilled longing: 'This at last is bone of my bones, and flesh of my flesh' (Gn. 2:23). The writer goes on to comment, 'Therefore a man leaves his father and his mother and clings to his wife, and they become one flesh.' The externality of the male genitals is also a key factor; loss of these excluded a man from the assembly of ancient Israel (Dt. 23:1), but not from the kingdom of heaven (*cf.* Mt. 19:12; Acts 8:26–39). A man's distinctive physical nature, specifically seen in his genitalia, is made to *connect with* one who is other, so that the two become one flesh.[6] In this way the notion of connectedness can be seen to be true of men as well as of women, but in a very different way.[7] The man 'leaves' in order to 'cling', pointing to a male search to find identity in communion with one beyond himself. Male embodiment entails searching for fulfilment outside oneself. It tends to be externally focused, even while being made for connection and communion with others.

Men's hobbies shed some light on this, even though most are today shared by women.[8] Some continue traditional male roles, such as hunting or fishing, or rely on the generally greater physical strength of men, in contact sports. Others reflect the world of work in miniature (Meccano, woodwork, mechanics or war games, for example), or make place at home for a creativity which is denied at work; the handyman syndrome is strong evidence of this. The latest hobby, computing, is dominated by men as a pastime; the computer clubs in which I have participated are almost exclusively male. The reasons for this are complex, including social conditioning; but it seems that a linear (rather than cyclic) approach to thinking occurs in men more than in women, so that many men take more readily to a form of thinking which is technical and external, in which the primary relationship can be with a machine as easily as with a person. Further, male social norms generally emphasize 'binary opposites', the distinction of things by way of contrast.[9] The precise 'yes/no' binary arithmetic which undergirds computer-related concepts thus concurs with the common cultural patterns of many men. Again, many men experience their embodiment in terms of relating to things external to themselves, as producers.[10] A man's physicality may lead to an approach which emphasizes that what is outside him is good, but there is much more to being a man that this only. Men as well as women belong to the human race, and it is in our inter-communion that what it means to be made in the image of God is discerned. Our distinctive female and male embodiments can assist each of us to contribute to this diverse communion, reflecting the unity in diversity of the triune God.

Manliness: achieved or split?

That a male human is manly simply by being male, and that this is good, seems obvious. Yet it is often not accepted as a given, a good gift which a man should be glad to receive and live out. Many men have an apparent need to *achieve* being manly, to 'prove' that they are men, typically expressed in a conquest approach to male sexuality. Roy McCloughry cites several examples of societies in which a young man must endure successfully a series of initiation rites or tests to be regarded as a real man.[11] Although few modern societies practise such rites formally, and none is recorded in the Old or New Testament, their contemporary equivalents abound, especially in institutional environments such as boarding schools and military establishments. Why this is the case is hard to say; identity is rarely an issue for members of a dominant culture. McCloughry suggests that part of the answer may be men's lack of a biological threshold to indicate puberty, such as the onset of menstruation; but many modern initiation rites occur well beyond the age of puberty, in military bootcamps, for example. It seems as if many men are unwilling to accept that they are manly until they have overcome some enemy, or at least proved that they are capable of doing so.[12] At its worst, men refuse to accept the reality of their physical strength, but need to have it constantly affirmed and reaffirmed, as if without repeated reinforcement a man cannot be assured about his manliness.

Why do many men seek refuge in an achievement-oriented approach to male identity? Physical factors are involved, but hardly seem sufficient. Formaini (following ideas first introduced by Freud) suggests that patterns of child-rearing are a more significant factor.[13] Boys and girls alike begin life with a close tie to the mother, but come to distinguish themselves from the mother in different ways. As a boy moves away from his mother, he comes to view her as enemy as well as loved, and turns to the father as a positive alternative. In many modern societies, however, the father is largely absent in a child's first years, so that the boy lacks a positive role model to identify with as a male. This distinctive combination of relationships and experiences, Formaini argues, introduces a split into the male psyche, leading to a damaging separation of a man's inner, intimate side from his outer, physical life. Life then becomes split into compartments, and this split is magnified by the modern separation of the public world of work from the private world of home. It leads to lack of confidence and ability in maintaining personal relationships, and places too much emphasis on external, physical realities.

Much feminist thought takes this analysis further, seeing this split as the root of a dualistic worldview, based on dividing things into contrasting opposites. This, it is argued, lies behind hierarchical forms of social organization, especially those which place women below men (i.e. patriarchal societies). Further, this split underpins the dominance of reason and technology (the masculine) over the imagination and relationships (the feminine) in much modern life. Masculinity is difficult to define, but in the light of the above ideas it carries very negative tones. Formaini comments, 'Whatever masculinity is, it is very damaging to men.'[14] She takes the term to mean the sum of roles which derive from the need to take the lead, to be assertive, to strive for dominance, or to prefer reason to emotion and the like. It is used in contrast to femininity, which embraces roles associated with passivity, prettiness, subservience, nurture, caring and gentleness. Such definitions are both used and accepted in much of the literature and conversation of modern times, but they form gross generalizations. Defined like this, both men and women clearly share masculine and feminine characteristics, but many men identify themselves as masculine, and many women likewise see themselves as feminine.[15]

The notions of masculine and feminine can be helpful, when used to recognize differing aspects of being human. But when used as divisive stereotypes, as typical categories into which we force ourselves and others, they are not only confusing, but dangerous. In particular, when a man emphasizes his masculinity, his physical strength comes to be used aggressively, to dominate and oppress, and to justify being a 'real' man. Men like this propound the false equation that male = masculine, though many resist the full implications of this. Formaini interviewed 120 men as part of her research into maleness, and found that not one 'feels himself to be masculine'. She nevertheless comments that 'women and men have become half-human: women have been designated the feminine part and men the masculine. But neither role allows a full humanity.'[16] It is thus important not to equate male and masculine, female and feminine. To do so leads to the damaging stereotyping of gender roles, and confuses further the question of what it means to be a man.

Dualism and submission

The strong emphasis on technology in much of the modern world is associated with a division between mind and body, theory and practice. Reason was elevated above the bodily passions, to the point where the equations women = nature, and men = culture, came to be taken for granted. In this light a male/female pairing came to be seen as related to mind/body and reason/emotion pairs; this kind of pairing continues to be influential, in both feminist and non-feminist thought. Colin Gunton, writing from a theological perspective, argues that this dominance of reason over imagination is related to the Enlightenment's strong preference for reason over and against revelation. In part this preference was motivated by the desire for human freedom from institutional captivity to revelation understood as an oppressive tool of the church. To the extent to which the Enlightenment sought liberation from God, however, Gunton contends that it furthered the subservience of women. This subservience was deepened as science and technology lost touch with Christian faith, and so were denied a sense of accountability to God for their actions. Loss of a sense of accountability fed the destructive impact of unrestrained industrial development, and promoted the split between the 'masculine' public world and the 'feminine' private world. It is therefore understandable why both feminism and Christian theology have questioned much of the dualist Enlightenment heritage of divisions between mind and body, thought and action, theory and practice.[17] Feminists in particular have come to question the supposed value-free objectivity claimed for science, emphasizing that all knowledge is 'situated, contextual and strategic'.[18]

Feminist rejection of such dualisms sometimes leads to monism or pantheism. These deny the basic Christian tenet that there is a fundamental, qualitative difference between God and creation, expressed in the strong rejection of any form of idolatry (cf. Ex. 20:1–6; Is. 40:11ff.; Acts 17:22ff.). This tenet can be stressed so strongly, however, that God comes to be regarded as distant and uninterested, beyond any possible living relationship with us (the view called deism). The reality of divine 'at-one-ment', and of the personal presence of God through the Spirit, need to be kept in close relationship with the notion of God's holiness. Classically this is expressed through the interactive concepts of divine transcendence and immanence, though the balance between them has not always been maintained in the Christian tradition.[19] A further problem is that the distinction between God and creation is sometimes depicted in male–female terms; Father God and Mother Earth, for example. The very concept of God is then rejected by some feminists because of the assumption that God is male, and so the male is God. In its place, the concept of connectedness comes to function in a pantheistic way, with reality needing no separate source for its existence and well-being.

Along with much scholarly feminism, Christian theology rejects dualistic imagery of a male deity and female creation. At a popular level, however, the idea that God is male flourishes, and feeds feminist rejection of any distinction between Creator and creature. The Judeo-Christian tradition insists on this distinction as fundamental, but its own false dualisms must be acknowledged before the rejection of any concept of God by some feminists can be faced with integrity.[20] The rejection of dualism by feminism provides a significant critique of these false dualisms: for example, between public and private domains, classes in society, or body and soul in the human person (see chapter 10 below). Even though Christian thought has placed severe limits on such uses, at a popular level these divisions have flourished, and have done a great deal of damage to human well-being, not least in male–female relations. The idea that the body, sexuality or the world of physical work is less 'spiritual' than the soul, feelings or relationships is common among Christians of every tradition, even though these ideas question the incarnation, and the physicality of the Scriptures, sacraments and common life.

In the light of men's frequent abuse of the idea of submission, especially as husbands, many feminists reject any submission to others as a remnant of patriarchal, dualistic, oppressive social forms. This rejection can extend to submission to God, especially if it is perceived to function as giving social legitimacy to oppression. This view is incompatible with the Judeo-Christian tradition, which asserts that there is a genuine dualism between obedience and disobedience to God (*cf.* Lv. 26; Dt. 28). As Paul puts it, Christians are to 'walk not according to the flesh but according to the Spirit' (Rom. 8:4), for 'the mind that is set on the flesh is hostile to God; it does not submit to God's law' (Rom. 8:7). This latter text has often been misunderstood in the Christian tradition as contrasting the physical with the spiritual, leading to a despising of material things. This interpretation is a dangerous dualism that questions the doctrines of creation and incarnation. 'Flesh' and 'spirit' in Romans 8 do not refer to what is material and non-material, but to different modes of life as material creatures. To 'walk according to the flesh' is to live for oneself only, whereas to walk according to spirit (as it may be translated) means active obedience to God, our maker and re-maker. It must also be acknowledged that despite Paul's insistence that Christian obedience is inseparable from freedom (*cf.* Rom. 8:2; Gal. 5:1; and the discussion in chapter 6 above), notions of obedience have been used to further oppression, for example in the way theological support was given to slavery in the nineteenth century, and to apartheid in the twentieth.

By contrast, submission is always portrayed in the New Testament as the voluntary act of a free, capable person, and is never forced.[21] We are to 'be subject to one another out of reverence for Christ' (Eph. 5:21). It is one thing to encourage submission to another as a responsible act, and quite another to authorize a 'ruler' to have power over others; for this there is no basis in the Scriptures (with the fascinating exception of 1 Tim. 5:14).[22] Forced submission entails sinful oppression, but the rejection of submission to God is the essence of sin. And, as noted in chapter 6 above, the paradox involved in Christian service is that submission to God is the only way in which human freedom can be recovered and sustained. The Christian tradition has often abused the notion of submission, transfer-ring to humans powers which belong only to God. Many, including feminists, rightly protest against this abuse, and seek to enable those who are subject to oppression to become conscious of their state, and to seek freedom from their chains. Christians should be in the forefront of such work, whether by care for the oppressed, raising their consciousness, or involve-ment in campaigns for change. But the rejection of submission in all senses is impossible for Christians. Our status as humans is tied to our being accountable to God as our sovereign, and our identity as Christians is inseparable from the confession that Jesus is Lord. Denial of this demolishes the Christian under-standing of what it means to be human.

Feminist protest against dualism therefore finds a solid echo in mainstream Christian faith, but it cannot be accepted uncritically. Christian faith entails a fundamental distinction between God and all else. It calls for obedience to God, an obedience whose shape is revealed in the 'new commandment' of Jesus, that 'Just as I have loved you, you also should love one another' (Jn. 13:34; cf. Rom. 13:10; Jas. 4:7–10). The integration of these false dualisms into a healthy harmony, embracing all that is good in the feminine and masculine aspects of being human, is a pressing need in the search for renewed humanity, not least in the area of male sexuality.

The circumcised phallus

Male self-understanding, especially in the environment of cultures distorted by sin, has often focused on the phallus (Latin for 'penis') as the symbol of male power and identity. Male physique, embodiment and sexuality have been discussed above, but their symbolic significance has only been touched on. Much thought, both past and present, links them with the penis as *the* symbol of all that seeks to domineer and invade.[23] This 'phallic consciousness' is seen most directly in the conjunction of war and rape, both in reality and symbolically. This symbolism functions widely, for example in the phallic associations given to swords, rifles, motorcycles and sports cars (often approvingly, in the case of some men), or to industrial chimneys, viewed by many as symbols of the rape of the earth.[24] In the light of this, it is not surprising that many men, Christians included, find themselves feeling guilty simply for being men. Male imagery has come to be bound up with masculinity; it badly needs redemption.

Phallic symbolism is widely used in most cultures, including those within which Israel lived. Most generally, it is closely associated with fertility rites. Israel was to cut down the 'sacred poles' (*'ăšērîm*) of Canaan, and strong sanctions were set in place against their erecting such objects themselves (cf. Ex. 34:13; Dt. 12:3; 16:21–22). The Scriptures thus use phallic imagery, but in anti-phallic ways, rejecting fertility-based religion. Where the notion that woman = nature holds, this rejection has been interpreted as anti-female, to the point where Israelite religion, and even the idea of a transcendent deity, have come to be regarded by some as male constructs.[25] Yet the opposition to fertility religion displayed in the Old Testament is as much a critique of masculine religion as it is of feminine. Both are condemned as abominations, oppressing men and women alike (*cf.* 2 Ki. 3:27, and the terrible purges of 2 Ki. 10 – 11). The idolizing of both womb and phallus was utterly rejected in Israel.

Perhaps the most striking transformation of phallic symbolism is the practice of circumcision. The Scriptures record it as commanded by God to Abraham, as the sign of God's covenant made (literally 'cut') with him and his descendants; circumcision of every male child is required of each succeeding generation (Gn. 17:9–14). Here the physical embodiment of male sexuality is cut, and its blood is shed, as a symbol of belonging to the covenant people of God. This act questions the notion that men are to find their identity and source of power in the penis, and directs them to relationship with God. The prophets appeal for Israel to 'remove the foreskin of your hearts' (Je. 4:4), since 'Israel is uncircumcised in heart' (Je. 9:26). In this vivid image lies a strong rejection of male dominance, an attitude continued in the New Testament. Circumcision is described there with particular relation to Christ, vividly emphasizing the significance of the shedding of his blood. He was circumcised on the eighth day in accordance with the law (Lk. 2:21), and his being 'circumcised in heart' was evident in his full submission to the will of God, especially seen in his 'circumcision' in dying on the cross, through which all believers receive 'spiritual circumcision' (*cf.* Col. 2:11–12). In theological terms, the shedding of Christ's blood is more commonly associated with sacrifice and the ritual of the day of atonement (*cf.* Rom. 3:25; Heb. 10:19ff.), but its shadow fell on the very beginning of his life through his circumcision. By his blood shed in his death on the cross, Jesus did all that was necessary to restore the broken relationship between God and the human race as a whole. His atoning work was operative for all people, not only for the male descendants of Abraham.

Gentile and Jew, women and men, alike benefited from the sacrificial shedding of Christ's blood; his 'circumcision' opened up to all a covenant relationship with God. In this light, it is not surprising that in the early church the continued requirement of circumcision for entry to the people of God was strongly debated (see Acts 15; Gal. 2:1–14; 5:2–12). Circumcision was clearly commanded in the Scriptures, yet it formed a barrier with Jewish (circumcised) male believers on the one side, and Gentile (uncircumcised) male believers and all female believers on the other. The decision not to continue with compulsory circumcision thus marked a key transition in the life of the Christian church. The replacement of circumcision by baptism opened the boundaries of the people of God to women and men alike, of all cultures (*cf.* Col. 2:12–13; Rom. 4:1–12; Gal. 3:28). In Christ, true circumcision is not something 'external and physical', but 'a matter of the heart' (Rom. 2:28–29). In time, the full opening of God's covenant to women as well as to men meant that circumcision ceased to function as an effective symbol, and in many places outside Judaism it has ceased as a practice. Nevertheless, its radical undermining of phallic symbolism is a strong argument for the symbolism to remain in the awareness of Christians. On the one hand it can be argued that circumcision ritualizes the rejection of male superiority, by symbolically shedding the blood of the penis. On the other hand, the rejection of circumcision as a prerequisite for membership of the people of God removes the penis from its gender-dividing role, so repudiating all claims to male spiritual superiority. Relationship with God, the key to true and full human identity, does not depend on being a woman or a man. Each and every barrier within the people of God is removed by the shed blood of Christ, a reconciliation now activated by the Spirit, and made visible in Christian baptism, our 'spiritual circumcision' (Col. 2:11–12; 1 Cor. 12:13).

Thus far I have avoided speaking about male sexuality directly, since beginning at this point leads to a false impression regarding its significance.[26] Freud's work demonstrated the importance of sexuality in human life, albeit from a male perspective, but gave it such a dominant place that every aspect of human psychology came to be explained in sexual terms. Likewise, D. H. Lawrence sought to demonstrate through his novels that sexuality, both male and female, is the driving force in human relationships and life. The Scriptures reject this idea, especially through the repudiation of fertility religions in which sexuality is given divine status (*cf.* Ex. 34:14; Dt. 7:5). The Christian tradition refuses to ascribe to any particular factor in life the all-encompassing integrative power which Freud,

Lawrence and many others attribute to sexuality. Human beings, made in the image of God, are too complex for such reductionist positions. Sexuality certainly plays a prominent part in life. Sexual relations are celebrated in poetry (especially the Song of Songs), and used to describe the relation between God and human beings (*cf.* Ho. 1 – 2; Ezk. 16; 20; 23). The power of sexuality in the lives of both men and women is acknowledged in the stories of people such as Dinah and Shechem, Delilah and Samson (Gn. 34:1–3; Jdg. 14 – 16). Its powerful vitality has led to sexuality itself becoming suspect, not only in the Christian tradition, but also in the light of feminist analysis of the damage done by misused and corrupted sexuality.

The significance of sexuality for males is shaped by the nature of male responses to sexual stimuli, remembering that sexual response is a welcome aspect of being human. Male sexuality is closely related to the sense of sight. Most men respond rapidly to seeing women or images of women whom they regard as attractive, and they do so irrespective of any relationship with the women concerned. Although closely related to the sense of sight, arousal is also easily accomplished through reading sexually explicit material, or fantasizing (as is also the case with women). Associated with rapid response to stimulus of the imagination is the ease with which a man can have an erection. This is occasionally an embarrassment, especially in the teenage years, when sexual self-identity and relationships are forming. Erection is in itself a good thing, and a sense of humour is needed rather than feelings of shame. It represents a profound aspect of male sexuality, and can occur for apparently non-sexual reasons. Many men need to learn that erection is not wrong in itself, even though it has come to represent much that is wrong with masculinity; but more of this below.

A second factor in male sexuality is the nature of the act of intercourse in male perspective. In the first place, it involves penetration by the man, as his distinctive mode of connecting with the woman. Male sexual activity as penetration has become a powerful metaphor for much male self-understanding (the word itself derives from 'penis'). The act has come to be associated with the notion of conquest, invasion, or even humiliation of an enemy. Indeed, the use of sexual metaphors for warfare, and *vice versa*, is a frightening side of male sexuality

207

as many men experience and practise it.[27] Yet to say there is something wrong with the act of penetration itself is another form of regarding sex as sinful. Such an idea distorts the relationship within which this deeply intimate act of communion between two persons takes place, as much as invasive views of male sexual activity corrupt the manner in which sexual intercourse takes place. To say this, however, is to stand over and against the dominant sexually explicit ethos of much of the world in which men live.

Another aspect of male sexuality is that sexual climax is definite, marked physiologically by the ejaculation of semen. Without this climax, the vast majority of men would regard the act of intercourse as incomplete, but its definite nature means that sexual climax is easily separated from the wider context of a loving relationship, including non-climactic sexual activity, within which sexual intercourse belongs.[28] Prevailing male cultures speak of male sexual activity as something which happens with little reference to the person with whom one is having intercourse. In this light, it needs to be once more affirmed that male sexuality, including male climax and the ejaculation of sperm, is good in itself. Given the prevailing climate of male socialization, the idea that sexual activity is more than a particular experience unrelated to other people, but is tied closely to human relationships, is something that many men need to learn. Again, the ejaculation of semen, the biological purpose of which is conception, has led to the association of male sexual activity with the idea of 'sowing seed', treating women as merely fertile soil. The wonder of conception, intended to be inseparably linked to an act of love, points to the goodness of sexual intercourse for both partners. Scriptural passages such as Genesis 2:15–24, and especially the Song of Songs, indicate that sexual activity, female and male, is a gift we are to receive with thanksgiving and careful delight.

Sin in men's experience

The negative side of being manly has already been touched on at several points. Men are as much caught up in sin as women, yet there are distinctive ways in which men are involved in sin. Physically, male sinfulness can be seen in the readiness of many men to resolve conflict through brute force, not only at the global or national level through war, or by intimidation in the workplace, but also in domestic violence within the family. Again, a man can come to regard his penis as outside, rather than part of, his own self. When this happens, the penis comes to be regarded as a tool to be used *by* his body, rather than forming part *of* his own body. Combined with the notion that male embodiment has an external focus, this both expresses and leads to living in a way that denies 'connectedness'. Men come to live as if they can relate to the world around them only in an instrumental, mechanical way. Such a way of life is profoundly debilitating. It depersonalizes a man, and all with whom he comes into contact. Male socialization generally pushes men, Christians included, towards objectifying sex.[29]

This observation serves to strengthen the hypothesis noted in the previous chapter, that women tend to sin by omission, and men by commission. The corruption of men's external focus leads to the attempt to dominate the outside world, and so to sin more by doing what is wrong than by failing to do what is right. A man is thus likely to see God in the first place in solely external terms, as distant and unrelated: 'deism', in formal terms. He may then view God as an external rival, whose claim to the man's allegiance is, as a consequence, resisted. Many men find it difficult to think of God as the intimate source of life in whom 'we live and move and have our being' (Acts 17:28). In its extreme form this can become monism or pantheism, but in essence it expresses classical trinitarian language about God, as Persons in relationship. The converse of relationship with God is one's concept of sin. In the classical typology of the seven deadly sins, pride, the sin of ultra-activity, is fundamental; its first place in the schema of sins may be due to the male life experience of most theologians! For many women, it may be sloth, the sin of culpable passivity, which is closer to being the centre of sin.

Whatever the understanding of the distinctive nature of men's sinning, lust certainly dominates many Christian men's consciousness of sin. Given the visual orientation and immediacy of male response to sexual stimuli, this is not surprising. Lust does *not* mean seeing a woman as an attractive person with a distinctive beauty, open to fully personal relationships. It means seeing her as a mere object of sexual desire, existing only to feed male appetites. The power of lust was well understood by Jesus, whose teaching speaks directly to men: 'everyone who looks at a woman with lust has already committed adultery with her in his heart' (Mt. 5:28). Here the act of adultery is seen to have its roots in the attitude of lustful desire. The Christian tradition has never underestimated this, but sometimes it has so overdone the danger of lust that sexuality itself has come to be questioned. When this happens, men feel themselves faced with a choice between denying the sexual side of their nature, or giving way to a promiscuous lifestyle that damages many women as well as themselves. Many Christian men feel caught in the middle of this invidious choice, especially when they live and work in cultures (such as the motor trade) where sexually explicit material is pervasive, yet belong to churches in which sexuality cannot be discussed. Techniques can be learnt which assist men to shun lust and affirm their sexuality, but it is no easy matter.[30]

Brotherhood

Men as we know them rarely live as brothers. We are sinners, and live in a world shaped and distorted by sin. Many patterns of brotherhood are shallow or demeaning: the favouritism of the old-boy network, or the boastful (and often fictional) locker-room tales of sexual conquest, for example. The Australian concept of 'mateship' illustrates the ambiguity of brotherhood: 'mateship' had profound origins in the shared suffering of convict life, pioneer struggles to survive, and especially war service. For some men it does enable a sense of solidarity and mutual loyalty to be sustained. But for others, and for most women, it is a sentimental shadow of brotherhood, little more than an excuse to get drunk with 'mates'.

Many men find the qualities needed for sharing life as brothers beyond their capabilities, especially those of friendship and intimacy. When these factors are seen in the light of the achievement-oriented perspective most men have towards their identity, sexual activity comes to be seen as a matter of performance, a stereotype which itself forms a highly oppressive part of male mythology. Some men, including Christians, have reacted against such a shallow worldview, sometimes by seeking spiritual meaning in sexuality itself, sometimes by rejecting sexuality altogether. Christians point to the need for a fuller understanding of the significance of love in human life, not only with regard to sexuality, but also for intimacy in the worlds of work and political life. Prevailing trends remain depressingly negative, however, given the sex-distorted environments within which most of us live.

It is good to be a man. Male physique, embodiment and sexuality are good in themselves. And it is good to be a man among men, to experience brotherhood. One of the psalms celebrates it: 'How good and joyful a thing it is, when brothers live together in unity' (Ps. 133:1, my translation). The first Christian communities are described as 'brethren', members of the one body in Christ, whose lives were to be shared together.[31] In the early twentieth century, the ideal of Christian theology and lifestyle was popularly termed 'the fatherhood of God and the brotherhood of man'. To use such a phrase today without being misunderstood is impossible, since it involves heavily gender-exclusive language, but the positive ideal behind the words is significant. It is good to be a brother, to both women and men.

10

THE WHOLE PERSON

To be human means to be made in the image of God. We are made for relationship with God our creator, with otherkind, and with our fellow human beings, both male and female. In previous chapters many aspects of these relationships have been considered; we now focus on the relationship each of us has with our own self, our wholeness as persons.

Whole salvation

Wholeness is an idea which has gained much attention in recent decades, particularly in the light of the split that many, especially men, experience in living (see chapters 8 and 9). Anything which contributes to holistic living is valued highly today, while dualistic impulses are vigorously avoided. The notion of the whole person is more than a passing fad, however; it has been the goal of systems of philosophy and the aim of many social systems. Christian faith points to Jesus Christ as *the* example of a whole life lived in full integrity, 'without sin'. The distinctive feature of the work of Christ is that he freely gave up his life, so that his wholeness might be offered to all. The scriptural word *sōtēria*, often translated as 'salvation', is helpfully rendered 'health', or 'wholeness'. Salvation in Christ brings healing from the consequences of sin, a healing whose fullness awaits our resurrection but is anticipated in the present through the work of the Spirit. A major question arises here: is a person saved as a whole, or only in part? The Scriptures are emphatic that we are saved wholly, looking for the 'redemption of our bodies' (Rom. 8:23), when our earthly self will not be unclothed, but 'further clothed' as our mortality is taken up into immortality (2 Cor. 5:4). Many Christians have thought otherwise, speaking of salvation in terms of the 'soul', 'spirit', or other immaterial aspect of human life. Ideas such as this are based on the notion that human beings are divided into a number of parts, usually body and soul, or body, soul and spirit.

The modern quest for wholeness has thus come about not only as a search in its own right, but in reaction to the idea that we are divided selves, an idea common in western Christianity. Many Christians assume that the idea that each of us has a self divided between body and soul and/or spirit is biblical. As will be argued below, strict forms of this cannot be sustained from the Scriptures, but are remnants of presuppositions about human nature imported into the way the Scriptures are read.[1] Many of our ideas about being human stem from the flowering of humanist culture in ancient Athens. Plato, Aristotle, Socrates and others began to wrestle with the instability and uncertainties of life. Where was reality to be found? They knew that the senses are uncertain, and form our greatest limitations; should not one seek reality beyond the material self? Plato came to view the body as the vehicle in which each person (soul) resides. Aristotle held a slightly different view, that the soul is the 'form' which shapes the material self to be the person, and is still viewed as separate from the body. Greek philosophy embraced a tendency to regard the body as an unfortunate restriction on the real self or soul. Death was seen as the release of the soul from its earthly prison, into an immortality (deathlessness) which was naturally its possession.[2] Common sense tells one that a person is somehow more than a corpse; 'breath' is what makes for life, and the word for it in Greek, Latin and Hebrew is what English often translates as 'spirit'. In Christian theology after the fifth century, the idea that the soul mediated between spirit and body was proposed, but firmly rejected. Such a view divided physical and spiritual aspects of reality as if they were opposed, so denying the Christian concepts of creation.[3] Some Christians nevertheless retain a threefold view of human nature, seeing spirit as the life force underlying both soul and body, as well as the more common distinction between body and soul.

In some circles, including early Christian ones, this thinking led to the notion that matter itself is evil. Formally the church rejected such ideas, since they deny that creation is 'good', and compromise the genuineness of the incarnation and resurrection. Jesus lived a holy life as an embodied self, and rose in transformed bodily form. Embodied life as we know it suffers from bodily temptations, and the New Testament writers speak of the need for a disciplined lifestyle in Christians (cf. 1 Cor. 9:27; Rom. 12:1; 1 Tim. 4:8; 1 Pet. 1:13–16). Berkouwer summarizes this teaching effectively; of Paul he writes: 'His concern is not with vilifying the body, but rather in seeing that sin is not master in the body (Rom. 6:12). His struggle is not against the body, but for the body, that it might be directed rightly.'[4]

As time went on, body-denying tendencies slowly made their way into the churches, producing some fanatics, but leading more generally to a deeply ingrained idea that 'spiritual' Christians avoided practical affairs, and were celibate. Such ascetic attitudes can be found in all traditions – East and West, ancient and modern, Protestant, Roman Catholic and Pentecostal, liberal, radical and conservative. New forms of asceticism are always springing up: for many Australian Christians, women can now wear lipstick, and men an earring, but neither should drive a sports car. A disciplined, simple lifestyle has a firm base in the Christian tradition, since believers are often called to deny themselves for Christ's sake, and reject false, empty and vain values. Yet the Christian hope has often been spiritualized, and the earthy hope of the resurrection of the body replaced by an amorphous wish about an immortal soul. The key concept in Jesus' preaching, the kingdom of God, is often understood as a private matter, to do with the 'religious' part of life.[5] These ideas need to be re-examined in the light of the Scriptures.

Body, soul, spirit, heart

Genesis 2 has been examined in several chapters above. Humanity (*hā'ādām*) is made from the ground (*hā'ādāmâ*); we are thus indisputably material beings. We also are living beings (*nepeš*) as a result of God's breath (*rûah*) being breathed into us (Gn. 2:7). But this does not speak of a 'soul'; *nepeš* is used of any form of living beings, such as animals. It is probably best translated 'self' or 'person', as the following examples show: 'Bless the Lord, O my [*nepeš*]', cries the Psalmist (Pss. 103:1; 104:1); and Ezekiel preaches, 'the [*nepeš*] who sins shall die' (Ezk. 18:20).[6]

It is thus truer to say that we *are* souls than that we *have* souls, or as Barth puts it with characteristic limpidity, the human person is 'bodily soul, as he is also besouled body'.[7] Structurally, the Hebrew Scriptures think of humans as made of flesh (*bāśar*) vivified by God's breath or spirit (*rûah*). At death the flesh returns to dust, which God has ceased to activate with the divine breath (*cf.* Gn. 6:3; Jb. 34:14–15). The notion that the person has a continuing autonomous existence is given little attention, since being human is tied up with relationship with God and other people, and is not seen as having its own independent life. The Hebrew Scriptures only occasionally hint at an afterlife (*cf.* Dn. 12:2); what mattered was that a person's name was perpetuated, as the sign of his or her relationship with God and his or her people. It is this concern which lay behind customs such as levirate marriage, in which a childless woman was given to her husband's brother so that his name might continue (Dt. 25:5–10; *cf.* Gn. 38:8). Israel believed not so much in life after death as in the Lord who gives both life and death (*cf.* Is. 45:4–7; Lk. 18:27–38). When someone is present at a death, it is evident that the dead corpse is the body of the person from whom life has departed, and Israel knew that all life was in God's hands. There thus developed the notion of 'Sheol', a shadowy world where a 'shade' of our self continues, yet not without God's Spirit (*e.g.* Pss. 139:7–8; 88:13; 94:17).

The key part of us, in Old Testament eyes, is not body, soul or breath, but 'heart'. When the heart stops, life ceases, and the heart is the pump for our life-blood. Life is linked closely with blood, which is not to be shed lightly, and never eaten (Lv.

17:10–14; Gn. 9:6 relates both to the image of God). The heart is thus significant as a physical reality, and is also depicted as the source of our attitudes and actions, whether evil (Gn. 8:21), joyous (Ps. 105:3), obedient (1 Ki. 14:8), courageous (Ps. 27:14) or repentant (Ps. 34:18), for example. God 'looks on the heart' (1 Sa. 16:7), not merely on outward appearance, and salvation is described as being given a new heart and a new breath/spirit, a 'heart of flesh' and not of 'stone' (Ezk. 36:26). This centrality of 'heart' indicates the unitary emphasis of the Old Testament on human life, and this continues into the New (*cf.* Rom. 2:5; 5:5).[8] We are clearly fleshly, but not only that: heart, kidneys, bowels and even the liver are spoken of as typifying various facets of human existence (Je. 4:19; Ps. 16:7–10 and La. 2:11 use all these terms in the Hebrew, though the translations render them differently). Throughout, the analysis of human nature is eminently practical, and though we are described in many ways, there is no dividing up of the human person into various parts. The concern of the Hebrew Scriptures is that we respond to God with our whole being, a wholehearted allegiance perhaps best expressed in the *Shema*: 'Hear, O Israel: the LORD is our God, the LORD alone. You shall love the LORD your God with all your heart, and with all your soul, and with all your might. Keep these words that I am commanding you today in your heart' (Dt. 6:4–6). Jesus describes this as the 'greatest commandment', reiterating its demand on the whole person even more fully by adding 'mind' to the list (Mt. 22:37–38; Lk. 12:29). It is in the full humanity of Christ that human wholeness is displayed fully, in response to God, in his relations with others, and in his own self. Jesus was clearly material, eating, drinking, sleeping, tiring and so on (*cf.* 1 Jn. 4:2). He had a full emotional life, rejoicing, being grieved, crying, loving and getting angry. He had a 'spiritual' life, a genuine relationship with God, expressed particularly in various types of prayer. It is therefore quite proper to speak of Jesus' being fully human as embodied and ensouled. The Athanasian Creed speaks of him as 'perfect God and perfect Man: of a reasonable soul and human flesh subsisting'. This is not viewed as a division, however, as is seen in the use of the expression a little later to illustrate the unity of deity and humanity in Christ: 'for as the reasonable soul and flesh is one man: so God and Man is one Christ'. The Creed thus emphasizes that Jesus was like us in every respect, sin excepted (Heb. 4:15), and, since he is whole, so is human nature intended for wholeness.

Paul uses the vocabulary of Greek thought in speaking about being human: body (*sōma*), soul (*psychē*) and spirit (*pneuma*). In each case the concepts are modified by the Hebrew perspective, and the whole humanity of Jesus. Thus 'spirit' is used of our relation with God, especially in adverbial phrases such as 'walk according to spirit', or in the adjective 'spiritual'. The contrast Paul makes in these phrases is not with matter, but with disobedience, the 'flesh' (*sarx*); and he relates them to 'life', 'mind', and 'spirit' in reference to the Holy Spirit (see especially Rom. 8:2–9). Similarly, 'body' means more than merely our physical side; it refers to the whole self, whether in sin, in Christ or in the resurrection, as Romans 8:10–13 makes clear. Paul's terms include a mixture of philosophical and scriptural concepts: mind, heart, the new or old humanity, our inner and outer nature, and so on (*e.g.* 2 Cor. 4:16 – 5:4; Phil. 1:23). It is impossible to produce a tight Pauline anthropology, partly because his concerns were for the practical needs of his readers, and partly because he himself was affected by the sin which distorts our nature (*cf.* Rom. 7).[9] As with ancient Israel, Paul's concern is with human beings in the reality of their existence. We are made to be whole, and are offered glimpses of what that means in Christ. Bultmann summarizes Paul's thought as follows:

> Man does not consist of two parts, much less of three: nor are *psyche* and *pneuma* special faculties or principles (within the *soma*) of a mental life higher than his animal life. Rather, man is a living unity. He is a person who can become an object to himself. He is a person having a relationship to himself (*soma*). He is a person who lives in his intentionality, his pursuit of some purpose, his willing and knowing (*psyche, pneuma*). This state of living towards some goal . . . belongs to man's very nature.[10]

The future orientation of human life is significant in this quotation: as was argued in earlier chapters, to be made in the image of God is in part a present reality, but it awaits its full disclosure at the return of Christ (*cf.* 1 Jn. 3:20). There are two New Testament texts which some claim as teaching that internal divisions are present by design in each human. In 1 Thessalonians we read: 'May the God of peace himself sanctify you entirely; and may your spirit and soul and body be kept sound and blameless at the coming of our Lord Jesus Christ. The one who calls you is faithful, and he will do this' (1 Thes. 5:23–24). The vocabulary here is certainly 'tripartite' – body, soul, spirit – but the stress is on the sanctification of the *whole* person, and that in the future coming of Christ. In popular thought, the point of making a sharp distinction between body and soul is the assertion that the body does not survive death, and people sense that something else must do so. This text from 1 Thessalonians, however, teaches that every aspect of being human is to be kept for the coming of Christ, which contradicts the reason for dividing human beings up. Paul is free to speak of being human from different aspects, but avoids any obscuring of the unitary reality we find in Christ, seeing it as headed towards greater fulfilment in Christ, not division.

The other text is from the letter to the Hebrews: 'Indeed, the word of God is living and active, sharper than any two-edged sword, piercing until it divides soul from spirit, joints from marrow; it is able to judge the thoughts and intentions of the heart' (Heb. 4:12). This text is even clearer about the issues: if a strict division between body and soul is held, so must a divide be made between joints and marrow! The obvious point is that the gospel of Christ finds its way to the very core of our being, our 'heart'. In order to speak of the gospel's effective work in sinners the vocabulary of division is used. But there is no thought of it reflecting our actual nature. It is sin which divides us from God, and brings the sense of division within each of us. It is thus not our material nature as such, but that nature as corrupted, which brings about the common distinctions between body, soul, mind or spirit. More, the fullness of divine salvation with regard to the restoration of human beings, though anticipated to some degree in the present, awaits the future coming of our Lord Jesus Christ.

Wholeness in division

Some have reacted to human divisions by insisting that any speaking about ourselves as other than holistic is wrong. To do this tries to anticipate the future promise too much in the present. The world as we know it, and in which we live, is sin-distorted, and perceived through sin-distorted lenses. In this present age, therefore, and given our own partial self-know-ledge, speaking of ourselves as having distinct aspects can be very important. A surgeon operating on a patient will do more for the good of that person by shutting out from thought and feeling everything but the anaesthetized body on the table; the more personal bedside manner belongs to another time and place. Similarly, a preacher needs to focus on people's relation to God in order to let the gospel challenge and illuminate every facet of their lives. There is often a need to think and act as if we had distinct 'parts', in order to protect the unitary vision of human life in the Scriptures. The traditional words used at the administration of the holy communion provide a useful example: the minister says, 'The body of our Lord Jesus Christ, which was given for you, preserve your body and soul to everlasting life.' From one point of view this could be seen as dividing the recipient into two parts, but even if this were the case, the point is that the work of Christ reaches out to heal and preserve both; the body of Christ was given so that every aspect of the faithful communicant might be healed and kept for the coming of Christ. We are made as whole beings, and look to the time when we shall be remade in Christ as whole persons, as members of the new humanity. In the present we anticipate that redemption through the Spirit, as members of the body of Christ, and so expect to see some evidence of this in the here and now, through physical healing, restoration of personalities and relationships, and especially in the forgiveness of sins.[11] All of us will die, nevertheless, and in this age some distinctions in human nature need to be accepted: to live as if the new age were fully present is to fail to appreciate the dire and deceiving effects of sin, and can be at least as dangerous as refusing to recognize the reality of sin.

Christians thus preach a gospel of wholeness, but this whole-ness will be fully seen only in the resurrection. We see now 'in a mirror, dimly', not only concerning God, but concerning ourselves, since we do not yet see the image of God renewed fully: then 'I will know [myself] fully, even as I have been fully known' (1 Cor. 13:12). There is a proper sense in which the tripartite and bipartite models are of practical use in the time before the resurrection. When we, with our limited and distorted perspective, try to treat humans as a unified whole, we end by reducing them to one facet. In past times this saw the physical aspect eliminated in favour of the 'soul', whereas in our day it has become all-embracing in materialistic views of humanity. Thus behaviourists regard humans as wholly explicable in terms of stimuli and responses, Marxists in terms of economics, and so on. To the extent that such reductionism is to be countered, and the richness and mystery of human existence affirmed, some distinctions are necessary.

The tripartite view is useful in so far as it acknowledges humans as made not only with a relation to God (spirit) and matter (body) but also for social and emotional relations (soul). It has been rejected in the church because of the mediating role ascribed to spirit; the mediation Christ wrought was not between body/matter and soul/mind, but between sin and holiness. Many theologians have therefore avoided tripartite views because they can sometimes shift the seat of our plight from sin to finiteness, but their usefulness lies in the way they open out our relationships in horizontal as well as vertical dimensions. The bipartite view has use when it is necessary to stress that our earthly ties (social, emotional, psychic, *etc.*) must be seen in the light of God: the vertical dimension. In such circumstances it is helpful to speak of a distinction between body and soul. Whether tripartite, bipartite or integrated perspectives are employed, body, soul and spirit function as models for particular aspects of humanity as we experience it, in a finite, fallen world. They must not be seen as watertight compartments in our being, for we then slip into false asceticism or improper materialism.

The idea of a soul can be useful as a model which points beyond a merely materialistic view of being human. It also raises problems, seen perhaps most clearly in the traditional discussion about the origin of the soul.[12] Plato taught that the soul is immortal, living in a transient human body, and this idea was taken up by some early Christian thinkers such as Origen.

Although influential, the idea of a sharp difference between body and soul was eventually rejected because of the implication that matter exists only because of sin, so that the body comes to be regarded as a prison, rather than as created 'very good'. Assuming that each person has a soul, as an essential part of being human, how does it relate to the body? Creationism holds that God creates a fresh soul for each human being. It is a view generally held in the eastern churches, and is regarded in others as supporting opposition to abortion. It certainly emphasizes the uniqueness of each human, but if the soul is regarded as the seat of sin, it makes God responsible for evil. The alternative view is traducianism ('pass-on-ism'), which holds that the soul is passed on by the parents to each child. This allows for factors such as heredity, but tends to a materialistic view of the soul and sin, and is seen by some as distancing God too far from the work of creating human life. How can one decide between these views, each of which can apparently be buttressed by scriptural texts (cf. Ps. 139:13, Je. 1:5)? The comment of Berkouwer is apposite, that 'the solution lies in another direction, namely, that the way of stating the problem in this influential dilemma is illegitimate'.[13]

Moltmann offers the insight that body and soul interact 'perichoretically', the term applied to the 'dancing in and around' one another of the Persons of the Trinity. There is a fellowship between our various aspects, marked by differentiation and unity. Any attempt to reduce the human person to a merely physical or an exclusively non-physical reality fails to account for the mystery of human nature. If we do define ourselves in terms of body and soul,[14] 'then the body "informs" the soul just as strongly as the soul informs its body. The body talks continually to the soul, just as the unconscious continually influences what is conscious.' The interdependence of the various aspects which make up the human person comes to the fore here. Put simply, my personality would be different if my nose was more crooked, my hair fell out, or I lost a limb. Conversely, my body-language changes with my moods. In the light of such observations, the holistic nature of the gospel is seen afresh. Jesus proclaimed and enabled not only the forgiveness of sins, but also the restoration of human relationships and personality, and the healing of body and mind. In whatever manner it is helpful to think of ourselves, God offers wholeness. It is a wholeness into which we are yet to enter fully, but is real nonetheless.

Soul and body have been the commonest categories in which the different aspects of the human person have been understood. 'Spirit' merits fuller attention, in the light of current interest in spirituality.[15] There are at least three distinct meanings of 'spirit' in the Scriptures. The primary metaphor is that of breath, hence life and dynamic power. In this sense we speak of a spirited speech, horse or performance, for example, while in physical terms spirits mean strong drink (and, in modern terms, strong chemicals such as spirits of salts). Secondly, its particular theological sense comes from applying 'spirit' to God; as the source of all life and power, God not only *has,* but *is,* spirit (*cf.* Jn. 4:24). In this sense, 'spirit'uality means 'godliness', and to be 'spiritual' means to be 'godly', whether in material concerns, social relations, or fellowship with God. 'Spirit' comes to have a very particular meaning when 'holy' and 'spirit' combine to refer to the 'Holy Spirit'. A third meaning is the idea of 'a spirit', a living creature existing without material embodiment. (It is crucial to realize that the Holy Spirit is in no sense a spirit in this sense, since that would make him a creature.) The sphere of 'spirituality' in this sense is the occult, and has no special relation to godliness; it is the more subtle side of creation, affected like the rest of it by sin, and so dangerous.

Modern usage often speaks of spirituality in a fourth sense, to mean whatever is left over after the doctor, social worker, psychologist, community education officer and psychiatrist have had a go. 'Spirit' is here the inexplicable part of being human. This type of usage revives the idea of the person having a spirit aspect, but without any reference to God. Spirituality in this sense forms part of the privatization of religion, regarding it as but one (rather insignificant) area of life, of interest to religious hobbyists. We can have an interest in our spiritual side if we wish, and learn appropriate techniques for doing so, but this exists quite apart from any concept of God. In an age of rush and bother such techniques may be of great benefit; there is much to be gained from the integration of personality, body and feelings. Yet to confuse this with growth in the knowledge of God (the Christian meaning of spirituality), is a gross and dangerous distortion of divine truth. The issues are essentially the same as those raised by mysticism: where it becomes a matter of techniques for inducing states of trance, rather than referring to growth into the triune Lord, the boundary between faith and works has been crossed, and an incarnational, holistic human perspective is threatened. When, as in some eastern religious thought, the divine is regarded as one aspect of reality (monism), concern for spirituality can appear to have reference to God. In actual fact, however, this is not the case, since by 'God' here is meant the spiritual part of the human person. There is nothing wrong with talking about a spiritual aspect to humanity; the problems arise when Christians confuse this with relationship with the triune Lord who transcends the created order.

The sensual person

The body is of such significance to wholeness that it merits separate consideration. As has already been noted, the range of bodily parts used to represent our feelings and relationships is immense. In modern terms, it is through the senses that we discern what it means to be embodied, and each sense provides us with a distinctive perspective on our perception.[16]

Hearing is the most pervasive sense in experience. Sound cannot be avoided by a person who can hear; we do not have 'earlids'. The vibrations we experience as sound surround us, forming a shared environment in which all within earshot cannot help but participate.[17] The sense of hearing is thus a passive one, about which we have little choice (*cf.* the discussion of vision below). A sound event is also intangible and fleeting (*cf.* a tactile event); a sound is never quite the same as a previous occurrence of it, whether in its own pitch or duration, or the context into which it comes. Sound is therefore particularly appropriate to communicate personal experience; it creates 'acoustic space' in which people who hear the same sounds participate. Sound is the only sense which both receives and initiates, through ears and mouth. Our ears can hear a vast array of sounds, and while our mouths can produce a more limited range, our capacity to speak, sing, laugh and cry is remarkable. The words we speak express something of who we are; the proverb 'an Englishman's word is his bond' acknowledges the connection between speech and person. The occasional nature of speech, sensed especially in conversation through the distinctive timbres of each voice present, combined with the interpretative capacity of language, fashions it to be a prime vehicle for the communication of meaning. In the light of this, it can be seen that hearing is the sense whose loss most badly affects our ability to develop relationships as fully as we might otherwise. Hearing and speaking are not isolated senses, however; a telephone conversation has a different quality from a face-to-face encounter, in which other senses may be involved.

In biblical thought, the notion of speech as a fundamental means of revelation is prominent, from the 'And God said . . . and there was' of Genesis 1, through the 'Thus says the LORD' of the prophets, to the concept of 'the Word made flesh' of John 1. John also notes that the words which Jesus speaks 'are spirit and life', and 'words of eternal life' (Jn. 6:63, 69). In this respect, the passive nature of sound is significant; we do not initiate what God would say, but can only be in the place where hearing of the divine Word is possible. As Paul emphasizes, 'faith comes from what is heard' (Rom. 10:17), made possible through the preaching of the gospel, because God's voice 'has gone out to all the earth' (Rom. 10:18). It is also striking that sin is often described by Israel's prophets as refusal to listen (cf. Ezk. 3:27), while open response to the gospel message is the way by which the word of God is received (cf. 1 Thes. 2:13; Acts 13:48–49). The speech-act of preaching is the vehicle by which the Spirit opens the sinful heart to hear and respond to the word of God (e.g. Acts 10:44–48; 1 Thes. 1:4–8).

If hearing is a more passive sense, *sight* is more active. Every human who can see has the choice of not seeing: eyelids play a vital role in human life. Moreover, not only *whether* but *what* we see is an active choice. The need for the eye to focus in order for the brain to understand what is seen entails the element of deliberate choice about sight which is absent from hearing. Sight is also an ambiguous sense; the meaning of what we see is not always obvious. It is precisely this property which enables the painter, sculptor, fashion designer or film-maker to be creative, but it also explains in part the resistance to visible symbols in the Judeo-Christian tradition. For a long time the visible depiction of any living thing was prohibited, and this continues in Islam. It was only in the eighth century that the use of icons was finally permitted in the church. The medieval West saw sight raised to prominence over hearing, as the language of the church, Latin, became an unknown tongue to the vast majority of the population. Although this led to the marvels of thirteenth-century stained glass, it also occasioned the rise of ignorance and superstition; it is not surprising that the recovery of the word in the Reformation went along with a widespread rejection of visible symbols. In theological terms, the word is fundamental, but it is more than words. Made flesh in Jesus Christ, proclaimed in the gospel of Christ, and accompanied by the power of the Spirit, the Word of God involves eye as well as ear, as does response to the Word (*cf.* 1 Jn. 3:18). In the modern world, in which coloured clothing, magazines and especially television surround us on every side, the significance of sight cannot be underestimated.

In biblical terms, seeing is regarded with greater ambiguity than hearing. It may be possible for human beings to hear the word of God in some sense (*cf.* Dt. 5:22–28), but God is strictly invisible, 'unseeable' (*cf.* Ex. 33:20; Ezk. 1:26–28). It is especially sight that is associated with the worship of idols, because human beings long to keep an eye on that which they honour as powerful (*cf.* Ex. 32:1–4). It is salutary to realize that blindness is a frequent metaphor for sin (*cf.* Jn. 9:39–41), and the eye is the only sense organ of which Jesus speaks in terms of being plucked out (Mt. 5:29; 18:9). It is quite obvious that having no eyes will not stop evil thoughts, but the drastic action of self-blinding underlines the significance of sight when it is corrupted by sin. Conversely, sight is also ascribed the greatest privilege of all the senses, as Jesus teaches: 'Blessed are the pure in heart, for they shall see God' (Mt. 5:8).

The mouth is active not only in speaking, but in *taste*. Eating and drinking are essential to the very existence of life, but mean far more. Their abuse, whether through gluttony or leaving others hungry, is condemned in the Scriptures (*cf.* Mt. 25:35; Jas. 2:15–16; 2 Pet. 2:12–13; 1 Cor. 11:21). Their godly enjoyment, however, is regarded as a great good, both in themselves (*cf.* Ps. 104:14–15) and especially because meals express and deepen relationships. The peace offerings and tithe celebrations of

Israel are examples (Dt. 12:7, 17–18), while the prophetic message becomes part of a prophet through 'eating' it (Ezk. 2:8 – 3:3; Je. 15:16). Feasts play a prominent role in Jesus' parables (Mt. 22:1–14; Lk. 14:15–24), and formed his typical activity with the disciples after the resurrection. The risen Lord was known 'in the breaking of the bread' (Lk. 24:35), and it is in the Lord's supper that Christians continue to have the privilege of communion with Christ, looking for the banquet of heaven. It is therefore not surprising that taste is used in the Scriptures as a metaphor of direct experience; the psalmist exclaims, 'Taste and see that the LORD is good' (Ps. 34:8), and speaks of the law as 'sweeter than the honeycomb' (Ps. 19:10; cf. 119:103).

The sense of *smell* seems less significant than the others; like hearing, it is passive and corporate, though by holding the nose an unpleasant odour can be temporarily avoided. While it may be less significant in its own right, smell is distinctive in that it augments the other senses; many of the pleasures of taste and sight are the scents associated with food, drink or personal beauty. Smell is also distinctive in that it is an activity attributed to God in responding to human action, but only indirectly used to depict human response to God (cf. 2 Cor. 2:14–16). God delights in the sweet smell of genuine sacrifice, symbolized in incense, but is deeply offended by the stink of injustice and immorality (e.g. Gn. 8:21; Lv. 1:9, 13, 17).

If hearing and smell are more passive (sensing stimuli offered to us), and taste and sight are more active (senses directed by the human will), *touch* brings both dimensions of human experience together. We both touch and are touched, with caring tenderness and in cruel hurt. Touch is the sense of feeling and being connected, and above all the others shapes and expresses personal relationships. More is conveyed in a hug, blow, kiss, handshake or massage than can be put in words; the intimate connection between a prophet and the LORD is expressed through touch (cf. Is. 6:7; Je. 1:9). The barriers which sin raises in human life are seen in prohibitions against touching, for example, the unclean and lepers; while the meaning of salvation is seen most dramatically in Jesus' touching the sick, including lepers and the unclean (Mt. 8:1–4; Mk. 5:25–41; Lk. 18:15).

To be human thus means being embodied, material creatures, yet made for life in more than material ways. Our smelling, tasting, touching, seeing, hearing and speaking are all often used as illustrations of this wider meaning of life, especially to reflect on our relationship with God. This does not diminish the wonder or significance of these senses in their own right, or the consequences for human life of their absence through physical disability, or their corruption through sin. It is good to be made in the image of God as embodied persons; but what it means to be truly whole we know only in part, even though we look for it with hope, through faith, in love. When Christ returns, we shall know in fullness what it means to be made in the image of God, and we shall know as we are known, not only as individuals but as part of a re-created humanity, delighting in the new heavens and new earth.

CONCLUSION

THIS SPORTING
LIFE

Being human involves a bewildering array of perspectives. Many
have been addressed in this book, but many remain untouched.
As an example, consider the significance of the cinema (or
movies, flicks, films or pictures, depending on your English-
language sub-culture). Though taken for granted in every part
of the world today, it is just a century old, and has become part
of everyday life only in the past fifty years. The influence of film-
making on the way we understand sight and sound, and its
impact on culture, are immense. Films such as *Gone with the
Wind*, *Mrs Miniver* and *Smiley* shaped a whole generation's idea
of what it meant to be a patriotic American, English or
Australian citizen, balanced by others critical of those perspectives: *Citizen Kane*, *Don's Party* and *Gallipoli* for example. Whole
categories of film now exist, each with strong followings, such as
science fiction, documentaries, horror, crime drama, and the
pornography industry. In part films reflect back to us what we
want to see, in part they shape our self-image: consider the effect

on modern cultures of *Star Wars, Raise the Red Lantern, They Shoot Horses, Don't They?* and *La Dolce Vita.*

A whole tradition of non-literary reflection has thus emerged in the past hundred years, for which there is little precedent. Film has enormous propaganda power, as totalitarian regimes such as Nazi Germany and Maoist China know only too well, and democratic governments keep a sharp eye on the mass media. The Australian film industry has flourished since 1972, for example, encouraged by tax breaks from successive democratic governments keen to promote a sense of independent national identity. Visual media have taken on even greater significance as television has brought the illusion of reality which is the very stuff of film media into millions of homes, while videos embody the essence of youth culture. Space forbids further consideration; I have made these comments in order to emphasize how much more reflection is possible about the wonder of human life than is written here.

There is one aspect of modern life about which it would be irresponsible not to write, however: sport. It has been touched on briefly in this book, but its enormous influence on human self-understanding in recent decades cannot be underestimated. The sport phenomenon, which has emerged in the last century, illustrates many of the interacting issues discussed in this book. At the personal level it displays modern fascination with the body, material life, and health, and its heroes exercise profound influence on young people. At the corporate level sport can function as the focus for community identity – witness the immense passion poured out over football teams – or national pride. The Olympic movement reveals both aspects; its ideals as expressed in the athletes' oath are about individual ideals, but its actual support and following derive from battles for national prominence. Sport also reveals aspects of gender difference; there are separate sports for women and men, and very different male and female subcultures exist in sports such as tennis and golf, in which men and women alike are involved. In association with mass media, sport plays a major function in shaping popular culture in many industrialized societies. There are more hours of sports on Australian television than any other programme type, and a typical news bulletin contains ten minutes' local news, five

229

minutes' overseas news, five minutes' weather – and at least five minutes' sports coverage.

With this in mind, the use of sport in the New Testament to speak of aspects of Christian life is striking. That sport is used at all in this way is surprising, since sport was not a feature of Jewish life, and was closely associated with Hellenism's glorification of the body, while Roman games were often barbaric and cruel. Despite this, it is a part of life which was seen as useful to illustrate Christian truths. Several aspects of these arise from the way in which sport is used. First, the assumption is made that every Christian takes part; although leaders are especially urged on (*cf.* 1 Tim. 6:11–12), no élitism is present in these texts. Sport as we know it is largely an activity for those who are young, in full health, and with leisure time available, the rest being mere spectators. In Christ everyone is a participant, and the only spectators are the 'great. . . crowd of witnesses' (Heb. 12:1) who have finished their course. Secondly, sport as we know it sees injuries as tragedies, often ending someone's career. In Christ injury, hurt and struggle are par for the course, since we follow a pioneer who 'endured the cross, disregarding its shame' (Heb. 12:2); disability is the norm for those who take part in the sport of Christ the crucified king. Thirdly, in sport it is today's victories that count; yesterday's winners are quickly forgotten. In Christ, the orientation is very much to the future; it is the prize to be received (1 Cor. 9:24) and the goal to be reached (Phil. 3:12) that concern Paul. Hebrews expresses this most clearly, in urging readers to 'run with perseverance the race that is set before us, looking to Jesus the pioneer and perfecter of our faith' (Heb. 12:1–2).

In all of this the sense that we are to look to what God is making us to be, rather than what we were or are, comes through clearly. Paul sums all of this up in his unforgettable words:

> I want to know Christ and the power of his resurrection and the sharing of his sufferings by becoming like him in his death, if somehow I may attain the resurrection from the dead.
>
> Not that I have already obtained this or have already reached the goal; but I press on to make it my own,

because Christ Jesus has made me his own. . . . this one thing I do: forgetting what lies behind and straining forward to what lies ahead, I press on towards the goal for the prize of the heavenly call of God in Christ Jesus (Phil. 3:10–14).

When we receive that prize, and know as we have been known (*cf.* 1 Cor. 13:12), our present double vision will come into full focus, in the love of Christ. Then we will know truly what it means to be human.

APPENDIX 1

THE TRANSMISSION
OF SIN

Sin is a desperately critical aspect of human life as we experience it. Major aspects of its place in Christian thought, including the concept of original sin, have been discussed in chapters 2 and 3. The basic concept of original sin is not difficult to grasp, namely that we sin because there is a fundamental flaw at the centre of our being, the 'origin' of sin. Sins are the fruit of sin, not discrete acts of evil independent of each other. Given the amount of suffering, pain, injustice and moral evil present in the world as we know it, the fact of each human's having a radical flaw, a corrupted 'root' at the core of his or her being, is not difficult to defend.

It is one thing to assert that human life as we know it – though not as God made it or intends it to be – is sinful in every respect. It is quite another to explain how it is that such a tragic state *comes about.* Note the present tense in this sentence; mainstream Christian faith ascribes the beginning of sin to the disobedience of human beings described in Genesis 3. However puzzling, inexplicable and stupid may be the riddle of beings made in the image of God rejecting their Maker, Christian theology can offer an answer to the question how this tragic state *came* about.[1] The question as to how this beginning of sins is passed on to the race as a whole is given a far less ready response. In short, the *reality* of sin and sins is not difficult either to grasp or to defend, but how sin and its origin are *transmitted* is an extremely complicated matter.

The following three propositions have been formulated to try to clarify the issues involved. Each one is held as true in Christian thought, and has been repeatedly discussed in this book. The problem is how to hold all three as true at the same time. A number of theories have been developed in order to do this, each of which has been significant at differing times in the history of the Christian tradition. The purpose of this appendix is to review these, in the light of the Scriptures, so that Christian life today may be lived with appropriate awareness of both the seriousness of sin and the wonder of our salvation from its power and consequences.

1. All humans are created in the image and likeness of God, to be like Christ.

2. All humans are affected by sin, which distorts their being at its root; the effects of sin are seen in every aspect of human life, in sins.

3. All humans are responsible for their actions, and liable for their consequences.

To deny the first statement undermines what it means to be human; as created, we are essentially 'very good'. Some Christians so emphasize the truth of the second statement that the first is obscured, forgotten or denied, while others have held too optimistic a view of humanity as we know it. The third statement is rarely denied, but frequently overemphasized, especially when the idea of free will is discussed without reference to the reality of sin; sin does not remove our will, but renders it incapable of doing the will of God. As can readily be seen, it is no easy matter to hold all three statements together. The core of the problem is how humanity as God intends it relates to humanity as we know it; the way in which the corruption of sin is transmitted has been the issue around which the debate has formed and re-formed.

234

The debates about the transmission of sin are complex. In particular, they affect the way in which the full humanity of Christ is understood. Though without sin, and so more truly human than any other, he took sin upon himself for the sake of those held captive to its power. The web of sin extends to every aspect of human life, and any who enter this world as we know it cannot avoid its entanglement. Jesus was not exempt from this, but lived without being caught in its net until his 'hour' came, when he freely gave himself up to be 'made . . . sin', according to the will of God (*cf.* Jn. 12:23–33; 2 Cor. 5:19–21). In so turning the other cheek to sin, taking on himself all its consequences, he absorbed all its poison and set humankind free from its power. In Jesus we see a truly and fully free will, continuing to pursue the will of God even when that meant coming under the curse of sin.

How then are these statements to be held together? At least eight theories have been formulated;[2] the two extremes are noted first.

1. *Pelagianism* overemphasizes the third statement, holding that if we have been given a command by God, we must be able to obey it. This denies the second statement entirely, so that sins are regarded as distinct acts, rather than as the fruits of sin. There is no origin of sin at all, and so nothing is transmitted.

2. The other extreme, going back to Augustine, is *realism*: each and every human being sinned in Adam, and this original sin is transmitted physically through conception and birth. Not only original sin is passed on, but also 'original guilt', the consequences of that sin, so that humanity is seen as a 'lump of perdition'. This certainly takes the seriousness of sin seriously, but renders the third statement almost meaningless. In practice it can also obscure the first statement, and has been responsible for much harm in Christian attitudes to sexuality.

In between these wholly opposed stands are several other theories. Three were formulated in the debates following that between Augustine and the Pelagians, but continue to have influence today.

3. The *deprivation* theory was formed by medieval scholastics who stressed the significance of the will, arguing that we are at least capable of preparing to turn to God. Sin is seen as depriving us of an original righteousness which Adam knew,

rather than depraving our being and rendering it incapable of turning to God. It is not so much that an origin of sin is transmitted, but that a positive goodness fails to be passed on, so leaving us open to the influence of evil. The problem here is that while the reality of sin is acknowledged, its effects are minimalized.

4. A slightly stronger view is called *semi-Pelagianism*: sin is a disease rather than a lack. We are sick and need healing, and without it we will die. Sin is passed on like a disease – which leaves us with problems similar to those of realism when it comes to the first statement.

5. The *nature-person* theory takes up both these ideas, yet strengthens the approach to the seriousness of sin. We not only fail to receive an original goodness, and are diseased, but human nature as a whole is corrupted. Each human being thus receives a corrupted nature, but is not thereby a sinful person until he or she commits actual sin. The pastoral usefulness of such a view is evident, and it can be seen behind Article IX of the Thirty-nine Articles. The distinction between nature and person is used classically in Christology as well as in terms of sin, which increases the attractiveness of this view, though the distinction has become difficult to defend in modern times.

6. Close to the last view, but expressed in quite different terms, is the perspective of *the eastern churches*.[3] There has been little substantial debate of these matters in the eastern Christian tradition, so that it is difficult to be precise. The main ideas of the three statements listed above are held, but related through death rather than sin. Adam fell from a state of 'undeveloped simplicity' rather than from a great height, and so 'is not to be judged too harshly for his error'. The main consequence of this act was the entry of death and corruption into the world: our 'inheritance is of death rather than of sinfulness or guilt'.

The Reformation period saw vigorous debates in these areas, initially over the capacity of the will to turn to God.[4] In terms of the work of Christ, justification came to be understood as 'imputation' rather than 'impartation'; we are in the right with God because of an external change in our status before God, rather than by an internal renovation. As Luther put, Christ is 'for us' (*pro nobis*) before being 'in us' (*in nobis*). Just as the concepts of nature and person had been used in classical Christology and anthropology, so the concept of imputation now came to be applied in the area of sin. In order to defend the priority of grace over and against Rome, the first generation of Reformers tended towards the realist view, though it came increasingly to be seen as problematic. As the Reformation consolidated, fierce debates over the extent of election and the nature of sin broke out in the Protestant churches. Some continued to hold to one of the scholastic views noted above, especially the last; but in Reformed theology two major views emerged.

7. The theory known as *mediate imputation* accepts the realist premise that we all sinned in Adam, but questions the notion that this sin is transmitted directly to us. With the scholastics, the fallen position of the race as a whole is acknowledged, though sin is not imparted so much as imputed to each member of the race. This last expression is used to avoid the implication that each human is sinful in essence; Adam's sin is imputed to each person because of his or her participation in fallen humanity, not directly so much as mediated. Corresponding to this, the righteousness of Christ is imputed to each person in Christ, mediated through the effectual preaching of the gospel, and sealed in baptism.

8. The other Reformed theory is known as *immediate imputation* or *federalism*: the sin of Adam is imputed to the race immediately, not mediated individually. Adam is thus our representative 'federal head', in whom we all sinned, and whose sin is passed on to all. This view comes close to the realist view, but is more subtle. There is some debate about whether the parallel between the imputation of Adam's sin and the imputation of Christ's righteousness can appropriately be made, partly because in this schema it would seem to imply universalism, and partly out of concern to differentiate the role of the will in sin and in grace.[5]

Having listed these theories, there is a very real danger that sin can come to be viewed as a mere theory about which Christians disagree. That idea would itself demonstrate the deceptive character of the effects of sin. It must be admitted that some of the debates were unseemly, and conducted with little sensitivity to the theological, anthropological and cultural presuppositions which cloud understanding, especially the different approaches to sin of women and men (see chapters 8 and 9 above).

Whatever theory of the transmission of sin and its origin we hold, the reality is that everyone who reads this book is a sinner. Each of us needs constantly to turn to Christ, admit our need for forgiveness and healing, renounce sin and evil, and so live gladly the life which the Holy Spirit brings to birth in us. Only in that way can the old humanity be killed off, and the fruits of the Spirit flourish (*cf.* Col. 3:1–17). Our prime concern is not with the transmission of sin, but the anticipation of our restored nature as we participate in the new humanity in Christ. In the terms of the eighth view above, we are not to look to Adam, but to cling to Christ as our 'head',[6] both now and in the ages to come.

APPENDIX 2

INCLUSIVE LANGUAGE
AND BEING HUMAN

Inclusive language is a significant issue in relation to what it means to be human today, at least in English-speaking societies. Where the full humanity of all people is taken with renewed seriousness, inclusive language is a subject which needs some attention. It is difficult to define precisely, but this careful formulation is used here: 'Inclusive language is language that respects and includes every person regardless of gender, race, age, physical ability, nationality, family, class or status.'[1] This definition emphasizes that inclusive language is not in the first place a theory, or an issue, or a problem, but a way of enabling people to communicate with one another with as few barriers as possible.

Inclusion and exclusion

Traditionally, the English language has used male terminology generically. It was commonly understood until recently that male terminology included the female. For many today masculine language has become exclusive, because the accepted conventions have changed and are changing. Continuing to use male terminology in an inclusive sense can therefore appear to exclude women from participating, and from being recognized and addressed, in church and life. Since in Christ 'there is no longer male and female' (Gal. 3:28), these exclusions are to be rejected by Christians. Though grounded in the use of gendered language, many other types of language can fail to include people, often unconsciously on the part of the speaker or writer concerned. For example, jargon excludes many from understanding a subject, and some colour references can leave racist impressions: 'the darkness of sin' hardly affirms that 'black is beautiful'. Family terms can be used in such a way as to exclude single people, while age-based language can needlessly ignore the old – or the young. More broadly, body language can encourage participation, or signal exclusiveness and rigidity; and which is which varies from culture to sub-culture. Seen in this way, it needs to be recognized that all language can function in an excluding manner. Yet we cannot avoid speaking. Inclusive language should be seen as one means by which mutual understanding and communication can take place, not as a new law of political correctness that ties our tongues.

Inclusive language and male experience

Often this subject is discussed as if it were only a women's issue. What's in it for men? Let me offer some perspectives, not as a final answer, but as a start at approaching a new issue. First, some may *feel* excluded by non-inclusive language, while others are not aware of the problem. Paul's words are apposite: 'If one member suffers, all suffer together with it; if one member is honoured, all rejoice together with it' (1 Cor. 12:26). Christian men ought therefore to feel the hurt of Christian women who feel excluded in church, and be willing to do something about it. It is not good enough merely to say, 'That's their problem'; whatever is another Christian's problem is to some extent my own. If the cause is right, it behoves all Christians to stand for it. The problem with causes is that they are often furthered by those who stand most to gain from them. In this case, the stereotype of 'angry women putting themselves forward' is easily allowed to become an excuse to do nothing. Christian men have a duty to campaign with all women affected by excluding language, while avoiding the paternalism which assumes that women are too weak to do anything for themselves.

Secondly, most people in my experience find it very difficult to express what it means to be a male human being (see chapter 9 above). It seems far easier to pin down what is distinctive about being a woman. By constantly using 'man' and 'men' to refer to both males and humans, what is distinctive about being male gets mixed up with what it means to be human.[2] When we say 'women', we know we are speaking of one distinctive type of human, but men lack a distinctive vocabulary by which to express male identity. By refusing to use male language generically, and by using male language only when men are referred to, a way of thinking and speaking about being male, as distinct from language about being human generally, may gradually emerge. This confusion may be part of the reason fewer men than women generally attend church regularly (at least in English-speaking societies). For women, despite the use of exclusive language, the experience of church may mean being more opened to a fuller humanity. For men it may appear as closing such opportunities, because it questions the identity of 'man' = 'male'. Women have the opportunity to start helping men discover their own identity, based on women's long awareness of the distinctiveness in being both human and female.

Language that includes

Having once become aware of the issues of language which excludes, it is difficult not to notice instances of its occurrence. The depth to which gender influences language is profound, so that there is no neat, simple solution. In order to employ language which includes, a range of strategies is needed, attuned to the situations addressed and the people involved. As a first step, 'invisible mending' can be done by minor word changes or by omissions which few would notice. For example, omitting 'men', or replacing it with 'one' or 'person', can often resolve the matter. Perhaps the best-known example is the omission of 'men' from the phrase 'for us men and for our salvation' in the Nicene Creed.[3] The strategy of omission can be helpful, and can avoid excluding women; but it may also leave them 'invisible', and so not necessarily seen or felt to be included.

Another aspect concerns pronouns. Avoiding 'he' and 'him' used generically by employing plural pronouns is useful, but may lessen the personal and particular impact of the singular, and sometimes alters the sense. Thus changing 'I will raise him up' (Jn. 6:54, AV *etc.*) to 'I will raise them up' (NRSV) reduces a personal promise of Jesus to a general state. In quoting such a text in a sermon, the text could be repeated, saying, 'I will raise her up; I will raise him up', to preserve the sense of the original. If sung, 'him' or 'her' could be used in alternate verses, or the men present invited to sing 'her', while the women sing 'him'. Such a strategy makes both women and men visible, and can function as a form of mutual encouragement. Affirming the particularity of women and men can also be assisted by speaking of 'daughters and sons' rather than 'children' always, 'men and women' rather than 'people' always, and the like. It soon becomes clear that the changes needed can entail a complete rewriting of a text, and this may be especially difficult in a song, where rhyme, metre and copyright are involved. Modifications should not appear so contrived as to be jarring, or mean that participants focus more on themselves than on God, by being more sensitive about what is said than what is meant. Nor should the net result lead men to feel excluded, for example by the elimination of traditional language (such as carefully used military metaphors) with which many men have traditionally identified. All these outcomes would themselves be non-including.

A key issue for inclusive language is the translation of the Scriptures. A number of recent versions take responsible account of inclusive-language concerns, of which the New Revised Standard Version (NRSV) is the best known, and it has been used for this book. It retains masculine pronouns and imagery for God, while using gender-inclusive terms for human beings. In most cases a more faithful rendition of the original languages results, since Hebrew and Greek are less gender-specific than English. Sometimes further changes have been made, including the limited use of plural pronouns, and terms such as 'others', 'one', 'people' where 'men' or 'man' was used formerly (*cf.* Ps. 1:1; Mt. 5:16; Gal. 6:10).[4] Another example of such changes is the translation of the Greek *adelphoi* as 'brothers and sisters' when it is clear that the intended audience included both men and women (*cf.* 2 Thes. 1:3), but not when only men are present (*cf.* Acts 22:1; 1 Cor. 10:1 with 9:5). These considerations should encourage preachers to work continually with the Scriptures in Greek and Hebrew: original-language work is of the highest relevance in such a key issue as language.

Perhaps the most difficult area is song. Ideas, images and feelings are inseparably mixed when we sing familiar words. Respecting the intention of the original will involve asking some people to tolerate language that excludes for some time to come, while existing hymnbooks continue in use. Many living authors have already revised their own work, and it is far better to use this than to attempt amateurish alterations, especially if made on the run. There are newer books in which the integrity of a text is respected while exclusive language is avoided (*Sing Alleluia* being one notable example), and many hymnwriters are producing high-quality work in non-excluding language.[5] The Psalter is a special case, since it is the songbook of the Scriptures. At many points its language employs gender-exclusive terms which are not easily altered; how is Psalm 8:5–7 to be rendered, for example, especially given its New Testament citation to refer to Christ (Heb. 2:5–9)? The issues are not simple.

Language and God

The most substantial theological area regarding inclusive language concerns the way we speak of God.[6] The Scriptures undoubtedly use masculine imagery of God, and to be faithful to their witness the church will have to continue to receive and use it. But there are also other images, and these should be explored further to widen our appreciation of the wonder of the divine nature, and to enable both women and men to think, speak and pray in ways which affirm God's ability to identify with their distinctive gender.[7] Language about God dares to speak of 'boundless riches of Christ' (Eph. 3:8), and to pray 'with sighs too deep for words' (Rom. 8:26). Embarrassment about some images may drive us to silence on occasion – but Christians cannot refrain from speaking about what they have come to know of God, or from praying. Too often we speak as if God and ourselves were on the same level, losing a sense of awe in the presence of divine majesty, mingled with childlike delight in the privilege of access to God, in whom 'we live and move and have our being'. Language about God is most effective when it evokes rather than prescribes, points rather than declares.

The term 'father' is a sensitive one in this respect, since each of us imports into the term her or his own experience of being fathered.[8] It is especially dear to Christians because of its familiarity through use in the Lord's Prayer, and in trinitarian language. It is discussed briefly here as an example of the type of rethinking which is taking place concerning gendered language for God.

'Father' used of God occurs comparatively rarely in the Hebrew Bible (ten times), but comes into frequent use on the lips of Jesus (at least 170 times). Here the particular nuances of the four gospels are worth considering.

1. *Matthew*, especially in the Sermon on the Mount, discloses God to be our 'Father in heaven'. We are cared for by one who sees, knows, rewards, feeds, forgives, and gives; to be the child of such a father means having a firm sense of security and love. This Father is no 'softie', however: the children of God are to be generous givers, sincere pray-ers, self-disciplined, single-minded and non-judgmental (Mt. 6:3, 6, 17–21, 24; 7:1).

2. In contrast, *Mark* only once speaks of 'your Father in heaven' (Mk. 11:26), and only once records Jesus as calling on God as Father (using the affectionate term *Abba*), in the garden of Gethsemane, the most stressful moment in Jesus' ministry (Mk. 14:36). Mark thus emphasizes that Jesus' obedience to his Father was a matter of love, not blind submission. Further, it is only on the cross that Jesus calls on God in prayer *without* saying 'father': 'My God, my God, why have you forsaken me?' (Mk. 15:34). Jesus' last hours were thus marked by intense awareness of both the closeness *and* the 'absence' of his Father. There is in Mark a reticence about Jesus' intimacy with God.

3. *Luke* is almost as reticent, yet emphasizes Jesus' experience of God as his Father at three critical moments: first as a boy in the temple, 'about my Father's interests' (Lk. 2:48–49, mg.), and

secondly in the middle of his ministry following the return of the Seventy (Lk. 10:21–22). Thirdly, Jesus prays for those who crucified him, 'Father, forgive them' (Lk. 23:34), and dies praying, 'Father, into your hands I commend my spirit' (Lk. 23:46). Jesus' grim experience of God-forsakenness was bracketed by these two prayers, one of care for others, one of trust in God's fatherly care for him. And it is Luke alone who records the parable of the waiting father, linking it with the pictures of God as the seeking shepherd and searching woman (Lk. 15).

4. *John* says nothing of the fatherly character of God, as does Matthew; nor does he record Jesus' *Abba* prayer, as does Mark. Neither are Jesus' 'Father' prayers on the cross noted (Luke's distinctive contribution). Rather, John defines the relationship between Jesus and God as that of Son to Father. The enfleshed Word is 'the Father's only Son' (Jn. 1:14); the Father 'loves', 'honours', 'sends', 'witnesses to', 'seals' and 'glorifies' the Son. John identifies Jesus as the Son of God – and God as the Father of Jesus: chapters 5, 6, 8, 10, 12, 14, 15, 16 and 17 are saturated with this motif.

Each gospel thus has its own distinctive emphasis. The variety of approaches to this key metaphor is striking, as is their undermining of any patriarchal use of the image. 'Father' is never used of God in an abstract way, however. The Scriptures do not teach that 'God *is* Father': no metaphor can be equated with God. Rather, they reveal that we have come to know, through the Spirit, 'God our Father and the Lord Jesus Christ' as Paul often puts it (*e.g.* Rom. 1:7). 'Father' is a *relational* term, as the church came to learn in the Arian controversy of the fourth century. This nuanced sense entered into the language of trinitarian theology; the technical credal terms ('consubstantial' or 'one in Being', 'uncreate' and 'proceeding') transcend the gendered language of 'father' and 'son'. Moreover, 'begotten' carries both female ('bring to birth') and male ('sire') senses, while 'eternally begotten' removes any limits implied in these gendered references.

The theological issues raised here lead to an exciting, if challenging, rethinking of the faith; what it means to be human interacts with how we think and speak of God.[9] There is a richness in the language of the Scriptures and Christian tradition which invites deeper exploration, undertaken in trust that the God who has spoken in Christ is not struck dumb by contemporary problems in language, and will continue to grant us the Spirit of Christ to lead us into fuller truth according to the Scriptures. All of this suggests that we are on a journey, or pilgrimage, with regard to language. As the people of God, we continue to receive the gospel of Christ, the testimony of the Scriptures, and the Christian tradition, but do so with an orientation to the future as well as to the past, as those who are on 'the Way' (the first name for Christians, Acts 9:2). We are often puzzled or grieved by our inability to speak as we might, yet we believe in the Holy Spirit, who translates our unutterable groanings and turns them into prayer fit for Christ to offer. We know that language can easily offend, and need to acknowledge the continual need for repentance and sensitivity in this area.[10] Yet we also know that we cannot but help speak of what we have heard, and that our common life of corporate listening, proclamation, prayer, and song cannot be put aside.

Notes

Introduction

[1] Philip Edgcumbe Hughes, *The True Image* (IVP, 1989) offers a recent exposition of 'the origin and destiny of man in Christ' from a thoroughly Christ-centred perspective. An Anglican theologian, grounded in and expert on the English Reformation, Hughes worked for the latter part of his life as a seminary professor in the USA.

[2] The extent to which accessible writing by Christians about being human is dominated by European-oriented male academics will soon become apparent – and I include myself on the list.

[3] Article 'Man', *Baker's Dictionary of Theology* (Baker, 1973), p. 339. Carl Henry is a leading American evangelical theologian, concerned to commend biblical faith in the public and academic arenas, a task exercised especially through his work as the first editor of *Christianity Today*.

[4] For further exposition of these next paragraphs, see C. H. Sherlock, *God on the Inside: Trinitarian Spirituality* (Acorn, 1991), especially chapters 1, 2, 4 and 8.

[5] A vigorous Australian dialogue on the significance of context for reflection on being human is *A Theology of the Human Person*, ed. Margaret

Rodgers and Maxwell Thomas (Collins Dove, 1992), especially pp. 21–34, 61–66, 79–81. This volume is a responsive collection of papers from the Doctrine Commission of the Anglican Church of Australia, written by women and men, ordained and lay Christians, including a range of theological perspectives.

Karl Barth, in his survey of the history of Christian understandings of humankind 'made in the image of God', *Church Dogmatics*, III/1 (T. and T. Clark, 1958), pp. 192–206, shows 'how each interpreter has given content to the concept solely from the anthropology and theology of his own age', as D. J. A. Clines, 'The Image of God in Man', *Tyndale Bulletin* 19 (1968), p. 54, summarizes it. Barth, the outstanding Reformed theologian of this century, taught in Germany, and then Switzerland during and after the Nazi period. Clines, an Australian of Christian Brethren background, has pioneered new approaches to Old Testament study at Sheffield, England.

[6] For a clear account of the shifts in thought described below, see Alister McGrath, *Christian Theology: An Introduction* (Blackwell, 1994), especially pp. 76–105. McGrath is a priest of the Church of England who teaches at Oxford; a prolific writer, he is an acute interpreter of human life.

[7] Kelsey goes so far as to say that in the 'turn to the self' of the modern period, 'the very idea of human nature became unintelligible', because a subject cannot be defined in terms of itself: David Kelsey, 'Human Being', in *Christian Theology: An Introduction to its Traditions and its Tasks*, ed. P. Hodgson and R. King (SPCK, 1982), p. 155. Kelsey teaches theology at Yale Divinity School, with particular interest in the way in which men and women actually use the Scriptures.

[8] The Ironbridge historical complex in Shropshire, England, demonstrates this: a Quaker burial ground lies close by the first smelter site, in close proximity to some of the first mass-production and co-operative housing facilities.

[9] J. Moltmann, *Man* (SPCK, 1971), chapters 2 and 3, and *God in Creation* (SCM, 1985), have helped me to understand the importance of these movements and their contemporary implications in the light of the Scriptures. Moltmann was raised in Germany during the Nazi period, and was a prisoner of war in England. A prominent theologian in Germany, he works in close partnership with his wife, with particular concern to relate mainstream Protestant theology to the issues of the late twentieth century.

[10] H. D. McDonald, *The Christian View of Man* (Marshall, Morgan and Scott, 1981), though completed as recently as 1980, makes only one reference to women as far as I can tell (p. 36), and none at all to feminism. Yet McDonald, an English theological teacher who has also worked in the United States, is consistent in discussing 'man' generically, and helpfully condenses a wide range of Christian perspectives on being human.

[11] For example, George Carey, *I Believe in Man* (Hodder and Stoughton,

1977). Carey is now the Anglican Archbishop of Canterbury, with a background in seminary teaching and parish ministry in the Church of England.

[12] Dorothy L. Sayers, *Are Women Human?* (1931; Eerdmans, 1971). Sayers, described as 'such a strange lady' by one biographer, was an English theological writer and novelist, closely associated with both the Oxford of C. S. Lewis and the practical world of advertising and journalism. She held together Christian orthodoxy, feminist sympathies and an eccentric lifestyle.

Chapter 1: The image of God in ancient Israel

[1] Clines discusses in detail the significance of the preposition here: does 'like', 'in', or 'as' the image best represent the Hebrew text? Clines argues effectively against 'like'. While he prefers 'as' to 'in' (the rendering adopted here), the sense of his conclusion, 'that man does not have the image of God, nor is he made in the image of God, but is himself the image of God' (p. 80) is followed in this and the following chapter.

[2] The translation of Gn. 1:26–28 and 5:1–2 is from the NRSV, reading the marginal version in the <pointed> brackets since this represents the actual Hebrew text. In particular, it should be noted that humanity is referred to using both singular and plural pronouns in 1:27.

[3] Clines' article summarizes work done up until the mid-60s; it has been updated by Gerald Bray, 'The Significance of God's Image in Man', *Tyndale Bulletin* 42.2 (1991), pp. 195–225. Bray is a Canadian conservative evangelical Anglican theologian who teaches at Beeson Divinity School, Birmingham, Alabama.

[4] Note also Dt. 4:15–18, and particularly the emphatic indirectness in the vision of God in Ezk. 1.

[5] Jews who came under Hellenist influence rejected this prohibition some time in the second or third century after Christ, as can be seen in the synagogues at Dura-Europos or Tiberias: see H. Shankel, *Judaism in Stone* (Harper and Row, 1979), chapter 10. This realization is the fruit of modern archaeology, however; the Jewish tradition generally has continued its staunch anti-images stance.

[6] Bray, pp. 196–197, notes that 'there is no obvious link between Genesis 1:26 and Exodus 20:4', and concludes 'that there is no exegetical evidence which compels us to believe that the Genesis passages were composed as part of a campaign against the worship of idols', though there is a clear theological connection between the two ideas (*cf.* Barth, *Church Dogmatics* III/1, pp. 200–203). Protestants commonly accuse Roman Catholics and Orthodox of idolatry, unaware of the 'iconoclastic' dispute of the ninth century, in which the key distinction was made between 'worship' (only of

God) and 'veneration' (for what points to God). All Christian traditions take the risk of using symbolic forms for divine action, though some endeavour is made in Protestantism to minimize them. All traditions are also aware of the possibility of the misuse of such symbols, especially in popular religion, though not all seek to address their abuses adequately.

[7] Hughes, p. 22. He cites Tyndale as preaching in the same vein.

[8] See Augustine of Hippo, *On the Trinity* (available in the Library of Post-Nicene Fathers), especially chapters 8–14, where the 'journey' of the Christian into the life of God is correlated with deepening analogies of ways of knowing the triune God.

[9] This is the AV translation, used here because it has become proverbial. Bray writes that 'we cannot use [this text] as part of our argument for developing a doctrine of the image of God in man' (p. 210), but fails to consider its significant negative force. Since without denial there is no clear assertion, a significant amount of 'negative' exegesis is often employed throughout the present book, partly to clear ground, and partly to open up imaginative approaches regarding the range of options within that ground.

[10] I have generally included footnotes only to theological expositions, especially those of Barth, Berkouwer, Westermann, Hughes and Moltmann, and the survey articles by Clines and Bray.

[11] Clines, pp. 62–69, provides a thorough survey of possibilities, updated by Bray, pp. 197–200.

[12] See Gerhard von Rad, *Genesis* (SCM, 1956), p. 57. Clines suggests that God may be addressing the Spirit here.

[13] *Cf.* Gn. 3:22: 'See, the man [$h\bar{a}'\bar{a}d\bar{a}m$] has become like one of us, knowing good and evil' (NRSV), though the Hebrew would be better rendered 'humanity has become like one of us'.

[14] K. Barth, *Church Dogmatics* III/2 (T. & T. Clark, 1960), pp. 184–196; P. K. Jewett, *Man as Male and Female* (Eerdmans, 1975), pp. 33–43; Moltmann, *God in Creation*, pp. 222–224. These exegetical insights owe a great deal to Barth's lifelong assistant, Charlotte von Kirschbaum, who was more open than Barth to feminist perspectives: Renate Kobler, *In the Shadow of Karl Barth* (Westminster/John Knox, 1987). Jewett taught for many years at Fuller Seminary, an evangelical seminary in California, and was an evangelical theologian concerned to consider the challenge and opportunities presented by feminist thought.

[15] See further Sherlock, *God on the Inside*, pp. 18–22.

[16] It is interesting to note that $h\bar{a}'\bar{a}d\bar{a}m$ is never used in the plural, indicating its corporate nature. The words "$n\hat{o}\check{s}$ and '$i\check{s}$ (feminine '$i\check{s}\check{s}\hat{a}$, and with plural form '$^a n a\check{s}\hat{i}m$) refer to a male individual, the former often carrying military connotations, though they are also used in the generic sense of 'a person' occasionally.

[17] The term 'person', with its echoing of the trinitarian 'Person', and its

relational emphasis, is preferred to 'individual', since the latter carries today a strong sense of autonomous independence. Though language is not the end of a matter, it is highly significant, especially at a point such as this. Its theological echoes can be sensed in the claim that human beings are made to live as a community of persons, not as a collective of individuals.

[18] *Church Dogmatics* III/1, pp. 195–196.

[19] Ray S. Anderson, *On Being Human: Essays in Theological Anthropology* (Eerdmans, 1982), pp. 106–107, usefully distinguishes gender (the conscious awareness of our differentiation as male and female) from sexuality (the expression of gender in sexual union) as 'meeting' and 'mating'. Anderson teaches theology at Fuller Seminary, California.

[20] Hughes, pp. 18–21; contrast Moltmann, *God in Creation*, p. 222, who notes that the sexual relationship is not tied to fertility in Genesis 1, since male and female humankind are commanded to 'be fruitful and multiply', which would otherwise be unnecessary.

[21] Von Rad, p. 58. He goes on to argue, citing Brunner, that 'the idea of man . . . finds its full meaning not in the male alone but in man and woman', an observation of 'lapidary simplicity' with which 'a vast world of myth and Gnostic speculation, of cynicism and asceticism, of the deification of sexuality and fear of sex completely disappears'.

[22] Claus Westermann, *Creation* (Fortress, 1974), pp. 17–28. Westermann is a German Old Testament scholar whose work has been closely associated with the University of Heidelberg.

[23] This analysis raises the question as to whether 'an argument can be made for homosexual orientation as a possibility fully equivalent to heterosexual orientation in terms of human personhood as created in the image of God' (Anderson, p. 128, who qualifies this in relation to pastoral counsel on p. 203). A full discussion of the issues involved here lies beyond the scope of this book; an Australian Christian contribution is David M. Clarke, 'The Development of Sexual Orientation and Identity', *Zadok Papers* S64 (1993).

[24] Clines summarizes data on image concepts from the ancient Near East, in which royal metaphors are prominent: the image of an Assyrian king was a statue which 'represents the king's present occupation of occupied land. To revile the royal image is as treasonable an act as to revile the king himself' (p. 83); see also Westermann, pp. 58–60. The notion of dominion is thus etymologically cognate with the image concept, and makes further sense of the death sanction against taking human life in Gn. 9:6: to take life is to act against God in whose image human beings are made.

[25] Westermann, p. 49.

[26] F. Schaeffer, *Pollution and the Death of Man* (IVP, 1973), prints White's essay in an appendix. See also Douglas J. Hall, *Imaging God: Dominion as*

Stewardship (Eerdmans/NCCA, 1986), pp. 24–26. Hall is a Canadian theologian who has also taught in the USA. He has a particular interest in stewardship.

[27] Article 'Man', *Baker's Dictionary of Theology*, p. 341.

[28] Clines, p. 85.

[29] Westermann, p. 54.

[30] Bray concludes his article by stressing the significance of relationships for our understanding of 'image', but then, surprisingly, restricts the reference to our relationship to God, excluding what has been described here as its 'downward vertical' and 'horizontal' dimensions (pp. 222–223). The 'upward vertical' relationship is certainly primary, but does not exclude the others.

[31] The three diagrams of this chapter are my own work, but owe a great deal to the sustained theological discussion in chapters 3 and 4 of G. C. Berkouwer, *Man: The Image of God* (Eerdmans, 1962), and Moltmann, *God in Creation*, pp. 216–234. Berkouwer was Professor of Theology at the Free University, Amsterdam, for most of his career, and was a neo-Calvinist theologian who maintained a significant dialogue with Barth on the one hand and Rome on the other.

[32] Westermann, pp. 74–78, notes that humanity's having its beginnings in the earth is a common motif in the ancient world, but that the biblical account refuses to give any definition of the mystery of human life. As von Rad (p. 64) puts it, 'man is quite directly responsible to God . . . and man, therefore, cannot seek his direct relation to God in the world, in the realm of nature'.

[33] Note also Gn. 4:17–26, which indicates that such tasks continue to develop beyond the garden: Westermann, pp. 81–82.

[34] The New Testament texts 1 Cor. 11:8–9 and 1 Tim. 2:13–14 emphasize the personal aspects of being human in both creation and sin, perspectives considered in chapter 2. These aspects are not to be denied, but are facets of human existence not brought out in Gn. 1 – 2.

[35] The popular citation of *'ēzer k^enegdô* as 'helpmeet' has no basis in any translation, but is derived from the AV's 'help meet for him'. 'Helpmeet' is a term which has gathered to itself so many stereotyped ideas about female (and male) roles as now to be unusable. Mary Hayter, *The New Eve in Christ* (SPCK, 1987), pp. 101–102, discusses the phrase fully. Hayter is an ordained Church of England minister, with pastoral experience in university settings.

[36] This interpretation is not a description of the production of gendered beings from a being originally androgynous (including sexuality) or hermaphrodite (sexless). Gregory of Nyssa seems at one time to have taught that original humankind was created sexless, like the angels (*cf.* Mt. 22:30), but that gender was added later, in divine foreknowledge of the fall.

Some feminist biblical scholars seem to read the text androgynously, in a modern literalistic sense: see Hayter, pp. 96–98; Jewett, pp. 24–29; and, with a wide range of suggestions and evidence from the tradition, M. C. Horowitz, 'The Image of God in Man – Is Woman Included?', *Harvard Theological Review* 72 (1979), pp. 175–206.

The interpretation offered here is best seen as a further act of 'separation' in the divine work of creation, the characteristic divine activity in Gn. 1, where light is separated from darkness (Gn. 1:4), upper from lower waters (Gn. 1:7), and day from night (Gn. 1:14), while the seas are 'gathered' to leave dry land separate (Gn. 1:10). Jewish exegesis has seen 'separation' as typical of God's work in creation and re-creation, undergirding the demand for Israel to live a distinctive lifestyle as a separate people. The idea of the separation of humankind into male and female is thus suggested here as a corresponding explication of another category in which we are to live in relationship, as persons who are distinct yet more like each other than any other creatures. Westermann, pp. 42–43, regards these separations as the presentation of the basic categories of time and space in which we are to live; *cf.* Moltmann, *God in Creation*, chapters V–VI.

Paul's allusion to Gn. 2:18 in 1 Cor. 11:7–12 shows a clear awareness of the difference between the men and women in the world of his day, and their intended relationship in creation, now renewed in Christ. This text is considered further in chapter 2 below.

[37] While claiming that both men and women are fully human, and co-responsible to God, some argue that Gn. 2 does teach a subordination of woman to man: see the careful debate in S. Lees (ed.), *The Role of Women* (IVP, 1983); *cf.* Jewett, pp. 120–128. These issues are taken further in later chapters.

[38] ARCIC-2, *Life in Christ: Morals, Communion and the Church* (SPCK, 1993), section E, is a terse, careful discussion of these issues. Its twenty members are all Anglican or Roman Catholic theologians, from England, the Continent, North America, Brazil and Australia (including myself); some are married, others celibate.

[39] Sexuality is not the result of this sin, but part of our created nature, and so 'good' (*cf.* Gn. 2:24). The fruit-eating was responsible for the distortion of sex, not for its existence: see further Jewett, pp. 24–33; McDonald, p. 55.

[40] Anderson, pp. 98–101.

[41] The issue of the image after the beginning of sin is considered further in chapter 3, but it should be clear even at this stage that it is by no means abolished. Bray discusses this issue with some panache, concluding, against the pessimistic trend of traditional Protestant theology, that 'the New Testament, like the Old Testament before it, says nothing about a loss, corruption or defacing of the creation image of God in man' (p. 222).

[42] See further W. Zimmerli, *Man and his Hope in the Old Testament* (SCM,

1971), who points especially to the sabbath, the weekly reminder of and participation in God's holiness: 'the real Genesis lies not at the beginning but at the end of the human story' sums up his perspective well (p. 61).

⁴⁵ In Hebrew, adjectives are rare; they are commonly formed by using the phrase 'son of'. Here 'son of humanity' means one who is merely human, hence the translation 'mortal'. 'Son' in this sense carries few if any male connotations, and the intention of the phrase, parallel to *hā'ādām*, is clearly inclusive.

Chapter 2: The image of God renewed in Christ

¹ Bray, p. 210.

² See the discussion and bibliography in Hayter, pp. 119–127.

³ The Greek text of Gal. 3:27–28 uses different terms for the three pairs, as the translation implies; race and class are spoken of in terms of opposition ('or'), while gender is spoken of in terms of partnership ('and').

⁴ *Katakalyptesthai*, the word here translated 'unveiled', more likely refers to 'hair let down', the sign of a prostitute. Men are criticized for being *kata kephalēs echōn* (1 Cor. 11:4), a puzzling phrase literally meaning 'over/down from head', and for having 'long hair' (*koma*, 1 Cor. 11:14). A woman's *koma*, however, is her *doxa* (11:15)! The meaning of the precise details of this text will probably never be known in this age, but the distinction between the genders is clear, as in the fact that both men and women participate actively in prayer and prophecy (1 Cor. 11:4–5, 13).

⁵ Whatever its implications for the relations between men and women, it is critically important that 1 Cor. 11:3 should not be interpreted so as to subordinate Christ to God, apart from the incarnation. To do so undermines the deity of Christ, and so the possibility and reality of Christ's saving work: see C. H. Sherlock, 'On God and Gender', *Interchange* 22 (1977), pp. 93–104.

⁶ Bray argues that Paul understands *doxa* (glory) as varying before and after the fall, and between men and women, so that 'within creation, therefore, *doxa* bears witness to order and hierarchy, but not to inequality or enforced submission' (p. 221). However, in the light of its clearly generic use in Rom. 1:23 and 2 Cor. 3:18, this conclusion is difficult to sustain; whatever 1 Cor. 11:7 may mean, to hold that 'a woman is the *doxa* of a man' does not deny her bearing the *doxa* (as well as the *eikōn*) of God. What content remains in 'hierarchy' if 'inequality and enforced submission' are excluded?

Hughes' main discussion of 'glory' (pp. 42–44) does not refer to 1 Cor. 11:7. Earlier (pp. 18–23) he supports the general tenor of Bray's interpretation, but speaks only of 'order', especially in the home, emphasizing that the 'imaging' of God by the husband is to be sacrificial (*cf.* Eph. 5:22–31): '1 Corinthians 11, then, is not a blueprint for male tyranny' (p. 23). If an interpretation on the lines of 'order' is to be held, that of Hughes states it as well as can be.

[7] When Paul wishes to give an example of individual sin, following Gn. 3 he correctly names Eve (2 Cor. 11:3; 1 Tim. 2:14). To read Adam here as primarily an individual would therefore be unusual. To put it another way, 'Adam' here includes both Eve and Adam: see further the discussion of Rom. 5:12–21 below.

[8] Anderson, p. 135. He goes on to argue that in the Old Testament, 'dying' is seen as part of the 'sixth-day solidarity' we share with the animals, whereas 'death is a more theologically-oriented word which denotes the judgement which accompanies the creaturely experience of dying' (p. 136); but he cites only New Testament texts to show this. See also Hughes' impressive chapter 10, which nevertheless also utilizes only New Testament material on death.

[9] The reference to 'living' or 'psychic being', alluding to Gn. 2:7, reinforces the sense that humanity as a whole, represented in Adam, is the subject of discussion here. Yet Paul goes beyond the text of Genesis in affirming that in and through Christ humanity is open beyond 'psychic' to 'spiritual' life.

[10] Some theologians (Bavinck, for example) have suggested that being 'earthy' points to our being sinful, or at least having an 'inducement' to sin. Such ideas cannot stand, or the 'very good' of Gn. 1:31 is set aside, and a search is made for an 'origin' of sin outside human action, that would relieve us of the need to confess our guilt: see Berkouwer, *Man*, pp. 340–342, and Appendix 1 below.

[11] Bray points out that it is the resurrection which gives the titles 'heavenly' and 'last' Adam their meaning, but from this deduces that 'the double occurrence of *eikōn* in v. 49 has nothing to do with the image of God in man as described in Genesis' (p. 213). Such a sweeping exclusion is hard to justify, though the text does not directly refer to Genesis.

[12] Hughes, pp. 228–230, provides a discussion full of insight. He cites Eric Mascall, who wrote: 'The question is whether the re-creation of human nature, which is the *Leitmotiv* of the gospel, is to be located in the union of human nature with the Person of the Word in the womb of Mary the Virgin or in the death of the Lord Jesus upon the Cross. Is it, in short, Lady Day [March 25, nine months before Christmas] or Good Friday that is the supreme commemoration of our redemption?' Hughes then comments that Mascall 'wisely answers this question by affirming that the one cannot be held in isolation from the other'. See also the stimulating treatment in G. C. Berkouwer, *The Work of Christ* (Eerdmans, 1965), chapter 2.

[13] The contrast between Moses' veiling and his earlier requirement for the Corinthian women to have 'hair up', or their heads covered, is fascinating. Paul here certainly assumes that Christian women no longer have Moses' veil on their understanding, since they have the Spirit, and that they reflect more than merely the glory of a man, but also (along with their brothers in Christ) the glory of God in Christ.

[14] Though it does not use precisely the same terminology, *cf.* Heb. 1:3: '[The Son] is the reflection [*hapaugasma*] of God's glory [*doxa*] and the exact imprint [*charaktēr*] of God's very being [*hypostaseōs*], and he sustains all things by his powerful word.'

[15] On this metaphor in the Scriptures, see L. L. Morris, *The Apostolic Preaching of the Cross* (3rd edn, Tyndale Press, 1965), chapter VII. Leon Morris is an Australian Anglican scholar with a long-term commitment to relating the message of the New Testament to daily life in a way that is open to new insights and accessible. He also taught me Romans and New Testament theology.

[16] McDonald, p. 57, provides a succinct account of the issues involved. See also Hughes, pp. 128–135, and G. C. Berkouwer, *Sin* (Eerdmans, 1971), pp. 443–448 and 491–545, especially 512–518 on 'corporate' sin.

[17] J. L. Gonzales, *The History of Christian Thought* (Abingdon, 1970), vol. I, pp. 128–144.

[18] By 'evolutionism' is meant the worldview that sees the meaning and nature of all reality in evolutionary terms. 'Evolution' embraces a family of ideas all of which use the same term in common. Its scientific use properly refers to theories of organic development in biological species in response to external stimuli or changed life situations or both. It is questionable whether the term makes sense in geology or astronomy, since inorganic matter is unable to respond to stimuli, while its use in history or sociology is dangerous. It was not uncommon, for example, to say that European civilization 'evolved' to a peak of grandeur in the nineteenth century. But when Europeans migrate to Australia and discover Aborigines who have not 'evolved' to the standard of European civilization, they are likely to regard them as less than human. From there it is but a short step to hunting down aboriginal human beings like animals – which is exactly what took place.

We are not to think that sin and salvation are inevitable evolutionary developments (see Hughes, pp. 99–101, 131). The vision that God wills all to be saved – an entirely scriptural and Christian 'universalism' – is true. But to treat universal salvation as something which is automatically going to come about is to line up with evolutionist religious philosophy. The consequences of sin and injustice, the cost of Christ's work, and the genuine nature of the human will are sacrificed. We come to think that salvation is going to go on and on because that is the nature of the way things are. This forms a wholly inappropriate way of thinking about salvation. I am not arguing that 'heaven' must entail 'hell'. It may be that all are saved because of Christ's death. But we cannot say, on scriptural grounds, that all *must* be saved.

[19] *Cf.* Hughes, p. 129: 'To postulate the non-historicity of Adam and the nontemporal character of the fall may be convenient to a certain type of the modern mind, but historicity is one of the foundation stones of Christian doctrine. It is plainly central to the argument developed in Romans 5:12ff.'

[20] The term 'fall' does not occur in the Scriptures, and thus needs to be used with care: it is best regarded as a model, in the scientific sense of a way of describing a reality which resists exact definition.

[21] Berkouwer, *Sin*, chapters 1–4, gives a full discussion. The question of how 'original' sin is transmitted, an issue on which there is no direct scriptural data, is considered in Appendix 1, 'The Transmission of Sin' below.

[22] W. H. Griffith Thomas, *The Principles of Theology* (Longmans Green, 1930), pp. 155–175, offers a cogent exposition of both Article IX and Rom. 5. Thomas, of Welsh origin, was a priest of the Church of England with a particular interest in eschatology. He taught in England, Canada, and in the USA at Dallas Theological Seminary, and had considerable influence in Sydney, Australia.

[23] The debate had been brewing for some time: McDonald, pp. 49ff., argues that its beginnings lie in a difference of emphasis between Justin Martyr, placing great weight on the freedom of the human will to secure our responsibility for sin, and Ireneaus, who stressed the universality of sin. This matter is taken further in chapter 3.

[24] This 'realist' view of original sin also holds that newborn children are guilty sinners, implying a close association between the baptism of infants and birth: *cf.* 'Decree Concerning Original Sin', section 4, of the Council of Trent, citing Rom. 5:12 (see J. Leith, ed., *Creeds of the Churches*, Anchor, 1963, pp. 406–407), and the opening address in 'The Baptism of Infants' of the 1662 *Book of Common Prayer*. If this association becomes an equation, the meaning of baptism becomes distorted, for (at whatever age it is administered) it is not a 'birthright' but a 'new-birth rite'. Article IX, in the Augustinian tradition, says that our corrupted nature 'deserveth God's wrath and condemnation', but refuses to conclude that this condemnation follows automatically. In this way the corruption of human nature is acknowledged, but its fate is distinguished from that of any particular person: see Griffith Thomas, p. 167; McDonald, p. 62; and Appendix 1 below.

[25] Bray, p. 214.

[26] H. Ridderbos, *Paul: An Outline of his Theology* (Eerdmans, 1976), pp. 80–

THE DOCTRINE OF HUMANITY

86. Ridderbos was a Dutch New Testament theologian, active in the Reformed churches of the Netherlands.

[27] G. C. Berkouwer, *The Church* (Eerdmans, 1976), pp. 78–91, from whom the perspective on union and communion is also drawn, and Ridderbos, chapter 9.

[28] Cornelius Platinga Jr, an American Reformed theologian who teaches at Calvin Theological Seminary, outlines the shape of this conclusion in a moving essay, 'Images of God', in *Christian Faith and Practice in the Modern World*, ed. Mark A. Noll and David F. Wells (Eerdmans, 1988), pp. 51–67.

Chapter 3: The image of God in Christian thought

[1] McDonald, chapters 4 (from the New Testament to Augustine) and 6 (medieval and Reformation periods), provides a survey in chronological order, while Anderson, pp. 216–224, surveys the development of the *imago Dei*. A useful recent survey of classical issues is Donald K. McKim, *Theological Turning Points* (John Knox, 1988) chapter 4, while Kelsey, pp. 152–166, offers an incisive discussion of modern approaches. A standard historical account is given in Emil Brunner, *Man in Revolt* (Scribners, 1939), Appendix 1.

[2] C. Ryder Smith, *The Bible Doctrine of Man* (Epworth, 1951), pp. 29ff. Clines, pp. 56–58, notes that Old Testament scholars such as Gunkel, Humbert and Wheeler Robinson held similar views, in reaction to overly 'spiritual' views of human nature that tended to exclude the body from the image.

[3] McDonald, pp. 112–113; Freud is discussed further in chapter 8.

[4] Gonzales, vol. 1, chapter VI, offers a theological account of his work; the major extant work is *Adversus Haereses*, available in *Early Christian Fathers*, ed. C. C. Richardson (SCM, 1954).

[5] The technical term is *anakephalaiōsis*, 'recapitulation', from Eph. 1:10; *cf.* McDonald, p. 50.

[6] On this text, see D. Cairns, *The Image of God in Man* (Collins, 1973), pp. 50–51. Often relegated to the sidelines in western theology, it has grown in significance in recent decades as the motif of communion or participation (*koinōnia*) has become influential.

[7] *Adv. Haer.* III.19.1. 'Man' in the translation cited here carries the generic sense of 'humanity'.

[8] V. Lossky, *The Mystical Theology of the Eastern Church* (James Clarke, 1957), pp. 133–134, the conclusion of his exposition of 'Image and Likeness'.

[9] See further Sherlock, *God on the Inside*, pp. 12–17, 88–105, 212–218.

[10] This topic has an enormous literature; the work of G. L. Prestige, *God*

in Patristic Thought (SPCK, 1936), remains a classic, while Robert W. Jenson, *The Triune Identity* (Fortress, 1982), chapter 3, is a more recent discussion. Gonzales, vol. I, pp. 46–59 and chapter IV, outlines historical development of Christian-Hellenist interaction.

[11] See further Cairns, chapters III and VIII, although he is overly negative to the Greek fathers, especially Athanasius and Clement (pp. 97–99).

[12] Carl Henry is a modern defender of the view that the image consists of 'rational content', but grounded in relationship with God: article 'Man', *Baker's Dictionary of Theology*, pp. 340–341.

[13] Some later theologians also took this line, for example Richard Hooker in the Elizabethan age in England: *The Laws of Ecclesiastical Polity* I.4 (Everyman edn, 1907), pp. 161–164. Berkouwer concludes his book *Man* with a discussion of the angels and humankind, about which 'everything is centered around the great mystery of the gospel "which the angels desire to look upon" (I Pet. 1:12)' (p. 362).

[14] See Cairns, pp. 99–107; McDonald, pp. 57–67; Gonzales, vol. II, chapter I; Moltmann, *God in Creation*, pp. 234–239.

[15] I am indebted in this section to a seminar on Augustine under Prof. Rowan Greer at Yale Divinity School in 1982; the argument comes from a paper written by myself for the seminar.

[16] This is certainly the case with W. G. T. Shedd's introductory essay in the Library of Post-Nicene Fathers version.

[17] This analysis also eases the charge that Augustine used only the 'psychological' analogy for the Trinity: it reveals that there is an element of the 'social analogy' in his spirituality: see Sherlock, *God on the Inside*, pp. 214–218.

[18] See David Powys, 'The Nineteenth and Twentieth Century Debates about Hell and Universalism', in *Universalism and the Doctrine of Hell*, ed. Nigel M. de S. Cameron (Paternoster and Baker, 1992), pp. 93–138, especially pp. 100–113.

[19] See Cairns, pp. 79–88, and chapter IX; Berkouwer, *Man*, pp. 67–69.

[20] Clines, pp. 90–91; Bray, pp. 196, 200–201; and Anderson, pp. 216–217, summarize exegetical opinion, which is that there are slight differences in emphasis between the terms, which mean 'representation' and 'imitation' respectively, but that they function as synonyms in Genesis.

[21] Cairns suggests, following Struker, that for Irenaeus the soul aspect is the image of God, the bodily aspect is the image of Christ, and 'spirit' is the distinctive new property brought by the Spirit through faith in Christ (pp. 81–83).

[22] Although Irenaeus held a strong doctrine of the universality of sin, as we have noted, his concept of the fall as an attempt to accelerate divinely intended growth has been given new impetus by theologians seeking to incorporate an evolutionary dynamic in their understanding of human-

kind, especially in relation to sin and evil. John Hick contrasts an Irenaean with an Augustinian theodicy, that is, a 'creation–growth–deification' model and a 'creation–fall–redemption' one: see *Evil and the God of Love* (Collins, 1966), Parts II and III, summarized on pp. 262–264. To the extent that such an analysis is seen as illuminating complementary macro-level models of salvation, this is helpful, but to set Irenaeus and Augustine sharply against each other makes neither historical nor theological sense. Hughes, pp. 228–231, takes up this issue with reference to Teilhard de Chardin; more widely, see Henri Blocher, *Evil and the Cross* (Apollos, 1994), pp. 50–64.

[23] Cairns, p. 123, defends Irenaeus against the charge of holding a dualistic, 'two-storey' view of reality, a concept which entered medieval scholasticism more from the influence of Aristotle than from the Christian tradition.

[24] Cairns, pp. 120–122, cites Aquinas as dividing the image into three stages: natural, in the mind (the Old Testament view, according to Cairns); by conformity to grace, albeit imperfectly (the New Testament view); and in perfection, according to the likeness of glory; *cf.* Anderson, p. 218; Moltmann, *God in Creation*, pp. 228–230. The present argument has some similarities to this, being influenced by Richard Hooker; but the fundamental perspective is taken from Christ and eschatology, rather than nature and grace, and is expressed in relational rather than scholastic categories.

[25] The *Decree Concerning Justification* of the Council of Trent, chapters V–VII, in *Creeds of the Churches*, pp. 409–411, formulated this teaching in the Reformation period. Aquinas was more careful: 'No previous preparation is required on the part of man if we are speaking of grace as the help of God, by which he moves him to do good': *Summa Theologica* 12ae Q. 112, 3, from *Aquinas on Nature and Grace*, ed. A. M. Fairweather (SCM, 1954), p. 176.

[26] Both Reforming and Roman Catholic theologians agreed that the image was affected by sin, but that in some sense it remained, and that Christ's work alone could bring forgiveness. Protestants sometimes fail to realize this, criticizing popular Roman Catholicism rather than its actual doctrine. C. Stephen Evans, 'Healing Old Wounds and Recovering Old Insights: Towards a Christian View of the Person for Today', in *Christian Faith and Practice in the Modern World*, ed. Mark Noll and David F. Wells, pp. 74–78, seeks to distil the core concerns of both Reformers and Roman Catholics behind the polemics of the times. P. Toon, *Justification and Sanctification* (Marshall, Morgan and Scott, 1983), contains an eirenic discussion of the wider issues.

[27] See Cairns, chapters X–XI; Berkouwer, *Man*, chapter 4; Anderson, pp. 218–220.

[28] *Institutes*, I.15.3–4; II.12.6–7; III.3.9; see Berkouwer, *Man*, pp. 38–51, relating the idea to Eastern Orthodox theology, and Moltmann, *God in Creation*, pp. 230–234.

[29] Another factor was the use of Latin for public worship when it had ceased to be in common use; this emphasized the separate roles of priest and people, and excluded most from active participation, thus leaving each individual to his or her own resources during the liturgy.

[30] *Liber de persona et duabus naturis contra Eutychem et Nestorium*, 3: 'A book about the person and two natures [of Christ], against Eutyches and Nestorius', cited in *A Scholastic Miscellany*, ed. E. R. Fairweather (Macmillan, 1970), p. 334.

[31] Vocabulary usage illustrates the issues involved. Modern usage tends to speak of the 'individual', but the Christian tradition speaks of human life as 'personal', and human beings as 'persons'. Such personal language echoes that used about God, especially the trinitarian confession of God as 'three Persons in one Substance'. The use of the capital 'P' here is no accident; it indicates that we do not – and cannot – know what the divine 'Persons' are. Because of the self-revelation of God in Christ through the Spirit, being made in the image of this personal God entails being personal. This way of speaking seeks both to include what is distinctive about each particular person, and also to emphasize that we are not isolated individuals, but made for relationship with others. See further Sherlock, *God on the Inside*, pp. 116–121, 197–202, and C. Schwöbel and C. E. Gunton (eds.), *Persons, Divine and Human* (T. and T. Clark, 1991), especially Schwöbel's opening essay.

[32] See Berkouwer, *Man*, chapter 5, especially pp. 162–175, and Mc-Donald, pp. 90–96. McDonald, pp. 96–100, continues with a discussion of Arminianism, using John Wesley as a case study; Berkouwer, *Man*, chapter 4, considers 'synergism' in the post-Reformation Lutheran tradition. Both controversies illustrate the major point being made here, namely that in terms of what it means to be human, focus on the individual continued to grow, even though the individual was seen in the first place in relation to God, rather than autonomously as in much Enlightenment thought.

[33] His tomb, in the church of St Germain, Paris, contains a fulsome tribute to his efforts in preserving the faith at a time of scepticism and doubt. Modern theological critique of Descartes's work commonly seems to forget his own Christian self-understanding.

[34] Berkouwer, *Man*, pp. 122–124.

[35] *Cf.* Kelsey, pp. 152–156; Moltmann, *God in Creation*, pp. 40–47.

[36] This discussion is taken further in the chapters of Focus 2a.

[37] Bruce Wilson, *The Human Journey: Christianity and Modern Consciousness* (Albatross, 1980), Parts I and II, offers a vivid outline of many of these

trends. Wilson, now Anglican Bishop of Bathurst, NSW, is a sociologist by training, and has pastoral experience in university, inner-urban and rural ministries.

[38] *Cf.* H. Berkhof, *The Doctrine of the Holy Spirit* (Epworth, 1964), pp. 14–17.

[39] Jewett, pp. 33–43, 69–85, provides an excellent summary and reflection on Barth's work, especially in its feminist dimension. Berkouwer shows evidence of Barth's influence in his emphasis on the need to live out our status of being made in the image of God: see *Man,* especially pp. 72–74, 87–101, 235–237.

[40] Barth's exegesis is in *Church Dogmatics* III/1, pp. 191ff.; his more general treatment follows in the whole of volume III/2. For von Kirschbaum's influence, especially at this point, see Köbler, chapters 11–12. This is more than a merely historical note; it serves to indicate that the nature of theological reflection on being human is immeasurably deepened by the contribution of a man and woman consciously working in relationship themselves.

[41] For example, in *Signs of the Spirit* (WCC, 1991), pp. 98–99, 270 (the Canberra WCC Assembly Report).

[42] A musical friend with a sense of humour renders this as 'pleased as punch with us to dwell'!

[43] I have sought to address some of these issues throughout *God on the Inside,* especially chapters 6–8.

Focus 2a: Preamble

[1] Hall describes these relationships as 'being-with-God', 'being-with-the-human-counterpart (*Mitmenschen*)' and 'being-with-nature' (*Imaging God,* pp. 123–132), emphasizing that these are 'interconnections', not distinct relationships.

Chapter 4: Human life in society

[1] To say the latter assumes that the incarnation took the form of the Word being joined to an already existent human life; that view is Nestorian, affirming that in Christ there subsisted two persons side by side, one human, the other divine. In this perspective the reality of divine identification with humanity is questioned; God may come *alongside* us, but stops short of full identification *with* us (*cf.* Heb. 2:14–18). See Gonzales, vol. I, chapter XVII.

[2] J. C. Beker, cited in H. Paul Santmire, *The Travail of Nature* (Fortress, 1980), pp. 189–190; *cf.* Plantinga, pp. 63–67.

[3] Gn. 12:1–9 tells the story of Abram's obedient faith, in leaving his homeland. However, his taking Lot, in partial disobedience of the divine

command, and later seeking an heir through Eliezer (Gn. 15:3) and Hagar (Gn. 16:1–3) rather than through Sarah (whose own significance in these stories is considerable), reveal an element of doubt, with painful consequences for all involved. Both aspects are significant in Abraham's representative role.

[4] See Rom. 4:6–8; 5:12–21; 2 Cor. 11:3; 1 Cor. 10:1–5; 1 Pet. 3:18–22; Rom. 9:6, 13 respectively. An interesting case is that of Peter. Was his confession of faith in Jesus primarily personal or representative (Mt. 16:13–19)? Roman Catholics have sometimes insisted that it was personal, to defend papal primacy, whereas other Christians have sought to exclude the personal sense in reaction to this view. In John's gospel, parallels are seen in the confessions of Martha (Jn. 11:27) and Thomas (Jn. 20:28), which function at both individual and corporate levels.

[5] Tony Walter, *A Long Way from Home: A Sociological Exploration of Contemporary Idolatry* (Paternoster, 1979), offers a Christian survey and critique of several such issues, from a perspective which (since Walter is both an English sociologist and a theologian) holds together Christian faith and sociology with a godly reverence and acute observation.

[6] See Ridderbos, p. 38; C. J. H. Wright, *Living as the People of God* (IVP, 1994), pp. 197–198.

[7] We are not *constituted* as sinners, but *live* as such, in every dimension of life, since sin affects our nature at its root (see chapter 2 above). In theological terms, we are *existentially* rather than *essentially* sinners, though sin touches the essence of our being.

[8] Reinhold Neibuhr, *Moral Man and Immoral Society* (Scribners, 1932, reissued 1960), p. xii.

[9] A simple, memorable phrase of Juan Luís Segundo, cited in Hall, p. 5.

[10] See further Walter, chapter 5, who notes the paradox of individualism co-existing with collectivity in the modern industrialized state, a two-tier society where the individual and impersonal mass society feed one another.

[11] W. Temple, *Christianity and the Social Order* (Penguin, 1942), p. 18. Temple recounts the history of Christian resistance to taking seriously the social order (pp. 8–10), and of the emergence of social principles in the western tradition (pp. 26–34).

[12] John Gladwin, *God's People in God's World* (IVP, 1979), p. 80.

[13] Similar examples are the future of nations grounded in the birth of Jacob/Israel and Esau/Edom (Gn. 25:23); Achan (Jos. 7); David's family (2 Sa. 12:10–12); and the manner in which the health of Israel or Judah was summed up in the evil or good of the king (*cf.* 2 Ki. 21:1–9).

[14] Frank Brennan, *Reconciling our Differences* (David Lovell, 1992), pp. 63–92, offers a Christian approach to these issues, focused in the issue of Australian aboriginal land rights.

[15] Friedrich Engels, 'On the History of Early Christianity', in *Marx and*

Engels: Basic Writings on Philosophy and Philosophy, ed. L. S. Feuer (Doubleday, 1959), pp. 168–194, traces these comparisons, based on an exegesis of the book of Revelation.

[16] Cairns, p. 217.

[17] Wilson, p. 133.

[18] *Ibid.,* p. 51.

[19] A Christian response which is strengthened by its author's pre-Christian Marxist sympathies is Alister McGrath, *Understanding the Trinity* (Kingsway, 1987), pp. 23–27, and *Christian Theology,* pp. 89–92. McDonald, pp. 115–118, offers a more traditional response to Marxist perspectives on being human.

[20] Both concepts of estrangement are set over against an optimistic view of individual human nature, as seen, for example, in secular humanism. Both also oppose views which assume that human beings are irredeemably selfish, such as undergird free-market capitalism. Temple (p. 42) neatly sums up a Christian position when he writes, 'The art of Government is in fact the art of so ordering life that self-interest prompts what justice demands.'

[21] Moltmann, who has sustained a substantial theological dialogue with Marxism for decades, offers a penetrating analysis of Marxism and heaven in *God in Creation,* pp. 175–181. It is important here to note that the Marxist denial of God began as a critique of religion, where religion was viewed as keeping people from seeing the truth about their condition (*cf.* McGrath, *Trinity,* pp. 20–23). This denial is based on Feuerbach's theory of God as the projection of human ideals, 'God made in the image of humanity'. Yet Marxism itself has a religious structure and meaning, and the 'classless society' can itself be regarded as a religious projection.

'Religion' is better considered in functional rather than substantive terms (see Wilson, pp. 84–92): by 'substantive' is meant a definition of religion in terms of a particular set of beliefs, morals and rituals, whereas a 'functional' approach defines religion as ultimate beliefs about meaning and about moral values. The latter approach allows atheistic faiths such as Buddhism and Gaia, ideologies such as Marxism or secularism, and socio-cultural sacred cows to be discussed in the way they function as holistic worldviews, appealing for commitment and generating lifestyle criteria (*cf.* Walter, pp. 9–22). This approach is also able to analyse how theistic faiths such as the varieties of Christianity are actually experienced, whatever their ideals may be.

[22] Cairns, p. 217.

[23] Walter, pp. 192–194, is scathing on Christian theologians (from Left and Right) who forget this and identify a particular social trend or programme with the kingdom of God, describing this as 'culture religion' (pp. 163–169).

[24] It is ironic that in contemporary language, the new term coined to

refer to this wider meaning, 'ecology', meaning 'study (*logos*) of the household', is etymologically almost cognate with 'economy'.

[25] This is not a critique of the stock market itself; I hold shares with a clear conscience. Where uncommitted monies are available for investment, arguably their best use is through support of businesses that utilize the resources of human skill and toil directly, rather than indirectly, for example through bank deposits which are then used 'second hand', as it were. Such involvement also offers the opportunity and challenge for contributions to be made at the policy level: *cf.* Ian Hore-Lacy, *Creating Common Wealth* (Albatross/Lion, 1985), pp. 26–32, 57–59.

There is much theological discussion of macro issues touching the public sector (in western societies), the needs of those excluded from any meaningful participation in society, and micro issues such as business ethics. But there seems to be little Christian reflection on private-sector issues at the macro level, especially business, even though in western countries most Christians who are employed work in this sector. John Atherton, 'The Individual and the Organization', *Expository Times* 105 (1994), pp. 356–362, offers a helpful survey of many of the issues. He makes the point that codes of business ethics, while useful, fail to recognize at the personal level the importance of developing the character of managers, and at the corporate level the overarching organizational context in which businesses function; trans-national corporations are an evident example of the issues involved.

[26] It was the medieval prohibition of usury among Christians, and restrictions placed on Jewish business by Christian authorities, that led Jews to specialize in money-lending; this is an example both of concern for the common good, and also of the corporate sin of anti-Semitism; see Temple, p. 31. Jewish friends inform me that religious Jews today do not charge interest to other Jews; there are complex legal arrangements about this matter, and other Mosaic laws such as the Jubilee, in the modern state of Israel.

[27] Temple, p. 34.

[28] A classic discussion of these issues is R. J. Tawney, *Religion and the Rise of Capitalism* (Pelican, 1948). Hore-Lacy, pp. 20–26, gives a summary of the historical discussion.

[29] Helpful surveys are Donald Hay, *A Christian Critique of Capitalism* and *A Christian Critique of Socialism* (Grove, 1975), focusing on the concepts of human 'dominion' in particular.

[30] Hore-Lacy interacts with a range of British, Australian and American, Protestant and Roman Catholic perspectives. The point of view is that of an Australian evangelical Christian in business, supportive of a capitalist economy, with a thoughtful critique of Christian approaches to the economics of development (pp. 55–56).

[31] This includes promoting attitudes of accountable trust towards and in politicians, who are (sinful) *people*. In many societies, not least Australia, they are frequently abused as a class, while regarded more positively as individuals. To write, as Hore-Lacy does (p. 34), of a particular statement about taxation, that 'it begs the question of whether people trust their politicians to spend money more wisely than themselves', is destructive of such trust. It encourages the divisive idea that politicians are opposed to the public, assumes that people generally do spend wisely, and implies that we might trust non-politicians such as business leaders to spend money for us, even though they are not accountable to the public, as politicians are. Hore-Lacy goes on to ask, 'Does "fairness" mean that those who produce nothing should consume nothing?' This question assumes that 'produce' and 'consume' are defined in monetary terms, and that distribution is to be primarily related to productivity, rather than to what promotes the growth of persons in relationship.

[32] I. M. Ramsay, *Models of Divine Activity* (SCM, 1982), chapter II, offers an insightful introduction to 'economy' as a theological model. I do not wish to cast aspersions on the modern study of economics; I was an economic statistician before I began to teach theology.

[33] On Monarchianism, see Gonzales, vol. I, pp. 146–149, 182–190. Prestige, chapter V, is a classic exposition of 'economy' in Irenaeus and Tertullian.

[34] Sherlock, *God on the Inside*, p. 194. The quotation continues, 'Tertullian thus developed the famous formula, "God is three Persons in one substance". The words "Persons" and "substance" later took on a more philosophical meaning. Yet they remained the standard Western, Latin formula for the Trinity. The original metaphor of a king, legal agents, and influence was sufficiently rich to be capable of gradual transformation and growth. God matters more than the words or images used.'

Here it is being suggested that the original metaphors 'economy' and 'monarchy' are capable of further stretching, to assist us in coming to terms with the interrelationship between the nature of God and human life in society. Robert Banks, *God the Worker* (Eerdmans, 1992), expounds the doctrine of God implied in the concept of a God who works.

[35] The motif *koinōnia* is coming to have increasing significance in Christian reflection on the pattern of human life for which we are to strive; see, for example, *Signs of the Spirit*, section III; ARCIC-2, *Church as Communion* (SPCK, 1990), and especially ARCIC-2, *Life in Christ*.

[36] This is the name of an ongoing interdenominational Christian campaign to ensure that the least privileged members of Australian society are kept to the fore in government policy. 'Fair share' echoes the Australian idiom 'fair go', which means something like 'reasonable opportunity'.

[37] 2 Cor. 8 makes a good case study of biblical perspectives on stewardship; note also Phil. 4:10–19.

[38] Temple, chapters IV–V and appendix, set out an example of both principles and details. Though penned over fifty years ago, much of what he states remains highly relevant to modern industrial societies; the main changes since his time are the mass immigration which has affected many countries, and changes in the roles of women. A recent Australian example is *Common Wealth for the Common Good* (E. J. Dwyer, 1993), a carefully shaped outline of principles and policies for Australia in the next decade, issued by the Roman Catholic bishops after extensive church and wider community consultation. In New Zealand a similar programme was undertaken in 1994 by all the churches, with special reference to the full participation of Maoris and other non-Pakeha (white) citizens, culminating in a three-day meeting between heads of government and Christian leaders.

[39] The Australian 'theology of everyday life' movement offers further resources for practical application in this area: see for example Robert Banks, *All the Business of Life* (Albatross/Lion, 1989); New Zealander John McGuiness's *The New Pilgrims* (Albatross, 1982); and the many papers produced by groups such as the Zadok Institute for Christianity and Society (Australia) the Shaftesbury Project and Christian Impact (England), EFICOR (India), and Evangelicals for Social Action (USA). Addresses for these and other bodies, and practical wisdom, are given in Roy McCloughry, *Taking Action* (IVP Frameworks, 1990). Walter's critique of many aspects of life today, including the family, work, housing and the media, offers a sharp theological perspective.

Chapter 5: Human life in creation

[1] A useful term I first encountered in Hall, *Imaging God.*

[2] Moltmann, *God in Creation*, pp. 185–188, gives a particularly clear exposition of these texts.

[3] Walter Brueggemann, *The Land* (Fortress, 1979), analyses biblical perspectives theologically, while Cavan Brown, *Pilgrim through this Barren Land* (Albatross, 1991) does so in terms of European Australian experience. Aboriginal Australians speak in terms such as 'the land owns us', rather than 'we own the land'.

[4] See further Moltmann, *God in Creation*, pp. 5–7, 31 and chapter VII.

[5] Birch and Rasmussen, cited in Hall, p. 170.

[6] Hall, pp. 15–16. The Canadian Hall, and I, an Australian, include our own societies in this unhappy confession. The Lynn White essay on ecology and the Christian tradition is cited in chapter 1, n. 20.

[7] C. Deane-Drummond, *Gaia and Green Ethics* (Grove, 1993), pp. 12–13, notes the distinction made between 'deep' and 'shallow' ecology: the

former gives prime value to the ecological system itself, while the latter acknowledges a distinctive role for humanity within it.

[8] C. Gunton, *Enlightenment and Alienation* (Eerdmans, 1985), p. 25.

[9] Deane-Drummond, pp. 9–11. Another consequence is 'biocentrism' (see pp. 124–127).

[10] Including the way in which we know it, which needs to be more 'integrative' than 'masterly': Moltmann, *God in Creation*, pp. 2–3, and more fully in chapter III.

[11] In *God on the Inside*, p. 213.

[12] J. Moltmann, *Man*, pp. 18–19, notes that it has been 'often the non-Christian, such as Marx and Nietzsche, who had to remind the Christians of the crucified Jesus and of the wretchedness of man'.

[13] Hall, pp. 195–196. *Cf.* the entertaining and challenging article by Martin Palmer about the response of (British) churches to ecological concerns: 'Ecology – Prophetic or Pathetic?' *Expository Times* 106 (1995), pp. 100–104.

[14] R. S. Anderson, *On Being Human* (Eerdmans, 1982), p. 22 (the phrase quoted is from Helmut Thielicke).

[15] Hall, p. 54; *cf.* Moltmann, *God in Creation*, p. 193.

[16] The question of the soul is taken up in chapter 10 below.

[17] Moltmann, *God in Creation*, p. 77, draws a further, more strictly theological conclusion: 'What distinguishes human beings is that they are made in the image of God. Whatever this may mean for human beings and their position in creation . . . what it means for God is that in creation he does not merely want to recognize his work; he also wants his work to recognize himself.'

[18] A standard text is that by the Australian philosopher, Peter Singer, *Animal Liberation* (Cape, 1976); a Christian perspective is outlined in R. Griffiths, *The Human Use of Animals* (Grove, 1982), while a fuller, more partisan approach is Andrew Linzey, *Animal Theology* (SCM, 1994). It is estimated that almost half the mammals originally extant on the Australian subcontinent have now been rendered extinct.

[19] Deane-Drummond, p. 9; *cf.* Moltmann, *God in Creation*, pp. 23–32.

[20] Hall, pp. 161–163.

[21] Moltmann, *God in Creation*, p. 28, though he later notes that the early Marx had a less aggressive attitude to nature (pp. 40–41). E. Echlin, *The Christian Green Heritage* (Grove, 1989), p. 13, cites anti-ecological examples from Thatcher, Marx and Engels.

[22] Cited in Echlin, p. 14. The use of male language here is no doubt intended generically, but discloses the ethos which has led to the overlap between the outlooks of feminist and ecological interests (see further in chapters 8 and 9 below).

[23] Thus a rescue of trapped dolphins or whales, creatures which have

caught the imagination of the mass media as typifying what is 'natural', is televised across the world, as if in saving them we are saving ourselves.

[24] For example, the papal encyclical on development, *Sollicitudo Rei Socialis* (London: Catholic Truth Society, 1988); this contains an analysis of 'dominion' similar to that expounded here, incorporating both personal and social dimensions. The ecumenical programme 'Justice, Peace and the Integrity of Creation' is another example; initially it tended to question the validity of the concept of dominion altogether, as reflected in the Seoul Conference in 1990, but recently it has turned towards a more theocentric perspective; see *Signs of the Spirit*, section I.

[25] A phrase of Bernard Häring, cited in Echlin, p. 19.

[26] A famous example is the dramatic speech-performance by Chung Hyun Kyung (at which I was present) at the Canberra Assembly of the WCC, published in *Signs of the Spirit*, pp. 37–46, especially 43–44. It is noteworthy that she links a 'change from *anthropocentrism* to *life-centrism*' with a change from '*dualism* to the habit of *interconnection*' (a feminist perspective).

[27] There is thus a need for a contemporary restatement of the 'sustenance' aspect of the doctrine of providence; see G. C. Berkouwer, *The Providence of God* (Eerdmans, 1952), chapter 3.

[28] See A. W. Reed, *Aboriginal Myths, Legends and Fables* (Reed, 1982), p. 10. The motif through which aboriginal perspectives on the solidarity of humankind and otherkind is expressed is described as 'the Dreaming', in which totemism is prominent. Hall makes a similar observation about North American Indian and Inuit cultures (pp. 96–98).

[29] See Morris, *Apostolic Preaching*, chapter III, especially pp. 126–128, who shows that blood is associated not with life in the abstract, but 'life ended in death', and so has strong sacrificial connotations. See further chapter 9 below.

[30] Von Rad, *Genesis*, p. 126.

[31] A phrase of Peter Berger, cited in Walter, p. 16.

[32] Durkheim described this as 'anomie', lack of social custom: it is a social and environmental problem, not merely an individual one (Walter, p. 17). Berger speaks of the individual in this setting as like a 'heretic', adopting ways of living that are rejected and even punished by the wider society: *The Heretical Imperative* (Collins, 1980), chapter 1.

[33] Walter, p. 17.

[34] Walter, pp. 104–109, points out that what is meant by 'Nature' must be taken into account: this varies from the 'red in tooth and claw' view of Tennysonian evolution, to the 'all things live in harmony' romantic optimism of popular ecologism, and 'survival' ideology. If the one justifies violent repression of the 'less fit', the others fail to take seriously the depth of human sin, and easily come to function as legitimations for self-centredness.

[35] *Cf.* Moltmann, *God in Creation*, pp. 46–47.

Chapter 6: Human culture

[1] D. B. Barrett (ed.), *World Christian Encyclopedia* (OUP, 1982), p. v, states that around 1980 the Christian church was found in over 7,000 languages, and more than 9,000 peoples – numbers which have grown since then. Statistics like these are comforting, but should be seen as a reminder of the generous breadth of God's grace, when we are tempted to view faith through culturally blinkered eyes.

[2] *Cf.* Westermann, *Creation*, pp. 20–22.

[3] See *The Garden of Many Colours* (Anglican Information Office, Melbourne, 1985), chapters 1–3; and Jim Houston (ed.), *The Cultural Pearl* (VCC, 1986). Houston, a former senior immigration officer, is an Anglican priest working in the highly multicultural northern suburbs of Melbourne. Christopher Lamb, *Belief in a Mixed Society* (Lion, 1985) discusses these issues in a British context.

[4] Walter describes a similar series of responses (extermination, assimilation, apartheid, romanticism, plurality) based on British and North American experience (pp. 125–133). He also notes the formulation of a political programme for a plural society, on the basis of theological work, by the Dutch school of Abraham Kuyper and Herman Dooyeweerd (p. 131). While such a programme may be a valuable contribution in a particular place and time, to derive a permanent political structure from Christian theology makes the mistake of generalizing from one situation. It also runs the risk of idolizing one pattern of life, by calling for commitment to it above all else. Such a process has not been uncommon in the church's history, not least the Anglican tradition in which I stand, but always with tragic effects; Anglicans ought not to forget their persecution of other English Christians in the years following 1662.

[5] Likewise, 'childhood' is a relatively recent phenomenon in western societies, with a specialized sub-culture of dress, literature and toys, seen for example in the Victorian age in Britain (I remain a member of the Meccano Guild!). 'Childhood' was largely brought about by the rise of compulsory education, defining life-stages in terms of pre-school, primary (pre-puberty) and secondary (post-puberty) education, and today is commonly romanticized (with financial implications) or ideologized (especially in debates over child care). Such patterns are quite different in societies where, for example, children are part of the labour force, or educated through folk tradition, or where marriages are arranged; Walter, chapter 3, discusses childhood in the context of family. Similar comments could be made about concepts such as middle age, which has come about only as life expectancy (at least in industrialized societies) has risen from around forty to over seventy years *during the twentieth century*.

[6] Wilson, chapter 8, gives a good introduction to these issues. A fuller treatment is Alan Race, *Christians and Religious Pluralism* (SCM, 1983).

[7] The plurality of cultures has been closely associated with the rejection of any foundations for truth, values and especially language in post-modernism: see McGrath, *Christian Theology*, pp. 102–105, and Lesslie Newbigin, *Foolishness to the Greeks* (SPCK, 1986), chapter 1.

[8] Walter, p. 134.

[9] Walter, p. 160, going on to describe 'sect', 'denomination' and 'national church' types of church, tending to be respectively against, related to, and identified with, the prevailing dominant culture.

[10] The other major tradition was Methodist, which although not having a 'national church' background, did approach Victorian society with a comprehensive ethos. The Uniting Church of Australia, formed in 1977 from all Methodist and Congregational, and a majority of Presbyterian, congregations, has maintained this ethos, but with an orientation to being self-consciously Australian and ecumenical. Interestingly, two decades down the track this ethos itself seems to have become a distinctive ecclesial culture.

[11] See *God on the Inside*, pp. 4–11. An example from the Scriptures is the serpent on a pole; originally it functioned as an instrument of salvation (Nu. 21:7), but it became a source of temptation, and had to be destroyed (2 Ki. 18:4–5). Nevertheless, it could still be used by Jesus to illuminate the meaning of his saving work (Jn. 3:1).

[12] Richard Niebuhr, *Christ and Culture* (Harper, 1951).

[13] I acknowledge gratefully here the work of George Crombie, whose thesis *Faith and Fate* (Australian College of Theology, 1987) was prepared under my supervision. There is a growing literature on Australian culture, of which David Millikan, *The Sunburnt Soul* (Lancer, 1981, based on an ABC television series) and Dorothy Hughes, Douglas Hynd and David Millikan (eds.), *The Shape of Belief* (Lancer, 1982), are pioneer works from a Christian perspective, while Richard White, *Inventing Australia* (George Allen and Unwin, 1981), and Hugh McKay, *Re-inventing Australia* (Angus and Robertson, 1993), are influential general works.

[14] I have heard all these styles used in public worship, and others beside. The only form I have never encountered is the Irish reel or jig, the basis of the Anglo-Celtic Australian folk tradition, even though I have played five-string banjo in various bush bands for over thirty years. A fascinating study of music in American Black experience is Jon Michael Spencer, *Protest and Praise: Sacred Music of Black Religion* (Fortress, 1990).

[15] See further Walter, chapter 3; C. H. Sherlock (ed.), *An Anglican Pastoral Handbook* (Acorn, 1989), pp. 35–37, 63–64; and Greg Forster, *Marriage before Marriage?* (Grove, 1988).

[16] On this section, see Jacques Pohier, *God in Fragments* (SCM, 1985),

THE DOCTRINE OF HUMANITY

especially pp. 193–200. Pohier is a former Dominican preacher, theologian and psychoanalyst who was unexpectedly stripped of his priesthood in 1979. His book is a careful, passionate reflection on key aspects of being human before God in the light of the experience of losing identity, focused around the classic topics of death, sexuality and guilt.

[17] That polyandry (more than one man married to one woman) is almost unknown raises questions about the validity of polygamy, in that it reveals multiple-partner marriage to be a gender-skewed phenomenon. Polygamy is culturally understandable if marriage is regarded as primarily reproductive in purpose; one man can impregnate several women, but it takes a year of a woman's life to bear a child. The closest cultural approximation to polyandry, however, is prostitution. The Lambeth Conference of 1988 considered polygamy in the light of the experience of African churches: *The Truth Shall Make You Free* (Church House, 1988), pp. 220–221.

[18] Does the qualification for a presbyter to be 'married only once' (1 Tim. 3:2) imply that other Christians could be polygamous or polyandrous? Biblical examples of monogamy are rare, as anyone who has sought material for a wedding knows: Adam and Eve are not obviously a married couple in Genesis 2 – 3. Traditional prayers are based on the only Old Testament example after Adam and Eve, that of Isaac and Rebekah, a marriage that had its moments (Gn. 27:1–17), though the problems of rival wives is far more commonly given attention (*cf.* Gn. 30:1–24; 1 Sa. 1:1–8). In the New Testament the only named couple is Priscilla and Aquila (Acts 18:2; 1 Cor. 16:19), noteworthy for their work in mutual partnership.

[19] ARCIC-2, *Life in Christ*, pp. 20–27, sets out this teaching in brief compass.

[20] Anthropologists trace a pattern of separation, boundary-crossing (liminality), and reincorporation in rites of passage such as marriage, a pattern that appears to cross many cultural varieties: see Victor and Edith Turner, *Image and Pilgrimage in Christian Culture: Anthropological Perspectives* (Columbia University Press, 1978), pp. 243–255. In the commonest Australian Anglo-Celtic case, this pattern would be engagement, wedding and reception.

[21] The literature on language is immense, as scholarly discussion now ranges interactively over translation issues (*e.g.* Nida, Kraft), philosophical concerns (*e.g.* Ayer, Flew, Wittgenstein, Derrida), linguistic analysis and hermeneutics (especially Chomsky, Ricoeur, de Saussure), feminism (so de Beauvoir, Maitland), as well as theological work (*e.g.* Ian Ramsey, Mascall, Soskice, Thiselton) especially from a feminist perspective (notably Letty Russell, McFague, Ruether, Elisabeth Johnston). In what follows the argument has been restricted to issues that directly affect what it means to be human.

[22] Appendix 2 above includes a discussion on the way 'father' language functions in relation to God.

[23] *Cf.* Eric Mascall, *Existence and Analogy* (Longman, 1949); Norman Geisler, *Philosophy of Religion* (Zondervan, 1975), Part III. The questions involved in theology and language are beyond the scope of this book. A forceful survey is Gordon H. Clark, *Language and Theology* (Presbyterian and Reformed, 1975). Linguistic philosophy has given way to deconstructive and reader-response approaches, now focused in literature more than in philosophy departments; a full survey is Antony C. Thiselton, *New Horizons in Hermeneutics* (Marshall Pickering, 1992). These approaches have had particular impact in relation to the actual use of the Scriptures, not least in liturgy, where Christians use words in hearing and responding to the Scriptures, and in prayer, praise and reflection on life, with conscious reference to relationship with God.

[24] Poetry is another whole area of human culture which space does not allow us to discuss here. The poetry (and other literature, music and drama) we like not only reveals our tastes, but gives access to the way we see the world; in this sense it is more than a private art, but offers a language which both transcends surface meaning, and builds subtle bridges between people, across both time and space. You will know a fair bit about me when you have read the poetry of G. Studdert Kennedy, read the novels of Dorothy L. Sayers, and heard the music of Slim Dusty.

[25] This category is chosen in part because of my Anglican heritage, but much more because the concepts 'sign' and 'signified' have become standard ways of speaking in contemporary perspectives on language, whether theological or philosophical.

[26] *Cf.* G. C. Berkouwer, *Holy Scripture* (Eerdmans, 1975), especially chapters 1 and 6; Barth, *Church Dogmatics*, I/2 (T. and T. Clark, 1956), pp. 512–537; and John Goldingay, *Models for the Inspiration of Scripture* (Eerdmans and Paternoster, 1994), section I. The doctrine of revelation has traditionally been the place where language is discussed; I would suggest that this key focus should be blended with reflection on language in prayer, a 'doxological' focus, as Berkouwer puts it.

[27] Paul de Man, cited in McGrath, *Christian Theology*, p. 104: this typifies the latent rejection of authority itself in postmodern emphases.

[28] This matter is taken further in Appendix 2. A challenging reflection on many of the issues involved in language and culture, especially in speaking about God, is Brian Wren, *What Language Shall I Borrow?* (SCM, 1989). Wren is English, a United Reformed Church pastor and significant hymnwriter.

[29] Linguists classify Australian accents into Cultivated, Standard, and Broad; there is minor geographical variation in pronouncing particular words, and some differences between rural and urban speakers. Immigra-

tion has brought changes, too; children growing up in inner-city Melbourne use 'Sydney Road' vowels, for example, due to Italian, Greek and Arabic influence. Radio and television announcers now include foreign as well as native accents.

[30] Lewis Carroll's *Through the Looking-glass*, chapter VI: in the New English Library edition (1960), pp. 186–187.

[31] A concept of Aristotle which has received widespread acceptance: see the remarkable book of Karl-Josef Kuschel, *Laughter: A Theological Reflection* (SCM, 1994), pp. 17–18, and 47–48, 117–118 on the dehumanizing effects of the absence of laughter.

[32] Kuschel, p. xvii.

[33] I regard *The Life of Brian* as both hilarious and full of insight, and not in the least blasphemous (except perhaps to humourless revolutionaries), but I am aware that other Christians do not agree with me here. How do cultural and theological presuppositions interact in such a way that there can be disagreement between Christians about the humour of a film?

[34] Jonathan Margolis, *Cleese Encounters* (Chapmans, 1992), p. 212, a reference given me by Jonathan Bright.

[35] Michael Frost, *Jesus the Fool* (Albatross/Lion, 1994), chapter 3, presents Jesus in terms of a 'jester', one whose transparent simplicity enables a prophetic critique of others, even the most powerful; Jesus is no 'clown'.

[36] Frost calls this 'reframing', discussed in his chapter 4, and developed throughout the remainder of the book.

[37] See the discussion of the good Samaritan, for example, in chapter 7 below.

[38] Frost, p. 100.

Chapter 7: The unique person

[1] *Cf.* Clines, pp. 80–85, and the literature cited there.

[2] Barth, *Church Dogmatics*, I/2, pp. 417–420.

[3] Cited in Cairns, p. 288.

[4] Kelsey, pp. 154–155, points out that this subject-oriented approach to being human means that 'the very idea of human nature becomes unintelligible'.

[5] The examples are suggested by Hughes, p. 144.

[6] *Cf.* Morris, *Apostolic Preaching*, pp. 179–183.

[7] Morris, *Apostolic Preaching*, chapter I, especially pp. 38–53, expounds the metaphor fully, in terms of atonement.

[8] C. H. Sherlock, *The God Who Fights* (Edwin Mellen, 1993), pp. 382–400, explores this further.

[9] This last passage has been taken by some as teaching 'sinless perfection', *i.e.* that we are able to live 'free from known sin'. This reading

not only contradicts the overwhelming testimony of the Scriptures, but fails to appreciate the eschatological context, set by verses 2–3.

[10] *Cf.* Anderson, pp. 79–81.

[11] The apostolic injunctions about slavery are careful, though they have been much abused. Paul speaks of himself in the first place as the slave of Christ and his readers (2 Cor. 4:5). He never requires 'slavery' from anyone else and, in speaking to those who are slaves in society, he puts this condition in a wider context, in which masters and slaves alike are called to be slaves of Christ (Eph. 6:5–9). John H. Yoder, *The Politics of Jesus* (Eerdmans, 1972), chapter 9, provides an insightful discussion.

[12] Kelsey, p. 153. Augustine's main work of relevance is *The Spirit and the Letter.*

[13] A number of controversies in the Christian tradition have centred around human freedom, not only between Augustine and Pelagius, but also between Luther and Erasmus, the teaching of Calvin and Arminius, and between Wesley and Whitefield: *cf.* McDonald, chapter 6; Griffith Thomas on Article X, and Berkouwer, *Providence,* chapter 6. The centre of these disputes has generally concerned the *limits* of freedom, however, rather than its *exercise,* which is the concern of many modern people.

[14] McDonald, pp. 94–95; Berkouwer, *Sin,* chapter 8, especially pp. 259–266.

[15] Jung objected to the notion of evil as 'privation of the good', not on the grounds that it took evil too seriously, but that it could be used psychologically to play down the reality of evil: Berkouwer, *Sin,* pp. 257–259.

[16] See further Sherlock, *The God Who Fights,* especially chapters 7–9.

[17] A popular saying had it that Christians should avoid sex because it might lead to dancing!

[18] McDonald, p. 112. He later cites Dewar as saying that Freud made 'the most deadly attack ever levelled against religion', but a great deal here depends on what is meant by 'religion', a concept regarded with great suspicion in the Scriptures. A significant critique of Freud is Jürgen Moltmann, *The Crucified God* (SCM, 1977), chapter 7, especially pp. 294–298 on the concept of religion in Freud (which comes perilously close to anti-Semitism).

Pohier, a trained psychoanalyst, offers in his Part III an account of guilt which seeks to integrate theological and psychological perspectives. This is not the place to detail the various technical terms of Freudian analysis, particularly as several have entered popular speech. Cairns, pp. 234–242, provides a succinct account.

[19] McDonald's swashbuckling summary of Darwin and Freud, at least as they are popularly understood (p. 113).

[20] Berkouwer, *Providence,* p. 20.

[21] Frost, pp. 94–100, offers an excellent perspective on this.

[22] *Cf.* Pohier, pp. 212–217.

[23] Sally Morgan, *My Place* (Fremantle Arts Centre, 1987, now published by Collins).

[24] There are paradoxes here: Melbourne is a world leader in embryo research, into which seemingly limitless funds are poured, while abortions are often justified on the basis of a mother's economic need. In part, this imbalance reflects the greater political influence and media acceptability of middle-class couples over poor single mothers. Nevertheless, a technologically driven approach to medicine seems to reinforce a quantitative view of human life, but it is the technology which attracts funding, not human need in itself.

[25] Jim Cotter, *Good Fruits* (Cairns, 1988), chapter 1, offers an insightful discussion with reference to homosexuality.

[26] A delicious description I once heard was of Lazarus being 'ontologically challenged'.

[27] For example, note the papal encyclicals *Rerum Novarum, Dignitatis Mulieris*, and more recently *Veritatis Splendor.* On the Protestant side, the Chicago Declaration (1974) is significant, while the Grove Ethical Studies now cover more than a hundred subjects.

[28] See Elaine Graham, *Making the Difference: Gender, Personhood and Theology* (Mowbray, 1995), pp. 4–6. On the distinction between sex and gender (a distinction first posited by Robert Stoller in 1968), see pp. 19, 123–126. Today most would deny that this equates to a pairing of nature and culture, since this view disables a transformative approach to gender issues. Graham is Lecturer in Social and Pastoral Theology at the University of Manchester, England. Her book is a veritable encyclopedia of material on gender studies in major disciplines, considered within the overall framework of mainstream Christian theology.

[29] Cited in Daphne Hampson, *Theology and Feminism* (SCM, 1990), p. 97. She continues: 'By gender I mean the construction of the "masculine" and "feminine" which has been imposed on the biological difference between male and female'. Hampson was an orthodox member of the Church of England, who through the process of seeking ordination became more and more disenchanted with the church, and then with faith itself. She continues to teach theology in Scotland from outside faith, but without watering down what mainstream belief entails. John Stoltenberg, an American secular humanist, in *Refusing to be a Man: Essays on Sex and Justice* (Penguin, 1990), writes, 'The penises exist, the male sex does not' (p. 30).

[30] The occurrence of physical gender-mixing, for example a baby born with both a womb and penis, is held to support this, as is psychological transsexuality, expressed in cross-dressing and sex-change operations. The concept of each person being a mix of feminine and masculine is deeper

and wider than these particular situations, however, and rests on the use of the terms as social constructs: see Graham, pp. 78–82, and Heather Formaini, *Men: The Darker Continent* (Heinemann, 1990), chapter 4. Formaini is a journalist of Italian background whose book is based on field research with a wide range of American men.

[31] Popular as well as serious exegesis of Eph. 5:21ff. shows this readily enough: see Jewett, chapter II.

[32] Erin White and Marie Tulip, *Knowing Otherwise: Feminism, Women and Religion* (David Lovell, 1991), p. 116. White and Tulip are Australian academics active in a number of Christian feminist networks, one from a Roman Catholic background, the other Uniting Church. Their book has helped me to listen to the life experience of some Australian Christian women, even though to me it tends to define female over and against male experience, and at points appears to set aside the fundamental Judeo-Christian dualisms of Creator and creation, grace and sin.

[33] See Graham, chapters 4, 5 and 9 respectively, for full accounts.

[34] *Theology and Feminism*, p. 31. Two seminal works are Simone de Beauvoir, *The Second Sex* (Penguin, 1953), and Betty Friedan, *The Feminine Mystique* (Penguin, 1963). Feminist thought has developed beyond these works in a wide range of directions, but the paradigm shift in understanding which it represents remains. Empathetic Christian perspectives are offered in Nancy Hardy and Letha Scanzoni, *All We're Meant to Be* (Word, 1974), and Elaine Storkey, *What's Right with Feminism?* (SPCK, 1985). A useful collection of essays by British evangelicals is Kathy Keay (ed.), *Men, Women and God* (Marshall Pickering, 1987), while a wider, more integrated book by American evangelicals is Mary Stewart van Leeuwen (ed.), *After Eden: Facing the Challenge of Gender Reconciliation* (Eerdmans and Paternoster, 1993), noteworthy for its inclusion of cross-cultural insights and full bibliographies.

[35] For example, Stephen Clark, *Man and Woman in Christ* (Servant Books, 1980); John Piper and Wayne Grudem (eds.), *Recovering Biblical Manhood and Womanhood: A Response to Evangelical Feminism* (Crossway, 1991); and at a popular level, Elisabeth Eliot, *Let Me Be a Woman* (Tyndale House, 1976).

[36] For example, the practically useful book by Anne Atkins, *Split Image: Male and Female in God's Likeness* (Hodder and Stoughton, 1989), begins with an exegetically highly doubtful defence of the use of the term 'man' to include women. Treating people without regard to their being male or female is significant, if they (usually women) are thereby defined in such a way as to oppress or deny their full humanity, but that is not the issue here.

[37] Graham, pp. 195–197, shows the influence of gender assumptions on the practice of science, revealing the falseness of claims to objectivity even in this apparently empirically based area of knowledge.

[38] See *After Eden*, chapter 9, and Graham, pp. 135–139.

[39] Planned parenthood is acceptable to all Christian traditions, as is the rejection of the 'contraceptive mentality': it is the use of what are deemed to be artificial methods of contraception that is disputed, not contraception *per se*; see ARCIC-2, *Life in Christ*, section D.

Chapter 8: Being a woman

[1] The only theological work on humanity that I have encountered which considers menstruation is that by White and Tulip, though the subject is frequently discussed in feminist works.

[2] On blood in the biblical tradition, see Morris, *Apostolic Preaching*, chapter III, who argues convincingly that its symbolic value relates to death through the non-voluntary taking of life, rather than to life directly.

[3] White and Tulip, p. 36; the discussion following owes a good deal to White.

[4] Daphne Hampson is most forthright about this: *Theology and Feminism* is so powerful precisely because she understands Christian faith and doctrine profoundly, yet has consciously left them behind.

[5] The rites of purification and redemption associated with birth are considered below. At this point it should be noted that though the cultic requirement for their performance has been lifted in Christ, the anthropological realities underlying them have not been abolished.

[6] The *Te Deum* also testifies to the 'noble army of martyrs', and affirms that the Lord's people are 'bought with the price of your own blood'. The text can be found in Morning Prayer in the *Book of Common Prayer*, or its modern versions.

[7] That Bathsheba conceives, even though David's initial sexual relations with her occurred during her purification, means that sexual relations continued between them for some time after the initial contact; it was more than a casual affair.

[8] Mary Douglas, *Purity and Danger* (Routledge and Kegan Paul, 1966), pp. 35–40 ('clean') and 51–54 ('holy'); *cf.* G. Wenham, *The Book of Leviticus* (Eerdmans, 1979), pp. 19ff. Note the importance of language here in 'constructing' the world of meaning: the same is true when it comes to terms such as 'masculine', 'gender' and 'nature'.

[9] *Cf.* Sherlock, *The God who Fights*, pp. 87–89.

[10] In a similar way, Graham emphasizes the need to move beyond theories about gender to making the difference in actual living, especially as Christians (pp. 187–191, and chapter 10). This entails moving away from the regulative approach represented by a binary-opposites way of thinking.

[11] The Greek words *koinos* and *koinōnia* have the same root, as 'common' and 'community' do in English. It is significant that the term 'fellowship' or 'communion' occurs in Acts 2:42 for the first time in the Scriptures with

reference to relationships between humans and God. The few earlier occurrences mean something shared between humans, for example 'deposit' or 'marriage'; the idea that humanity and God could 'share' anything is one of the radically new concepts resulting from the coming of the Spirit, following the finished, atoning work of Christ.

[12] A much larger debate is involved here; my approach here is to affirm the distinction and equal standing in Christ of female and male, without drawing out the implications of this for other subjects: see further van Leeuwen (ed.), *After Eden,* especially chapter 1, and the discussion in chapters 1 and 2 above.

[13] Jairus is also liberated here, whether by the haemorrhaging woman's example, or the emergency situation. He invites a (now unclean) strange male into his home, and allows him to visit a dead female with no women present. There are thus many levels of the transformation of taboos in this story.

[14] White and Tulip, p. 53. A similar learning of Jesus from a woman is possible in the healing of the daughter of the Canaanite (*viz.* Gentile) woman from Tyre and Sidon, who may well have been the human means of opening Jesus' eyes to a mission wider than that to the house of Israel (Mt. 15:21–28).

[15] This is not to defend the idea that Mary herself was free from sin (the dogma of the immaculate conception). It merely indicates that those who accept this dogma do so while accepting that she underwent the 'atonement' ritual prescribed.

[16] The precise details of these rituals are the subject of much scholarly debate, but the main point is uncontested, *i.e.* that the Lv. 12 ritual does not imply that childbirth was sinful: see the article 'Sacrifice, 1', *Illustrated Bible Dictionary,* vol. 2 (IVP, 1988).

[17] Tensions around childbirth are most keenly felt when a longed-for child dies before birth or soon after, especially when conception has been delayed (as is common in industrial societies) or has taken place only after considerable medical treatment. In Australia, cemetery officials tell me that the graves of infants or stillborn children continue to receive flowers for up to seven or eight years, whereas most other graves are rarely treated in this way for more than a year or so.

[18] My own city, Melbourne, is a world centre for such work, which has brought not only great joy to some, but also significant ethical problems, and disillusionment; the rate of marriage break-up following unsuccessful fertility treatment is much higher than the average, for example. Further, such research is criticized as not taking sufficiently seriously the masculine ethos of much scientific work: *cf.* Graham, chapter 9.

[19] Note that it is temptation which is under discussion here, not psychosexual development: *cf.* Graham, chapter 5.

[20] For example, Formaini, chapter 13.

[21] Lavinia Byrne, *Woman Before God* (SPCK, 1988), pp. 5–6, cites examples from Tertullian, Aquinas and John of Damascus. The balancing idea of Mary as the new Eve, common in medieval reflection, may be poetically imaginative, but nevertheless tends to reinforce the notion that Eve, and so woman, bears the brunt of the blame for sin.

[22] For example, statements by John Paul II, including his teaching in *Ordinatio Sacerdotalis*, are particularly clear on both the full dignity of women and their equality with men, as well as their admissibility to holy orders.

[23] *After Eden* and *Men, Women and God* offer Christian perspectives and resources in these and other areas.

[24] The phrases are deeply familiar to Anglicans from the General Confession of the *Book of Common Prayer* (1662) and most of its derivatives.

[25] This analysis seems to have been made first by Valerie Saiving, in an article originally published in 1960, 'The Human Situation: A Feminine View', reprinted in Carol P. Christ and Judith Plaskow (eds.), *Womanspirit Rising* (Harper and Row, 1979). See also *After Eden*, pp. 172–177, relating sin, women's experience and ecology; and Ann Carr, *Transforming Grace: Christian Tradition and Women's Experience* (Harper and Row, 1988).

[26] Another way of putting this would be to say that whereas men may be called to self-denial, women may be called away from it. Many feminist theologians, characterizing women's sins as self-negation and passivity, regard grace as correspondingly having to do with enabling liberation and granting wholeness, more than forgiveness for 'active' sins, and reject the concept of grace as the gift of self-sacrificing love: see Carr, p. 8.

[27] Graham, in chapter 9, notes the significance of 'writing the body' for some schools of feminism, as a strategy to correct the mind-oriented focus of much Enlightenment thinking (which can be taken up by men as well).

[28] See further Naomi Wolf, *The Beauty Myth* (Vintage, 1991); and *After Eden*, chapter 9, which includes a discussion of similar issues in men's experience. In recent times there has been a strong growth in male beauty products, and eroticism of the male body in the media, especially in sport. This trend may change men's attitudes to women, but seems more likely to reinforce the 'hegemonic masculinity' in the media (*After Eden*, p. 263). Christ rejected lust and idolizing the body and its needs, for both men and women (Mt. 6:25–33).

[29] White, p. 46.

[30] *Cf.* Graham, pp. 11–14, 42–43, 61–64, 174–185; she is especially sensitive to post-structuralist feminist critiques of patterning life in terms of 'binary opposites'.

[31] See Romans 8 especially, where walking according to the flesh is contrasted with walking according to spirit. At a popular level, meta-

physical dualism is seen in treating the devil and God as practically co-equal, but this denies the sovereignty and oneness of God. The question of dualisms in the human constitution, such as body and soul, is considered in chapter 10 below.

[32] *After Eden*, pp. 83–88, gives examples from Saudi, Indian, and black American women. The Indian Veena Das points out that modern western housing and courtship patterns have the effect of isolating women from the mainstream of life, without offering a distinctive woman's culture in return.

[33] This comment reveals that in a mixed group, as well as with men only, I sense that I am an active participant. Many women in a mixed group feel themselves to be spectators, because of the strong social bias towards male dominance in many group relationships, a bias which I find extremely difficult to remove from my own attitudes.

Chapter 9: Being a man

[1] Roy McCloughry, *Men and Masculinity* (Hodder, 1992), p. 4. Roy McCloughry is an evangelical social activist who works in England through the Kingdom Trust, and teaches part-time at St John's College, Nottingham, in which city he has taken part in a men's group for some years.

[2] See further Appendix 2, 'Inclusive Language and Being Human'.

[3] *Cf.* Graham, chapters 3 and 4, summarized on p. 190.

[4] Robert Bly, author of *Iron John: A Book about Men* (Element, 1990), develops a lively poetic 'mythology' about life as a man based on an eclectic range of sources. It is focused in the story of 'Iron John', who epitomized the 'Wild Man' in each man which needs to be let out – and wounded – before reigning. Due to its imaginary nature, it is difficult to respond to it at the strictly rational level (which is probably a good thing!): my concern is chiefly that Iron John seems too close to a caricature of Christ for comfort, and that military metaphors predominate. His work has become influential (and misunderstood) in the USA at a popular level, but it re-embraces the notion of a manly 'essence', thus perpetuating the dualistic tradition: *cf.* Graham, pp. 28–31. A movement with a similar ethos, but working within explicitly Christian parameters, is Promise Keepers; it is too recent a development for an evaluation to be made, except to note that it also appears (unfortunately) to stand for an essentialist view of gender.

[5] Cited in McCloughry, *Men and Masculinity*, p. 32.

[6] The term 'other' seems the most appropriate to use at this point. However, I do not want to be heard as supportive of the notion that woman is 'the Other', defined in terms of what men 'lack', as in neo-Freudian thought.

[7] See further Richard Holloway, *Who Needs Feminism? Men Respond to*

Feminism in the Church (SPCK, 1991) and James Nelson, *The Intimate Connection: Male Sexuality, Masculine Spirituality* (SPCK, 1992), both offering perspectives which partly develop and partly complement McCloughry's.

[8] Although distinguishing the results of long-term socialization ('nurture') from male physicality ('nature') is difficult, and perhaps impossible, the general trends are, I believe, useful to illustrate and analyse – but not to determine – what it means to be male: see Graham, chapter 3.

[9] See Graham, pp. 12–13, for an illuminating list of such pairings.

[10] Correspondingly, many women experience their embodiment as reproducers. Participation in reproduction is a great privilege, but (as noted in chapter 8) to define women's lives exclusively in such terms is damaging to all concerned. See *After Eden*, pp. 9–50, on Marxist analysis of women and men in terms of productivity.

[11] McCloughry, *Men and Masculinity*, pp. 28–31, summarizing the work of David Gilmore. He notes that there have been a few societies, generally where food is plentiful and easily found (such as Tahiti), where men seem to express little concern about being manly in aggressive ways.

[12] This need appears to be a principal attraction in Bly's 'Iron John' for many men, though Bly himself seeks to transform it into a positive self-understanding.

[13] *Men: The Darker Continent*, especially chapters 1–3. Chapter 8, 'Violence', lacks any reference to male physical strength, a surprising omission from the book as a whole. Graham, chapter 5, offers a detailed critique of neo-Freudian perspectives on gender and development, and on pp. 172–182 analyses francophone psychosexual studies (especially Lacan) in their post-structuralist context (especially Irigaray).

[14] Formaini, p. 13.

[15] This is related to Jung's concept of *animus* and *anima*, the masculine and feminine sides in each person.

[16] Formaini, p. 19.

[17] Gunton, *Enlightenment and Alienation*, especially chapters II and V. A parallel analysis of the development of capitalism was made by R. H. Tawney in *Religion and the Rise of Capitalism*, which argued that although its modern form began in Calvinism's sense of the divine vocation of each person, capitalism became distorted when the sense of accountability before God was lost. The 'Protestant work ethic', which says that hard work is its own reward, thus corrupts rather than furthers Protestant ideals: see further chapter 5 above.

[18] Graham, p. 211.

[19] Their close interrelation corresponds to the inseparability of creation and redemption, as noted in the previous chapter, and the connections between general and special revelation (using Reformed terminology), the spheres of nature and grace (as Augustinian concepts) or the notions of

nature and supernature. The Reformation regarded these as having become so distinguished in the medieval period as to constitute distinct secular and sacred realms, and protested against the dualistic worldview implied, a protest that today is echoed in much feminist rejection of dualism.

[20] *Cf.* White and Tulip, pp. 37–44, and especially *After Eden*, pp. 164–168.

[21] As noted earlier, Yoder's concept of 'revolutionary subordination' is helpful: see *The Politics of Jesus*, chapter 9.

[22] *Cf.* the discussion of dominion in chapter 5. An exercise which I have used in discussing passages such as Eph. 5:21 – 6:9 is to ask those present to put their hands over their ears until (by visual sign) their category is mentioned. In relation to Ephesians, all hear 5:21, only wives hear 5:22–24, only husbands hear 5:25–33, only children hear 6:1–3, only fathers hear 6:4, only slaves hear 6:5–8, only slave masters hear 6:9 – and all hear 6:10ff. The effect of this is to help participants to appreciate the particularity of different forms of submission, and seek to act on the form which applies to them. It also denies, for example, the sinful tendency of a husband to want to tell his wife how she is to submit to him, rather than setting about loving her; the form of her submission is her business, not his. A similar approach taken on Romans 13 illustrates the role of submission at the level of government.

[23] Graham, pp. 174–175, notes that recent work in Freudian circles distinguishes the phallus from the penis, using the former term to refer to male power as symbolized in the penis. In order to avoid giving an overly medical sense to the argument, this convention is adopted here.

[24] Phallic symbolism is perceived not only in objects which are long, thin and hard, but also in powerful objects seen as isolated sources of power, which lack relatedness; mobile phones are a recent example.

[25] *Cf.* the utterly inadequate discussion in Formaini, chapter 13.

[26] I have said nothing directly about female sexuality in chapter 8, in part because its abuse has done much less damage to humanity than male sexuality, but more because my maleness precludes useful reflection. I have written little also about the many ethical and pastoral issues involved in sexuality, since these lie outside the scope of this book, but have found Lewis B. Smedes, *Sex for Christians* (Eerdmans, 1976), a helpful resource.

[27] See further Wren, especially chapter 3; *cf.* Stoltenberg, pp. 77–89. Wren is an English United Reformed pastor and theologian, who has written many hymns that bring biblical and contemporary imagery together in faithful vividness.

A related issue is the link between rape and violence; feminists emphasize that rape should be seen as primarily an act of violence against women, rather than an act of sexual gratification. Some men, influenced by feminist critique of male lifestyles, have come to regard 'nonpenetrative' sex as the ideal; this is not only unrealistic, but denies the biblical concept of becoming 'one flesh', and the integration of sexual intercourse with procreation.

[28] Masturbation, whether by men or women, can offer an outlet to people under sexual pressure, but sexual climax is cut off from any other person, except as they exist in the mind of the one masturbating: *cf.* Smedes, pp. 160–164.

[29] Stoltenberg, Part I, spells out this objectification vividly, deliberately using crude language which reveals the depth of the effect of false male understandings of sexuality on others, especially women.

[30] In my experience, a key factor is having real relationships with the women I know; to regard as a mere object someone one knows as a friend is quite difficult.

[31] 'Brethren' was an inclusive term, today translated as 'brothers and sisters'. The positive sense it gives to 'brotherhood' must not be obscured by its rejection in a generic sense, but rather broadened to acknowledge that women as well as men share filiality in Christ. In this sense it is no surprise that one Christian group has chosen to call itself 'the Brethren'.

Chapter 10: The whole person

[1] McDonald, pp. 75–79, outlines major positions taken in the Christian tradition, and notes that humans are composed of both body and soul/spirit, not one or the other, but he fails to examine the presuppositions involved. As he shows, the first direct evidence of Christian dichotomy or trichotomy in the human person is in Tertullian and Justin, not the Scriptures. Anderson, pp. 207–214, offers a fuller and more nuanced appendix on 'Body, Soul, Spirit'.

[2] Despite continuing belief in this 'natural immortality' among Christians due to the ongoing influence of Platonic ideas, the New Testament 'portrays immortality as a natural property of God, and of God alone (1 Tim. 6.16), but for Plato immortality was an inherent characteristic of the rational "part" of the human soul ... From the New Testament perspective, since immortality is intrinsic to God and so extrinsic to man, it may come to man only as a divine gift': Murray J. Harris, *Raised Immortal* (Marshall, Morgan and Scott, 1983), pp. 201–205. Murray Harris is a New Zealand New Testament scholar who has taught in the USA and Britain as well as in his native land.

Modern abandoning of the concept of a distinct 'soul' entails a reconsidering of the functions which it has played in much traditional Christian theology. Some of these functions, such as enabling speculation about our state between death and resurrection, have been let go with a sense of relief; others, such as seeing the soul as the aspect of human being which relates to God, have been replaced by wider understanding of relationship; but others, such as regarding evangelism as consisting exclusively of 'winning souls', or excusing false asceticism, need to be rejected. I am grateful to Brian Edgar for some of these insights; he is an Australian who teaches at the Bible College of Victoria, and his doctoral thesis from Deakin University considers in detail the functions of the soul. *Cf.* John Cooper, *Body, Soul, and Life Everlasting: Biblical Anthropology and Modern Debate* (Eerdmans, 1989), which defends the notion of a distinct soul.

[3] Berkouwer, *Man*, pp. 209–211.

[4] *Ibid.*, p. 207.

[5] The translation of Lk. 17:21 as 'the kingdom of God is within you' (AV) is often misunderstood in this private way, because the 'you' in English can be heard as singular. It became a slogan for a body-denying, soul-oriented view of human nature in the nineteenth century especially; the translation 'among you' clarifies the meaning.

[6] See further Anderson, pp. 209–210.

[7] Barth, *Church Dogmatics*, III/2, p. 350: the translator, G. W. Bromiley, should be given due credit for the English phrase.

[8] In Christian liturgy, 'heart' has a prominent place. Cranmer's holy communion service, taken up into the *Book of Common Prayer*, begins with the recognition that before God 'all hearts are open', and prays that 'the thoughts of our hearts' may be cleansed. The Commandments evoke the response, 'Lord, incline our hearts to keep this law', concluding with the petition that God would 'write all these thy laws on our hearts'. The prayers include the request that all present may receive God's word 'with meek and obedient hearts'. The climax of praise is reached in the call 'Lift up your hearts!' and the communion itself, where we 'feed on' Christ in our hearts 'by faith'. Finally, the blessing prays that the peace of God may 'keep your hearts and minds in the knowledge and love of God'. In this and similar liturgical texts the centrality of 'heart' in the Christian tradition of prayer can readily be seen.

[9] Ridderbos, pp. 114–120, offers a good survey of Pauline anthropology, but from the perspective of 'The Corruption of Man'. A stimulating exegesis of the many relevant Pauline texts is R. Bultmann, *Theology of the New Testament*, vol. I (SCM, 1952), pp. 190–239. Bultmann is (in)famous for his 'demythologization' project as regards the New Testament; his reinterpretation of human life in existential terms is a part of his work which has enduring value.

[10] Bultmann, p. 209; note that the German uses the generic *Mensch* for 'man'.

[11] See further Moltmann, *God in Creation*, pp. 270–275, on the concept of 'health'.

[12] McDonald, pp. 68–74.

[13] Berkouwer, *Man*, p. 285; his chapter 8 is a full discussion of the issues.

[14] Moltmann, *God in Creation*, p. 260.

[15] I have discussed this more fully in *God on the Inside, passim*, and especially pp. 9–17, 212–218.

[16] That women and men experience embodiment in distinctive ways is evident. This factor is not taken into account in this chapter, given the limits of space, but the discussions in chapters 8 and 9 should be seen in this light.

[17] On this paragraph, see Edward Foley, 'Toward a Sound Theology', *Studia Liturgica* 23/2 (1993), pp. 121–139.

Appendix 1: The transmission of sin

[1] This topic moves into the question of the problem of evil, which lies beyond the scope of this book. A terse, realistic treatment is Geisler, Part IV. Geisler is an American evangelical philosopher who has engaged in public discussion of many issues of social morality.

[2] Contemporary systematic theologies do not often discuss these theories in detail: an older but full discussion is Charles Hodge, *Systematic Theology*, vol. II (1871; Eerdmans, 1952), chapter VIII. A useful work which seeks to relate grace and sin to pastoral concerns such as self-esteem, and surveys carefully the historical debates, is Neil Ormerod (ed.), *Grace and Disgrace* (E. J. Dwyer, 1992). Ormerod teaches theology at St Paul's Seminary, Sydney, and is known for clear thinking about Christian faith in its Australian contexts.

[3] See John Chryssavgis, 'Original Sin – An Orthodox Perspective', in Ormerod, pp. 197–206, from whom both quotations in this paragraph come. Chryssavgis, an Orthodox deacon, teaches at St Andrew's Seminary, Sydney, and is known for seeking to build bridges between the Orthodox and churches of an English background.

[4] Berkouwer, in *Sin*, chapters 12–14, discusses these matters in some detail, and with pastoral sensitivity.

[5] These two theories also came to be associated respectively with traducianist and creationist views of the soul, since the transmission of sin was discussed in relation to transmission of the soul; see chapter 10 above.

[6] See Henri Blocher, *Original Sin: Untangling the Riddle* (Apollos, 1997), the Moore College (Sydney) lectures for 1995.

Appendix 2: Inclusive language and being human

[1] Kathleen Hughes, 'Inclusive Language: An Issue Come of Age', *Liturgy* 90 (May–June 1993), p. 9.

[2] As noted previously, the confusion over 'man' used generically reflects an assumed male superiority. 'Real men' are male, while women are rather second-rate approximations. As Henry Higgins asked in *My Fair Lady*, 'Why can't a woman be more like a man?' This is simply sexist prejudice. Conversely if 'men' means both 'humans' and 'males', how do men know what is distinctive about being male?

[3] This amendment raises other issues, such as whether 'for us' will be understood as 'us present'. Nevertheless, after careful consideration it has been adopted for the standard text of the Creed, as recommended by the English Language Liturgical Consultation: see *Praying Together* (Canterbury Press, 1991).

[4] It is worth recalling that the Authorized Version adopted the convention of printing added words, especially pronouns, in italics, thus indicating (at least to a reader) something of the gender base of the original text.

[5] Examples include Brian Wren (England), Elizabeth Smith (Australia), Thomas H. Troeger (United States), and John Bell and Graham Maule (Scotland). Paradoxically, at greatest fault are many new choruses, but these can be avoided in favour of better material.

[6] The best introduction I know is of Brian Wren, *What Language Shall I Borrow?* Further literature is cited below.

[7] A striking example is the mutually interactive gender language of the Song of Songs; see Robin A. Payne, 'The Song of Songs: Song of Man, Song of Woman, Song of God', *Expository Times* 107 (1996), pp. 329–333.

[8] *Cf.* my *God on the Inside,* chapters 6–7; D. Tennis, *Is God the Only Reliable Father?* (Westminster, 1985); and especially Wren, Part II.

[9] The literature is growing rapidly; careful discussions include D. G. Bloesch, *The Battle for the Trinity: The Debate over Inclusive God-language* (Servant, 1985); Graham Leonard, Ian Mackenzie and Peter Toon, *Let God be God* (Darton, Longman & Todd, 1989); Rosemary Radford Ruether, *Sexism and God-Talk* (SCM, 1983); and Janet M. Soskice, *Metaphor and Religious Language* (Clarendon Press, 1985).

[10] It is in this spirit that for the past decade I have not used male pronouns for God in my writing, including this book.

Bibliography

All the standard textbooks of Christian theology discuss anthropology, as do articles in theological dictionaries, especially *ādām* in *Theological Dictionary of the Old Testament*, vol. 1 (Eerdmans, 1974), and *anthrōpos* in *Theological Dictionary of the New Testament*, vol. 1 (Eerdmans, 1964). The following select bibliography lists only works which pay major attention to the issues involved in the doctrine of humanity.

General works on being human
R. S. Anderson, *On Being Human* (Eerdmans, 1982)
G. C. Berkouwer, *Man: The Image of God* (Eerdmans, 1962)
G. Carey, *I Believe in Man* (Hodder and Stoughton, 1976)
D. Cairns, *The Image of God in Man* (Fontana, 1973)
P. Hughes, *The True Image* (IVP and Eerdmans, 1989)
W. G. Kummel, *Man in the New Testament* (Epworth, 1963)
H. McDonald, *The Christian View of Man* (Crossway, 1980)
J. Moltmann, *Man* (SPCK, 1974)

M. Rodgers and M. Thomas (eds.), *A Theology of the Human Person* (Collins Dove, 1992)

C. Schwöbel and C. E. Gunton (eds.), *Persons, Divine and Human* (T. and T. Clark, 1991)

Other theological works with a distinctive contribution to the discussion of being human

K. Barth, *Church Dogmatics* III/1, III/2 (T. and T. Clark, 1956–)

G. C. Berkouwer, *The Providence of God* (Eerdmans, 1952)

G. C. Berkouwer, *Sin* (Eerdmans, 1971)

V. Lossky, *The Mystical Theology of the Eastern Church* (James Clarke, 1957)

J. Moltmann, *God in Creation* (SCM, 1985)

N. Ormerod, *Grace and Disgrace* (E. J. Dwyer, 1992)

E. Schillebeeckx, *Christ: the Experience of Jesus as Lord* (Crossroads, 1990), Part IV

C. H. Sherlock, *God on the Inside: Trinitarian Spirituality.* (Acorn, 1991)

C. Westermann, *Creation* (Fortress, 1974)

Works on particular areas in Focus 2a

J. Gladwin, *God's People in God's World* (IVP, 1979)

C. Gunton, *Enlightenment and Alienation* (Eerdmans, 1985)

D. Hall, *Imaging God* (Eerdmans and Friendship, 1986)

K.-J. Kuschel, *Laughter: A Theological Reflection* (SCM, 1994)

R. Niebuhr, *Moral Man and Immoral Society* (Scribners, 1932)

J. A. Walter, *A Long Way from Home* (Paternoster, 1979)

B. Wilson, *The Human Journey* (Albatross, 1981)

Works on particular areas in Focus 2b

J. Cooper, *Body, Soul and Life Everlasting* (Eerdmans, 1989)

E. Graham, *Making the Difference: Gender, Personhood and Theology* (Mowbray, 1995)

H. Formaini, *Men: The Darker Continent* (Heinemann, 1990)

D. Hampson, *Theology and Feminism* (Blackwell, 1990)

M. J. Harris, *Raised Immortal* (Marshall, Morgan and Scott, 1983)

P. K. Jewett, *Man as Male and Female* (Eerdmans, 1975)

K. Keay (ed.), *Men, Women and God* (Marshall Pickering, 1987)

R. McCloughry, *Men and Masculinity* (Hodder and Stoughton, 1992)

J. Piper and W. Grudem (eds.), *Recovering Biblical Manhood and Womanhood* (Crossway, 1991)

J. Stoltenberg, *Refusing to be a Man* (Meridian, 1990)

M. Stewart van Leeuwen (ed.), *After Eden: Facing the Challenge of Gender Reconciliation* (Eerdmans and Paternoster, 1993)

E. White and M. Tulip, *Knowing Otherwise: Feminism, Women and Religion* (David Lovell, 1991)

Indexes

Scripture references

Non-English terms

Names

THE DOCTRINE OF HUMANITY

Subjects